# TWENTIETH-CENTURY ANALYTIC PHILOSOPHY

AVRUM STROLL



MOTILAL BANARSIDASS PUBLISHERS
PRIVATE LIMITED • DELHI

*Reprint : Delhi, 2017*
*First Indian Edition : Delhi, 2007*



ISBN: 978-81-208-3143-8 (Cloth)
ISBN: 978-81-208-4111-6 (Paper)

MOTILAL BANARSIDASS
41 U.A., Bungalow Road, Jawahar Nagar, Delhi 110 007
8 Mahalaxmi Chamber, 22 Bhulabhai Desai Road, Mumbai 400 026
203 Royapettah High Road, Mylapore, Chennai 600 004
236, 9th Main III Block, Jayanagar, Bengaluru 560 011
8 Camac Street, Kolkata 700 017
Ashok Rajpath, Patna 800 004
Chowk, Varanasi 221 001

*MLBD Cataloging-in-Publication Data*
Twentieth-Century Analytic Philosophy
by AVRUM STROLL
ISBN: 978-81-208-3143-8 (Cloth)
ISBN: 978-81-208-4111-6 (Paper)
Includes Index, References
I. Philosophy II. Western III. Analysis
IV. Stroll, Avrum



*Printed in India*
by RP Jain at NAB Printing Unit,
A-44, Naraina Industrial Area, Phase I, New Delhi–110028
and published by JP Jain for Motilal Banarsidass Publishers (P) Ltd.,
41 U.A. Bungalow Road, Jawahar Nagar, Delhi-110007

*For Mary*

## Table of Contents

# Acknowledgments

Given the span of more than a hundred years that this study covers, and the complexity of much of the material, I would have found it impossible to write this book without abundant expert assistance. I therefore wish to thank Zeno Vendler, Robert Rowan, Henry Alexander, Pieranna Garavaso, A. P. Martinich, and John Collins for their invaluable comments. Each of them read the entire manuscript and, mirabile dictu, presented me with *written* criticisms, as well as detailed recommendations for improvement. My appreciation for the labor they expended is boundless. I also owe a debt of gratitude to the editor of the *Journal of Philosophy*, who allowed me to include in this work part of an essay, "Proper Names, Names, and Fictive Objects," that I published in the *Journal* in 1998. I owe a similar debt to an editor at MIT Press for permission to use part of a chapter from my *Sketches of Landscapes: Philosophy by Example* (1998). These materials appear in the last sections of chapter 8. With those exceptions, the book contains only new writings.

I wrote much of the manuscript during two stays at the American Academy in Rome, and without the hospitality and generosity of the then director, Caroline Bruzelius, and the assistant director, Pina Pasquantonio, it would have taken me much longer to complete this work. Finally, no expression of thanks will do justice to the acute observations on the text made by my wife, Mary. Her careful reading of the manuscript greatly improved its style, organization, level of argument, and content. That she took so much time away from her own current research on twelfth-century papal politics is indeed an act of supererogation. For her help, and, of course, for other reasons, I dedicate this book to her.

Chapter One

# The Solera System

The rapidity with which major movements suddenly appear, flourish, lose their momentum, become senescent, and eventually vanish marks the history of twentieth-century analytic philosophy. Examples include idealism in its absolutist and subjectivist variants, sense-data theory, logical atomism, neutral monism, and logical positivism. These defunct "isms," and their living congeners, such as "reductionism," "pragmatism," and "naturalism," form the subject matter of this study and will be explained for the general reader in due course. There are, of course, exceptions to the pattern of birth, flowering, and decline. In ontology various forms of materialism continue to enjoy widespread support, and naturalized epistemology—developed by W. V. O. Quine and expanded by his followers—shows no signs of abatement.

Indeed, if anything, the prestige of science has intensified in the twentieth century. Scientism, the doctrine that *only* the methods of the natural sciences give rise to knowledge, is today widely espoused in epistemology, metaphysics, philosophy of language, and philosophy of mind. In 1918 in *Allgemeine Erkenntnislehre* Moritz Schlick, the founder of the Vienna Circle, formulated the doctrine in this way: "Since science in principle can say all that can be said there is no unanswerable question left." Patricia S. Churchland's *Neurophilosophy* (1986) contains a later expression of the same position: "In the idealized long run, the completed science is a true description of reality: there is no other Truth and no other Reality."

Contemporary philosophers have reacted to the impact of science in three different ways, two of which are forms of scientism. The more radical of the two asserts that if philosophy has a function it must be something other than trying to give a true account of the world, because science preempts that prerogative. In the *Tractatus*, for example, Ludwig Wittgenstein writes: "Philosophy is not one of the natural sciences. . . . The result of philosophy is not a number of 'philosophical propositions', but to make propositions clear." A variant of this view is to hold that philosophy should deal with normative or value questions, as opposed to science, which is a wholly descriptive, fact-finding activity. A second less radical reaction is to maintain that philosophy, *when correctly done*, is an extension of science. It is contended that both disciplines are committed to the same standards of evidence and logical cogency but that their subject matters are different. According to Quine, there is a division of labor among investigators. For example, professional scientists use numbers in constructing theories, and philosophers analyze the concept of number as it is used in such contexts. More generally, some scientistically oriented philosophers hold that the task of philosophy consists in analyzing the foundations of knowledge, including the main concepts of science. Finally, a variety of approaches reject scientism and in different ways defend the autonomy of philosophy; their proponents hold that philosophy has a descriptive function and can arrive at nonscientific truths about reality. G. E. Moore, Ludwig Wittgenstein, J. L. Austin, O. K. Bouwsma, Norman Malcolm, and Gilbert Ryle, inter alios, can be assigned to this last category.

The question about the relationship between science and philosophy leads to another major contrast. This is the issue, much debated in the twentieth century, of whether philosophy should be dedicated to the construction of theories about the world and its various features. The controversy cuts across the scientism/autonomy distinction at an angle, since many committed to scientism as well as many of their opponents (such as traditional metaphysicians) feel that philosophy should engage in theory construction. There are also those who espouse and those who reject forms of scientism yet deny that the business of philosophy is theorizing. Wittgenstein is perhaps the most famous example of a philosopher who espoused scientism in his early work, the *Tractatus* of 1922, and disavowed it in his later writings, such as the *Philosophical Investigations*, published in 1953. Nevertheless, from beginning to end he consistently rejected the notion that the aim of philosophy is theory construction. In the *Tractatus*, for example, he states: "Philosophy is not a theory but an activity" (4.112). Virtually the same words occur in the *Investigations*: "It was true to say that our considerations could not be scientific ones. . . . And we may not advance any kind of theory. . . . We must do away with all *explanation*, and description alone must take its place" (1958:109).

These two distinctions (scientism versus autonomy, and theorizing versus nontheorizing) raise a profound problem that we shall address at length in this study. What is philosophy? What is (are) its task (tasks)? What kind of information, illumination, and understanding is it supposed to provide if it is not one of the natural sciences? Within the so-called analytic movement this is one of the sharpest issues that divides practitioners about the point and purpose of doing philosophy.

One thing we have surely learned from studying the preceding period is that contemporary analytic philosophy is intimately tied to its history. In this respect it is less like science and more like history and literature, although there are important differences even here. But the contrast with science is more striking. Why this is so is complicated. Partly it is due to the difference between empirical and conceptual activities. Aristotle's cosmological theories are not of current interest to most scientists. Insofar as his problems were susceptible to experimental treatment, they have been solved. Insofar as they were metaphysical, they remain immune to scientific analysis and indeed may resist solution altogether. The early discoveries of Galileo and Newton are no longer in the forefront of scientific attention because they have been absorbed into routine investigative procedure. When such absorption occurs, science moves on without much memory of its predecessors.

But this is not true of philosophy. Plato and Aristotle have never died, even though their ideas have become part and parcel of present practice. We still read Thucydides and Gibbon on the use and abuse of political power and Shakespeare and Jane Austen for their penetrating insights into human character. Despite frequent references to "scientific philosophy" today, there is no doubt that philosophy is essentially a humanistic activity. And this is shown by its ties to the past. Even though most analytic philosophers are not exegetes of ancient texts, the problems posed by venerable thinkers are still as vivid now as they were centuries ago. Many issues we presently deal with first surfaced eons ago: How it is possible to speak meaningfully/truly about the nonexistent? How with consistency can one deny that something exists? How is it possible for two true identity sentences to differ in meaning? Is existence a property? Yet despite their older origins, all these questions have been of pressing centrality in the work of Gottlob Frege, Bertrand Russell, Saul Kripke, and Quine, to name a few. Shall we then conclude that no progress has been made in this discipline? I do not think we should. But if there is progress, it cannot be identical with that made in science, which often achieves definite solutions. Yet philosophy exhibits something like advancement: there are improvements in the techniques used and new schemes for resolving traditional issues.

Thus, in a sense difficult to articulate, the contemporary turf is both familiar and alien; we seem to recognize it as terrain we have traversed in the past, and yet it somehow now looks quite different.

It is thus difficult to answer the question about progress without taking account of the role that the past plays in contemporary analytic philosophy. In trying to find a figure of speech that would provide a picture of this complex relationship, I originally thought I would call this chapter "New Wine in Old Wineskins." The new wine would be the philosophy I will be describing in this book, and the old wineskins would be the tradition that, stemming from the Greeks, often sets the problems and sometimes the outlines of the solutions to them. But the analogy is not quite right. Contemporary philosophy is perhaps a kind of new wine, but traditional philosophy is not an old wineskin. You can drink wine but not a wineskin. We need a conceit in which traditional philosophy is like old wine that intermingles with a new vintage. I suggest a metaphor that captures this relationship. Sherry makers call it the "solera system."

In his *Encyclopedia of Wines and Spirits*, Alexis Lichine describes it in these words:

> The most interesting thing about Sherry (apart from the mysterious *flor*) is the peculiar system by which it is kept at its best. A very old, very fine Sherry has the power to educate and improve a younger one. Because of this, the old wines are kept in the oldest barrels of what the growers call a *solera*. This is a series of casks graduated by age. A series is made up of identical butts. The oldest class in a *solera* is the one called the Solera. The next oldest is the first Criadera, the next the second Criadera, and so on. When the wine is drawn from the Solera, it is drawn in equal quantity from each butt. Then starts a progressive system by which the Solera is refilled by the first Criadera and that in turn by the second Criadera, etc. The magic result of this system is that the oldest casks remain eternally the same in quality. A cask of 1888, for instance, may retain hardly a spoonful of its original vintage; but each replacement poured back into it over the years will have been educated to be 1888, and replacements still to come will be schooled to the same standard. By this system, it is possible not only to preserve the same quality and character of wine over the years, but also, by constantly refreshing the Fino types with younger wine, to keep these from losing their freshness. (1971:492)

In this system of pipes and barrels we find a way of describing the relationship between traditional and contemporary philosophy. Borrowing Lichine's phrase, we can say that old philosophy has the power to educate and improve new philosophy. And new philosophy not only preserves the quality and character of old philosophy but has the capacity to refresh it. Intermingling, preservation, and refreshment are thus the characteristics that define the relationship between present philosophy and its history. But now the question is whether the solera metaphor fits the facts. Is twentieth-century analytic philosophy like new wine? Or is it like old wine that has lost its freshness?

The issue is compounded by the fact that it is difficult to give a precise definition of "analytic philosophy" since it is not so much a specific doctrine as a loose concatenation of approaches to problems. The century begins with a book, G. E. Moore's *Principia Ethica* (1903), that emphasizes the importance of "analysis" in attempting to understand the nature of moral deliberation. Moore argues that the predicate "good," which defines the sphere of ethics, is "simple, unanalyzable, indefinable" (p. 37). His contention is that many of the difficulties in ethics, and indeed in philosophy generally, arise from an "attempt to answer questions, without first discovering precisely *what* question it is which you desire to answer." Questions thus require "analysis" to unpack them and to know what they mean. Moore's monograph unquestionably sensitized his contemporaries and nearly all his successors to the importance of becoming clear about the questions they asked and the kinds of answers that would be appropriate.

But it would be a misreading of history to think that the idea of philosophical analysis begins with Moore. There is a much longer tradition of analysis whose lineage can be traced to the ancient Greeks. Socrates, for instance, can be construed as trying to capture the ordinary meaning of the concept of justice in Books I and II of the *Republic*. The dialectical method he uses, which consists of proposed definitions and counterexamples to them, with a sustained effort to arrive at the essence of justice, is not much different from Moore's approach in *Principia Ethica* with respect to the notion of "good." Similar remarks apply to Aristotle's characterization of truth in the *Metaphysics*, which prefigures Alfred Tarski's semantic conception in *Der Wahreitsbegriff in den formalisierten Sprachen* of 1935. There is clearly an analytic streak embedded in David Hume's voluminous writings, as exemplified by his explication of the notion of causation. It is thus plausible to argue that something like analysis has always been part and parcel of philosophical practice.

Still, even today there is no consensus on what analysis is. The history of the topic is replete with suggested definitions. In "Logical Atomism," published in 1924, Bertrand Russell writes: "The business of philosophy, as I conceive it, is essentially that of logical analysis, followed by logical synthesis. . . . The most important part [of philosophy] consists in criticizing and clarifying notions which are apt to be regarded as fundamental and accepted uncritically" (1956:341). C. D. Broad regarded analytic philosophy as a kind of science: "Thus there is both need and room for a science which shall try to analyze and define the concepts which are used in daily life and in the specific sciences" (1924:78–79). In the *Origins of Analytical Philosophy* (1993), Michael Dummett proffers a two-part characterization: "What distinguishes analytical philosophy, in its diverse manifestations, from other schools is the belief, first, that a philosophical account of thought can be attained through a philosophical account of language, and, secondly, that a comprehensive account can only be so attained" (p. 4).

The two most extensive, recent discussions of this notion appear in P. M. S. Hacker's *Wittgenstein's Place in Twentieth-Century Analytic Philosophy* (1996) and in Hans Sluga's critical notice of Hacker's book, "What Has History to Do with Me? Wittgenstein and Analytic Philosophy," in *Inquiry* (1998). Hacker gives a brief survey of the modern use of this concept and draws several illuminating distinctions, such as those between logical and conceptual analysis, and reductive and constructive analysis. His ultimate decision is to take the term "analysis" to "mean what it appears to mean, namely the decomposition of something into its constituents." As he explains:

> Chemical analysis displays the composition of chemical compounds from their constituent chemical elements; microphysical analysis penetrates to the subatomic composition of matter, disclosing the ultimate elements of which all substance is composed. Philosophical analysis harboured similar ambitions within the domain of ideas or concepts which are the concern of philosophy. Accordingly, I take the endeavours of the classical British empiricists to be a psychological form of analytic philosophy, for they sought to analyse what they thought of as complex ideas into their simple constituents. This method of analysis, they believed, would not only clarify problematic, complex ideas, but

> also shed light upon the origins of our ideas, as well as upon the sources and limits of human knowledge. Taking 'analysis' decompositionally, twentieth-century analytic philosophy is distinguished in its origins by its non-psychological orientation. (Hacker 1998:3–4)

Sluga's essay opens with a lengthy discussion of what might be meant by "analytic philosophy." After a careful evaluation of various historical options, he concludes as follows:

> The outcome of all this is that it may be hopeless to try to determine the essence of analytic philosophy, that analytic philosophy is to be characterized in terms of overlapping circles of family resemblances and of causal relations of "influence" that extend in all directions and certainly far beyond the boundaries we hope to draw. So our question should not be: what precise property do all analytic philosophers share? But: how can one draw the boundaries of analytic philosophy most naturally and most usefully and to what uses are we putting the term when we draw them in one way rather than another? (p. 107)

I think Sluga is right in saying "it may be hopeless to try to determine the essence of analytic philosophy." Nearly every proposed definition has been challenged by some scholar. It has been denied that analysis is a science, that the notions being analyzed are those that are accepted uncritically, that analysis seeks to give a philosophical account of thought, that what is being sought is a comprehensive account of anything, or that "analysis," as Hacker contends, is always the decomposition of a concept into its elements. On this last point J. L. Austin's account in "Three Ways of Spilling Ink" (1970b) of the difference between doing something intentionally, deliberately, or on purpose is an example of the analysis of the concept of responsibility that does not involve the decomposition of the concept into its constituents. Such actions are not constituents of responsibility in the way that atoms of hydrogen and oxygen are constituents of a molecule of water.

Let us accept Sluga's suggestion, with a slight modification following Moore, that we are dealing with a family resemblance concept. Many scholars would agree with Sluga that there is no single feature that characterizes the activities of all those commonly known as analytic philosophers. Yet most commentators would concur with Moore that, however much the work of particular practitioners differs, it is directed toward articulating the meaning of certain concepts, such as "knowledge," "belief," "truth," and justification." A guiding assumption for this emphasis is that one cannot make a judicious assessment of any proposed thesis until one understands it and its constituent concepts. This is essentially what Moore takes the function of analysis to be. But there are many different ways of pursuing such an end, from the strict formal approach of a Frege or a Tarski to the aphoristic example-oriented technique of the later Wittgenstein. Therefore, rather than trying to define the concept by looking for some common feature that all instances of analytic philosophy exhibit, I shall concentrate on the contributions of a cluster of individuals who are generally regarded as analytic philosophers. This group includes Gottlob Frege (1848–1925), Bertrand Russell (1872–1970), G. E. Moore (1873–1958), Ludwig Wittgenstein (1889–1951), Rudolf Carnap (1891–1970), J. L. Austin (1911–1960), Gilbert Ryle (1900–1976), and W. V. O. Quine (1908–). Not all commentators agree on who should be included in such a list. Hacker, for instance, holds that Quine is not an analytic philosopher. Still, this is a minority view and most commentators would place Quine in the category.

Most of the major achievements in this field are due to these persons. They are the initiators of philosophical doctrines, styles, approaches, or outlooks that become codified and form the rough equivalent of schools. Such approaches set the fashions and attract numerous followers. Among such twentieth-century doctrines are logical atomism, commonsense philosophy, pragmatism, ordinary language philosophy, logical positivism, and the semantic conception of truth. Many of these thinkers have transformed or extended older traditions in new ways (e.g., Quine's holistic empiricism), but some (e.g., Austin) have developed new and unique approaches to philosophical questions. Without a doubt, the most influential philosopher of the era has been Wittgenstein (1889–1951). His writings—nearly all published only after his death—dominate the contemporary scene and seem destined to be of central importance in the foreseeable future. A fruitful way of surveying the period is thus to concentrate upon the contributions of this distinguished set of individuals. I shall do this chronologically. But it should be added that from the 1930s to the present, other thinkers have also made noteworthy contributions. This assemblage includes Karl Popper, P. F. Strawson, Roderick Chisholm, Donald Davidson, David Lewis, Hilary Putnam, Ruth Barcan Marcus, Paul and Patricia Churchland, John Searle, Zeno Vendler, Tarski, Bouwsma, Dummett, and Kripke. This list is not complete by any means.

Unfortunately, because of space limitations I cannot deal with the work of each of these persons, though I will deal with some. This study is not so much a survey of the period as a depiction of what I regard as some main philosophical ideas in the twentieth century.

The creation of symbolic (or mathematical) logic is perhaps the single most important development in the century. Apart from its intrinsic interest, and its significance for computer studies and artificial intelligence, it has exercised an enormous influence on philosophy per se. Though there are anticipations of this kind of logic among the Stoics, its modern forms are without exact parallel in Western thought. It quickly became apparent that an achievement of this order could not easily be ignored, and no matter how diverse their concerns nearly all analytic philosophers have acknowledged its importance. This was especially true when the new logic, with its close affinities to mathematics, was recognized to be fundamental to scientific theorizing. Many philosophers regarded the combination of logic and science as a model that philosophical inquiry should follow. Logical positivism—a doctrine that flourished in the 1930s and '40s—was a paradigmatic expression of this point of view. In the latter part of the century, the theories of meaning and reference developed by Carnap, Quine, and Putnam have similar antecedents. As we shall see, this mélange of science and logic dominated American philosophy from the time of the early pragmatists, such as C. S. Peirce, who was writing at the beginning of the century, to the present.

But symbolic logic itself, apart from its scientific affiliations, served as a role model. Many philosophers felt that its criteria of clarity, precision, and rigor should be the ideals to be emulated in grappling with philosophical issues. Peter Simons, David Kaplan, Quine, Davidson, Lewis, Marcus, and Kripke are contemporary well-known representatives of this point of view. Yet other thinkers, and especially the later Wittgenstein, rejected this approach, arguing that treating logic as an ideal language, superior to natural languages, such as English or German, led to paradox and incoherence. Wittgenstein's later philosophy consisted in developing a unique method that emphasized the merit of ordinary language in describing the world. As he says: "What *we* do is to bring words back from their metaphysical to their everyday use." In particular, his method avoided the kind of theorizing and generalization essential to logic.

Despite the manifest influence of symbolic logic, I do not believe that a command of its technical detail is necessary in order to understand its philosophical impact. An analogy may be helpful here. One can understand a discussion about the effects of the automobile on the atmosphere without knowing how the internal combustion engine works. In this study, therefore, I shall make no effort to write the equivalent of a short logic text. Similar comments are apposite with respect to the discussion of modal logic in chapter 8.

In those sections of the book where there is a close affinity between technical logical notions, such as quantification theory, and philosophical doctrines, such as the theory of descriptions and the direct reference treatment of proper names, it is generally possible to explain the technical logical notions in ordinary English, and this is the policy I will follow. I thus believe the reader can understand the philosophical issues without a grounding in modern logic. With this stipulation in mind, let me now describe how and why these philosophers responded to the new discipline in the different ways that they did.

# Chapter Two

# Philosophical Logic

We can begin by describing, in this and the next chapter, two positive reactions to modern logic: the philosophies of logical atomism and logical positivism. To set the background for the discussion, I shall focus on the work of Alfred North Whitehead and Bertrand Russell, the authors of *Principia Mathematica* (vols. 1–3, 1910–1913). They had two important aims. The first, following Gottlob Frege, was to show that mathematics is a branch of logic, in the sense that number theory (arithmetic) can be reduced to propositions containing only logical concepts, such as constants, quantifiers, variables, and predicates. This was called the "logistic thesis" and we shall speak about it in a moment. The other was to show that mathematical logic was an ideal language that could capture, in a purely formal notation, the large variety of inference patterns and idioms, including different types of sentences, that are found in ordinary discourse. In doing the latter they also wished to show how vague expressions could be made more precise and how sentences susceptible to double readings could be disambiguated in such a way as clearly to expose the basis for the equivocation.

This latter purpose was brilliantly realized in their theory of descriptions, which diagnoses subtle but philosophically profound ambiguities in sentences whose subject terms lack a referent, such as "The present king of France is not bald." This sentence could be read either as saying, "There exists at present a king of France who is not bald," or as saying, "It is false that there presently exists a king of France who is bald." (The distinction is clearly expressed in the symbolic language of quantification theory. The first sentence is written as [(∃x) (-Fx)] and the second as [~(∃x) (Fx)]). The former is false because it claims that a French king now exists, adding that he is not bald, whereas the second is true because it denies that anything is now both a French king and bald. The difference is to be accounted for in terms of the scope of the negation sign. In the first sentence it applies only to the predicate and in the second to the whole sentence. The concept of scope was to have a lasting impact on the work of many later philosophers, such as Marcus, Kripke, and Quine. It became a key notion both in philosophy of language and in modal logic.

Such impressive results made a strong case for the proposition that the regimented language of *Principia* is an ideal language for solving conceptual problems. Whitehead and Russell contend that its range of application in philosophy is at least as great as any of the natural languages and, moreover, because of its perfect clarity, lacks their disadvantages. Frege had a similar aim. In "On the Scientific Justification of a Conceptual Notation," he states that ordinary language can be used to express emotions and certain nuances of meaning but that it is inadequate for a system of demonstrative science. Unlike Russell and Whitehead, who saw formal logic as an extension and perfection of ordinary speech, Frege believed that, despite certain overlaps, there is a basic incompatibility between the two and that for logical purposes ordinary language is to be avoided. As he wrote: "Certainly there should be a definite sense to each expression in a complete configuration of signs, but the natural languages in many ways fall short of this requirement" (Frege 1949:86). And in a footnote on the same page he states: "These fluctuations in sense are tolerable. But they should be avoided in the system of a demonstrative science and should not appear in a perfect language." A little later he adds:

> Now, it is a defect of languages that expressions are possible within them, which, in their grammatical form, seemingly determined to designate an object, nevertheless do not fulfill this condition in special cases. . . . It is to be demanded that in a logically perfect language (logical symbolism) every expression constructed as a proper name in a grammatically correct manner out of already introduced symbols, in fact designate an object; and that no symbol be introduced as a proper name without assurance that it have a nominatum. (pp. 95–96)

For Russell and Whitehead the development of an ideal language for the analysis of ordinary discourse and the attempt to prove the logistic thesis are compatible; in pursuing the former goal they believed they were at the same time pursuing the latter. Let us look at these twin aims, beginning with the logistic thesis.

## The Logistic Thesis

It is, of course, obvious that arithmetic employs numbers and allows familiar operations on them, such as addition and subtraction. In the nineteenth century, mathematicians showed that the concepts used in algebra and what was then called "the infinitesimal calculus" are definable exclusively in arithmetical terms. In effect, they "arithmetized" these branches of mathematics by reducing their basic concepts to the natural numbers and the familiar operations on them. For example, instead of accepting an imaginary number, say, the square root of minus one, as a mysterious entity, they showed that it could be defined as an ordered pair of integers (0, 1) on which such operations as addition and multiplication can be performed. Likewise, an irrational number, for example, the square root of 2, could be defined as the class of rationals whose square is less than 2. But Whitehead and Russell wished to do even more; they wished to demonstrate that *all* arithmetical concepts—in other words, number theory itself—can be derived from the principles of logic alone.

Number theory was based on a set of five postulates formulated by the Italian mathematician Giuseppe Peano in 1889 and 1895. These postulates state and organize the fundamental laws of "natural" numbers (i.e., the positive integers) and thus are the core of all mathematics. Here are the postulates:

1. Zero is a number.
2. The successor of any number is a number.
3. No two numbers have the same successor.
4. Zero is not the successor of any number.
5. If any property is possessed by zero, and also by the successor of any number having that property, then all numbers have that property.

Russell and Whitehead set about the derivation of Peano's postulates, starting from a set of their own axioms, all stated in a wholly logical notation. Using these axioms as a base (plus *modus ponens* as a principle of inference), they created a series of calculi (formal subsystems) of growing degrees of richness. At the end of this process they were able to derive Peano's postulates. The result was presumably a proof of the logistic thesis.

I say "presumably" because the system of *Principia* transcends elementary logic and includes set theory. Sets are collections of objects, and collections are abstractions that are neither physical nor concrete. That set theory is really logic in a narrow sense has been seriously challenged. It is clearly not logic in the way that Frege views logic, which is as a formal theory of functions and properties. Nor is it logic in a later, narrower sense, that is, as whatever concerns only rules for propositional connectives, quantifiers, and nonspecific terms for individuals and predicates.

With regard to this later conception, some logicians deny that identity (typically denoted by the symbol '=') is part of logic. The majority of logicians have assumed that it is. Still, set theory engenders a large number of nonphysical, nonperceived abstract objects that do not belong to logic in almost any narrow, formal sense; thus, according to some critics, the derivation of Peano's postulates has not been achieved purely by "logical" methods. Accordingly, Whitehead and Russell's results with respect to proving the logistic thesis were disputed and still are. Still, their achievement is of the highest importance and has had a lasting effect on subsequent work in logic and mathematics.

But the creation of these calculi had another important consequence that was more philosophical than mathematical. Russell and Whitehead also show that a close tie exists between logic and ordinary language. They show that the theorems of the different calculi correspond to different kinds of statements and to the inference patterns they allow in ordinary discourse. This tie is what led to the notion that *Principia* is the ideal language for philosophical analysis. The scope of the Whitehead-Russell program was thus even larger than proving the logistic thesis. I shall have more to say about this matter later.

*Principia* employed five axioms. The Harvard logician H. M. Sheffer later showed that these could be reduced to one, namely, to the proposition that p is incompatible with q. Sheffer symbolized this concept as p/q, and it was known as the "Sheffer stroke." From this concept one can derive the other connectives and from them the usual theorems of *Principia*. From p/p (p is incompatible with itself) one can derive p/p = ~p. This follows because, if p is incompatible with itself, p is false, and therefore p/p = not p. Likewise, p ⊃ q means that p is incompatible with the falsity of q, and this can be represented as p/(q/q), and (p and q) can be represented as (p/q)/(p/q), since, as we have seen, this formula means that both p and q are true.

Peano's postulates were situated at the highest point of the system. Given the machinery developed in the various calculi, the postulates could be formulated as propositions of formal logic and then validly derived within the system. The outcome was that arithmetic was shown to be a proper part (subbranch) of logic. As previously mentioned, this discussion oversimplifies the historical situation, which required problematic axioms (the "axiom of reducibility" and "the axiom of infinity") in order to derive the postulates. Those who rejected the axiom of infinity, such as Frank Ramsey (1903–1930) and Luitzen Egbertus Jan Brouwer (1881–1966), tried to develop a kind of logic in which only finite and no transcendental methods would be permitted. These ideas were later to influence Wittgenstein—but this is a complexity we cannot explore here.

Each calculus of theorems corresponds to certain kinds of sentences found in ordinary discourse. Theoretically, every type of English sentence and all the inference patterns their structures permit could be captured by the system of *Principia*. For instance, the propositional (sentential) calculus consists of theorems whose constituents are propositions (i.e., declarative sentences), such as "The streets are wet" and "J. R. Jones is tall." Various transformations are effected upon combinations of these propositions through the use of the axioms and *modus ponens*; the results are compound sentences that are true in all state descriptions, that is, tautologies. The law of simplification is an example of such a theorem. In symbolic language it is $(p \wedge q) \supset p$. What it states (in English) is that if both p and q are true, then p is true.

It is interesting to compare and contrast *Principia* with Scholastic logic. The latter was a logic of terms. Each term was taken to denote a class, such as the class of men, the class of mortals, and so on (Socrates was interpreted as a class containing only one member). *Principia Mathematica* provides a separate calculus for classes; technically, it belongs to set theory. It deals not only with the notion of inclusion, as Scholastic logic in effect did, but also with the notion of membership in a class, a concept not found in the earlier logic. The four canonical sentences of Scholastic logic—"All S is P," "No S is P," "Some S is P," and "Some S is not P," whose English equivalents would be "All men are mortal," "No men are mortal," "Some men are mortal," and "Some men are not mortal"—are treated as part of quantification theory and thus belong to the functional (first-order predicate) calculus. The words "all," "no," and "some" and certain equivalents, such as "there is" and "there are," in modern logic are called "quantifiers."

Quantification theory (the "predicate calculus") is a theory about the inference patterns of sentences containing quantifiers. Sentences like "Jones and Smith were acquainted" belong to the calculus of relations, and those like "The first president of the United States was George Washington" are part of the calculus of descriptions. Through these ascending calculi the system became progressively "richer" until it arrived at the point where Peano's postulates could be expressed in logical terms and were derivable from the system.

The concept of "richness" was later to play an essential role in Kurt Gödel's proof in 1931 that a logical system sufficiently rich to entail Peano's postulates would be incomplete. What Gödel demonstrated is that in a language, L, of that degree of richness, it would be possible to construct a well-formed formula (in modern logic abbreviated as *wff*) that can be proved to be true and also would not be a theorem of L if L is a consistent system. This result is sometimes called Gödel's "first theorem" and is distinguished from a related thesis, namely, that the consistency of a formal system adequate for number theory cannot be proved within the system. This corollary is sometimes also referred to as "Gödel's theorem" but more often as "Gödel's second theorem." Moreover, he proved that it would be impossible to develop another system, having other axioms and rules, and sufficiently rich to derive Peano's Postulates, that would be complete.

The point of Gödel's first proof is that *any* axiomatic system sufficient for number theory is essentially incomplete. This result entails that the ideal that the early mathematical logicians entertained—of providing a complete axiomatization of the whole, or even of a considerable part, of pure mathematics—had to be abandoned. This limitation upon the scope of the axiomatic method is considered the most important theorem in twentieth-century mathematical logic. Gödel's theorem is often construed as having important philosophical implications with respect to the relationship between the human mind and artificial intelligence machines, for example, that human beings can construct and know mathematical truths that no computer, such as a Turing machine, can capture. In wittily concurring with this point of view, a well-known logician once stated that what Gödel's theorem demonstrates "is that the human brain is definitely useful."

## Logic as the Ideal Language

In the second lecture of "The Philosophy of Logical Atomism," Russell states that *Principia* is an ideal language and formulates the criteria that any such language must satisfy:

> I propose now to consider what sort of language a logically perfect language would be. In a logically perfect language the words in a proposition would correspond one by one with the components of the corresponding fact, with the exception of such words as 'or,' 'not,' 'if,' 'then,' which have a different function. In a logically perfect language there will be one word and no more for every simple object, and everything that is not simple will be expressed by a combination of words, by a combination derived, of course, from the words for the simple things that enter in, one word for each simple component. A language of that sort will be completely analytic, and will show at a glance the logical structure of the facts asserted or denied. The language which is set forth in *Principia Mathematica* is intended to be a language of that sort. . . . Actual languages are not logically perfect in this sense, and they cannot possibly be, if they are to serve the purposes of daily life. (1956:197–98)

According to Russell, the system of *Principia* is closely related to natural language in the sense that it could capture its welter of differing types of sentences and expose them to an endless set of logical transformations, thus generating new theorems. It also represents a perfection of ordinary speech by eliminating ambiguity and vagueness. And finally, because it is an instrument of razor sharpness, it can solve certain enduring philosophical problems. Via the theory of descriptions, for example, it can explain why the ontological argument is not valid. This famous argument was discussed for centuries with varying degrees of perspicuity and success but without any agreed-upon solution. The best-known version of it is due to St. Anselm of Canterbury (1033/34–1109). We shall consider a simplified variation of it.

Let's begin with an assumption, namely, that no being can be greater than God. This assumption can be accepted without any existential implications. It leaves it open whether there is a god. It merely states that conceptually we cannot imagine anything that could be greater than God. Let us assume, second, that God does not exist, which is the converse of what we wish to prove. The proof is thus what is called an "indirect proof." It starts with the negation of the conclusion to be established and eventually shows that this assumption is false. If that is so, it follows that the negation of the assumption is true, in this case, that God exists. From those starting points the argument unfolds as follows: It is possible to conceive of a being that has all the properties normally attributed to God (omniscience, omnipotence, ubiquity, benevolence, etc.) but who has one additional property—existing. This being would then be greater than God. But by our initial assumption no being can be conceived that is greater than God. It follows that the assumption that God does not exist is false. Therefore God exists, Q.E.D.

According to Russell, the argument presupposes that existence is a property (or, in Russell's terms, a logical predicate). But as the theory of descriptions demonstrates, it is not; rather, the concept of existing functions as part of the apparatus of quantification. When one says, "Lions exist," one means, "There is something that is feline, usually of a tawny color, often six or more feet in length, and roars." In logical notation this would be written as $[(\exists x)\ (Fx \land Tx \land Sx \land Rx)]$. Likewise, one who claims that "God exists" is asserting, "There is something that has the properties of being omnipotent, omniscient, and benevolent." The phrase "There is an x, such that . . ." does not denote a property but is a way of affirming that something has such and such properties. Thus the basic move in the ontological argument that God would not be perfect unless He possessed the property of existing is fallacious because existing is not a property. It is expressed instead by the apparatus of quantification or, in terms of English grammar, by an indefinite pronoun, such as "someone," or "something." The sentence "God exists" could thus be rendered in English as "Something is omnipotent, omniscient, and benevolent." The word "something," unlike the words "omniscient," "omnipotent," and "benevolent," does not denote a property or attribute. This analysis is widely accepted today but not unanimously. There is an abundant literature on the question of whether existence is a logical predicate, and several well-known philosophers have disagreed with Russell on this point.

There were three other worries about existence and identity that the theory of descriptions was able to resolve. I shall consider the first of these now and the other two immediately thereafter. From the time of the Greeks on, philosophers had puzzled about the nature of nonbeing, without coming to any successful resolution of the issue. The classical question was "How can nonbeing be thought about or even referred to, since nonbeing is nothing at all?" In the twentieth century, this problem took the following form. We are able to make significant, and indeed sometimes even true, statements about nonexistent "entities" such as the greatest natural number, Santa Claus, Medusa, the present King of France, the round square, the mythical island of Atlantis, and so forth. It is surely true to say, "The present king of France does not exist." Or, again, when we say, "Hamlet murdered Polonius," that sentence seems to be true. But true of what?

According to the standard correspondence theory of truth, a sentence, p, is true if and only if it corresponds to a particular fact in the world. But the world does not contain the fact that Hamlet murdered Polonius because that putative event never occurred. Moreover, according to the most simple and intuitive theory of language, it seems plausible to hold that words get their meanings because they correspond to certain sorts of objects. Thus the word "dog" in the sentence "Some dogs are white" is meaningful because there are objects in the world, dogs, that it picks out or denotes. Yet "the present king of France," "Hamlet," and "Atlantis" all seem to be meaningful, even though there are no existents that they denote.

In the twentieth century, the problem of nonbeing surfaced in the work of the Austrian logician Alexius Meinong (1853–1920), who advanced the thesis that "there are objects that do not exist." In 1904 Russell accepted this theory but by 1907 had rejected it. Meinong argued that such things as the fountain of youth, the present king of France, Santa Claus, and Hamlet—which ordinary people regard as nonexistent—must exist in some sense or other. For some of these objects he coined the word *Bestand*, or "subsistence." These objects do not exist but subsist. Other objects, such as contradictory objects like "the round square," neither subsist nor exist but nonetheless have some sort of being. Meinong was led into this position by an argument that can be rephrased as follows:

1. The phrase "the present king of France" is the subject of the sentence "The present king of France is wise."
2. Because the sentence "The present king of France is wise" is meaningful, it must be about something—it must be about the present king of France.
3. But unless the king of France exists, the sentence would not be about anything and hence would not be meaningful at all, because one of its essential constituents, "the present king of France," would not be meaningful.

4. Because "the present king of France is wise" is meaningful, it therefore must be about some entity, namely, the present king of France; hence, such an entity must exist (or subsist).

## The Theory of Descriptions:

For Russell, this argument was not only fallacious but lacked—as he put it—the "robust sense of reality" that one should expect in good philosophy. As he says about Meinong:

> One of the difficulties of the study of logic is that it is an exceedingly abstract study dealing with the most abstract things imaginable, and yet you cannot pursue it properly unless you have a vivid instinct as to what is real. I think otherwise you will get into fantastic things. I think Meinong is rather deficient in just that instinct for reality. Meinong maintains that there is such an object as the round square only it does not exist, and it does not even subsist, but nevertheless there is such an object, and when you say 'The round square is a fiction,' he takes it that there is an object 'the round square' and also there is a predicate 'fiction.' No one with a sense of reality would so analyze that proposition. He would see that the proposition wants analyzing in such a way that you won't have to regard the round square as a constituent of that proposition. (1956:233)

According to Russell, Santa Claus is not a creature of flesh and blood, and no object is now or ever was king of France in the twentieth century. There is thus no sense in which such putative entities have being or exist. The theory of descriptions exposed the fallacy in the argument. According to that theory, one must draw a distinction between proper names and descriptions. A definite description is a phrase containing the word "the," modifying a singular noun, such as "the computer I am using now," or "the chairperson of the department," and it can be used to mention, refer to, or pick out exactly one person, thing, or place. A proper name seems to have many of the same functions as a definite description; according to Russell, it always picks out or denotes a particular individual. Yet unlike a description, which has no meaning in isolation, a proper name does have independent meaning, and its meaning is the individual it names. Thus in the sentence "Clinton is tall," the term "Clinton" both picks out and means the actual person, Clinton.

Though definite descriptions and proper names may sometimes denote the same individual or place, Russell argues that their logical functions are entirely disparate. Thus a speaker who in the year 2000 asserts, "The president of the United States is tall," might be using the definite description "the president of the United States" to refer to Bill Clinton. But that phrase is not Clinton's name; it could be used on different occasions to refer to different individuals. If Bill Clinton were replaced as president in 2000 by another tall person, that phrase would mention someone other than Clinton. Indeed, descriptive phrases can be used meaningfully without picking out anything. "The greatest natural number" does not pick out anything, since there is a strict proof that no such number exists. "The present king of France," if intended to refer to a twentieth-century monarch, would also lack a referent.

Russell's career as a philosopher stretched over seven decades, and in nearly all of these he produced modifications of the theory of descriptions. In its earliest versions he drew a sharp distinction between proper names and descriptions. A proper name was what in ordinary speech would be regarded as a proper name, such as "Jones," "Russell," or "Moore," whereas a definite description was a phrase of the form "the so and so," such as "the present king of France," or "the first person to step on the moon." In some of his middle period writings (as in "Knowledge by Description and Knowledge by Acquaintance," published in 1912), and in "The Philosophy of Logical Atomism," first published in 1918, the theory took an epistemological turn.

Russell now stated that a name was something that applied only to an object with which one was directly acquainted. Such demonstrative pronouns as "this," and "that," uttered on particular occasions, became proper names, whereas a grammatically proper name, such as "Julius Caesar," was not a logically proper name because nobody alive today was or could be directly acquainted with Caesar. Everything we know about Caesar we know from descriptions found in books, such as Livy's *History of Rome*. Therefore "Julius Caesar" was a covert or abbreviated description, not a real name. This continued to be Russell's view until quite late in his career. But from about the time of the Second World War to his death in 1970, Russell reverted to his original view in which "Scott" was a name in contradistinction to the definite description "the author of *Waverley*."

Complicating matters, we can also state that throughout his career Russell consistently held the position that the so-called names of fictive characters are not real names but are abbreviated descriptions. "Odysseus," "Hamlet," "Santa Claus," and the like fall into this category; they are not the names of persons but appear in history, mythology, or literature via legends, stories, or literary accounts. In the play, *Hamlet*, Shakespeare gives us a description of a certain character. In that drama the apparent name "Hamlet" is thus an abbreviation for a longer phrase, such as "the main character in a tragedy called *Hamlet* by William Shakespeare." Russell also consistently held that, no matter how the distinction between proper names and descriptions is drawn, it can be demonstrated that sentences containing proper names and sentences containing descriptions mean different things. And this can be shown by translating the respective sentences into an ideal language, such as that of *Principia*, where the difference becomes perspicuous and takes a purely symbolic form.

Thus "Bill Clinton is tall" is of the logical form "Fa." This is a singular sentence, containing a logical constant, "a," which stands for a proper name, and a predicate term, "F," which stands for a property. When the constant and the predicate are given descriptive meaning, as in the sentence "Clinton is tall," we see that both sentences are ascribing a certain property to a particular individual. Both are thus logically singular sentences. They can be contrasted with "the present king of France is tall," which is grammatically a singular sentence but which when translated into logical notation is not of the form "Fa." It has a completely different form. In English it means the same as "At least one person and at most one person is now male and monarch of France, and whoever is male and monarch of France is tall." It is thus not logically a singular sentence but a complex general one. In symbolic notation it would be expressed as a conjunction of three sentences, one of them asserting the existence of a French monarch.

1. $[(\exists x)\ (MFx)]$—At least one thing is now the male monarch of France.
2. $[\{[(x)(y)]\ \{[MFx \wedge MFy \supset (x = y)]\}]$—At most one thing is now the male monarch of France.
3. $\{[(x)]\ [(MFx) \supset (Tx)]\}$—Whoever is now the male monarch of France is tall.

In the English sentence "the present king of France is tall," the word "the" expresses singularity, referring to one object as monarch of France. Singularity (the concept of *the*) is captured by sentences 1 and 2. To say that one and only one object is the present king of France is to say that at least one such object now exists and also that not more than one does. If there is such an object, then sentences 1 and 2 are true, and if the object has the property ascribed to it, then the whole sentence, "The present king of France is tall," is true. The whole sentence is false under any one of three conditions: If there is no such object, then sentence 1 is false; if there is more than one such object, sentence 2 is false; and finally, if there is exactly one such object, but it does not possess the property of being tall, then 3 is false. But in logic if any conjunct of a compound sentence is false, the whole sentence is false. So in this case if any of the three conjuncts is false, the sentence "The present king of France is tall" is false. But if either true or false, it is meaningful. This analysis shows both how powerful and subtle an ideal logical language can be.

Apart from arguing that names and descriptions are to be analyzed differently, Russell throughout his long career proposed a host of arguments to demonstrate this point. As he writes in *Introduction to Mathematical Philosophy* (1919):

> A proposition containing a description is not identical with what that proposition becomes when a name is substituted, even if the name names the same object as the description describes. "Scott is the author of *Waverley*" is obviously a different proposition from "Scott is Scott": the first is a fact in literary history, the second a trivial truism. And if we put anyone other than Scott in place of "the author of *Waverley*" our proposition would become false, and would therefore certainly no longer be the same proposition. (p. 174)

The point of the argument is to show that "Scott is Scott" and "Scott is the author of *Waverley*" are different propositions and that this is so because the proper name, "Scott," and the description, "the author of *Waverley*," play logically different roles. Russell's argument has found widespread acceptance among philosophers of language, and until recently it was regarded as sound. But in my judgment it is not. Consider the following counterexample:

1. The author of *Waverley* is the author of *Waverley*.
2. The author of *Waverley* is the author of *Ivanhoe* is a fact in literary history.
3. If we put anyone other than the author of *Waverley* in place of "the author of *Ivanhoe*," then sentence 2 would become false.

This argument is a mirror image of Russell's. One can see immediately that "the author of *Waverley* is the author of *Waverley*" and "the author of *Waverley* is the author of *Ivanhoe*" differ in meaning in that the first is trivial and the second is not. The latter proposition is not trivial since one might not know that the author of *Waverley* also authored a book called *Ivanhoe*. Yet, in contrast, it is a trivial truth that the author of *Waverley* is the author of *Waverley*. One can also agree with Russell that in general there is a difference between proper names and descriptions. "The first-born child of John Smith" may refer to Robin Smith, but that locution is not her name.

If my counterargument is correct, his analysis of why the two propositions differ in meaning is flawed. The difference clearly does not turn on the difference between names and descriptions since the counterargument arrives at exactly his distinctions yet uses only descriptions. There is thus something wrong with Russell's line of reasoning. Frege offers a different solution to the problem to which this objection does not apply, in terms of the distinction between *Sinn* and *Bedeutung* (which I explain shortly), but it has its own difficulties. Nonetheless, even if Russell's argument does not succeed, there are other reasons for thinking that the theory of descriptions is unquestionably a major achievement. Frank Ramsey expressed the consensus of the analytic community when he described it as "that paradigm of philosophy." Among these reasons are the four that follow.

First, it shows that an ideal language can not only articulate the ordinary sentences of natural languages but also that it can reveal distinctions that such languages conceal.

Second, this fact implies that one must distinguish surface grammar from a deeper logical grammar that expresses the real meaning of such sentences. According to this deeper grammar, definite descriptions are not names, and sentences containing definitive descriptions are not singular but general sentences. This finding has direct philosophical import. It clears up a second puzzle about existence, namely, how it is possible, with consistency, to deny the existence of something. Suppose an atheist says,

"God does not exist." It would seem that the atheist is presupposing by his very words that there exists something, a God, that does not exist, so he seems to be contradicting himself. Russell shows that in this sentence "God" is not a name but an abbreviated description for (on a Judeo-Christian conception) "the x that is all powerful, all wise, and benevolent." The atheist's sentence can now be read as saying: "There is nothing that is all powerful, all wise, and benevolent." The apparent name, "God," has disappeared from the atheist's sentence. The analysis thus allows a philosophical position to be expressed without falling into inconsistency. This result has similar implications for skepticism. It allows a radical skeptic to deny that knowledge is attainable without presupposing that there is such a thing as knowledge.

Third, if one looks at the preceding analysis of the sentence "the present king of France is tall," one will see that the phrase "the present king of France" no longer appears as a single unit in any of the three sentences that, taken together, give its meaning. This means that the phrase "the present King of France" has been eliminated and replaced by a complex of quantifiers, variables, and predicates. If it were a proper name, it could not be eliminated. Because they can be eliminated, Russell calls definite descriptions "incomplete symbols." His theory of descriptions is thus a theory about the nature and function of incomplete symbols.

Fourth, each of the analyzing sentences is a general sentence and each is meaningful. This fact is key to understanding how a sentence whose subject term lacks a referent can be meaningful.

In the light of this account, one can summarize Russell's objection to Meinong's argument. Meinong was essentially confusing definite descriptions and names. Once one sees that "the present king of France" is a description, then there need be nothing that the phrase refers to; therefore, given that a sentence containing the phrase is meaningful, it does not follow that its grammatical subject term denotes anything. There is thus no need to posit the existence or subsistence of such "entities" as the present king of France, Hamlet, Medusa, and Santa Claus.

## Frege: Identity Sentences and Descriptions

The new logic was also able to solve a third problem—a puzzle about the nature of sameness or identity. This is an issue with a long history. It is central to a number of major perplexities, among them the ancient problem of change that challenged the Greeks and a conundrum about personal identity that bothered seventeenth- and eighteenth-century thinkers. Both difficulties stem from questions about the nature of identity. The two most highly regarded solutions to the problem are those offered by Frege and Russell. There is a serious controversy today within philosophy of language about which approach is preferable, and each has widespread support. Among the important contemporary writers who have contributed to the debate are Hilary Putnam, John Searle, David Kaplan, Keith Donnellan, Marcus, Quine, and Kripke.

Frege's solution is to be found in a paper, "*Über Sinn und Bedeutung*" (translated by Herbert Feigl as "On Sense and Nominatum"), that was originally published in 1893 and received little recognition in its own time but was rediscovered after World War II and has been influential ever since. Frege begins by affirming that the idea of sameness challenges reflection. Anticipating Russell, he formulates the problem about sameness (identity) in the following way. Consider two true identity sentences: "Venus = Venus" and "Venus = the morning star." The first is trivial, a tautology that communicates no new information. But the second is not trivial. It represents an extension of our knowledge. But if both sentences are saying of a particular object that it is identical with itself, how can the second sentence be significant whereas the first is not? In identifying the same object twice, are we not merely repeating ourselves?

Frege solves this problem by drawing a tripartite distinction between linguistic expressions, what they mean, and what they refer to. In effect, he is making the point that the concept of "meaning" is ambiguous: sometimes, in speaking about the meaning of a linguistic unit, one is speaking about its connotation or sense and sometimes about the reference or object it is referring to or mentioning. Accordingly, he invented a technical vocabulary to discriminate between these two uses of the term. The connotative use he calls "Sinn" and the referential use "Bedeutung." In ordinary German they are often used as synonyms for "meaning." But they are sharply different in Frege's technical use.

The difference can be brought out intuitively as follows. The term "the greatest natural number" has a certain connotation, or *Sinn*. We can grasp the sense it expresses and, accordingly, we can translate what it means into a different language. But there is no greatest such number, so it has no referent, or *Bedeutung*. In contrast, the phrase "the morning star" has both a

*Sinn* and a *Bedeutung*. The sense it expresses is that of an astral body that appears in the morning sky. Its *Bedeutung* is the planet Venus.

Frege's basic idea is that every meaningful expression has a *Sinn*, and many also have a *Bedeutung*. But the important point, as the example of "the greatest natural number" illustrates, is that some may not have a *Bedeutung*. Scholars have translated Frege's distinction between "*Sinn*" and "*Bedeutung*" into English in various ways. "*Sinn*" has been rendered as "sense," "meaning," "concept," "intension," "connotation," and "designation." "*Bedeutung*" appears in the literature as "meaning," "referent," "nominatum," "object," "extension," and "denotation." In what follows we shall use "intension" and "extension" as corresponding to the German expressions "*Sinn*" and "*Bedeutung*," respectively.

With this distinction in hand we can see why the two identity sentences differ in significance. In stating that Venus is the morning star, one is doing more than repeating oneself. One is adding new information, namely, that this is the celestial object that first appears in the morning sky. Everyone knows a priori that Venus is Venus, but it was an astronomical discovery by the ancient Babylonians that Venus is identical with the "star" that first appears in the morning sky. It is the knowledge that one is referring to the same planet under a special description that makes the sentence significant and not trivial. Frege's solution was that both terms, "Venus" and "the morning star," are identical in meaning in the extensional sense but not in the intensional sense, and it was the latter difference that made the second sentence significant.

This was a brilliant insight that he generalized into an entire philosophy of language that applies not only to words but to larger units of language as well, such as descriptions and sentences. Each can be said to have a *Sinn* and, depending on the state of the world, a referent, or *Bedeutung*. In the case of whole declarative sentences their normal intensions are propositions, and their extensions are The True or The False, depending on whether they are true or false. Descriptive phrases express a sense and have a denotation if something exists that they pick out. All individual words or grammatically correct combinations of words he called "names." Thus a declarative sentence is a name in his account and, if true, names The True. All names in natural languages have an intension, but some, as I have noted, may lack an extension. This is true of fictive names, such as "Odysseus." Frege regarded this fact as a defect of natural languages and as one important reason why philosophy should be done in an ideal language. In his regimented language the defect is repaired. Each term has both a *Sinn* and a *Bedeutung*, even if in some cases, as with respect to "the greatest natural number," the *Bedeutung* is an artificial "entity," such as aleph-null or A*.

Russell, differing from Frege, denies that genuine proper names like "Venus" possess intensional meaning. According to him, they mean only the object they denote. The bearer of a proper name is the meaning of the name in this account. This seems to raise a profound difficulty for Russell's view. Since both "Venus" and "the morning star" denote the same object, both locutions would presumably mean the same thing; if that is so, the view could not explain how "Venus = Venus" is trivial whereas "Venus = the morning star" is not. His solution to the problem is unexpected and ingenious; in effect, he denies that "Venus" and "the morning star" have the same meaning. Indeed, in his view "the morning star" means nothing at all in isolation, whereas "Venus" does. Therefore, because "the morning star" is a definite description, the sentence "Venus = the morning star" is not an identity sentence in which two names are flanked by the identity sign, but a complex general sentence that should be analyzed according to the theory of definite descriptions. The two sentences thus differ in meaning for that reason, as their differing analyses show.

The two accounts can be evaluated as follows: Frege's is generally supported on the ground that it captures the grammatical form of the English sentences, allowing both to be identity sentences, whereas Russell's theory analyzes what to the ordinary grammatical eye is a singular sentence, "Venus = the morning star," into a set of general sentences. This seems clearly counterintuitive. But the Fregean position has some disadvantages as well. For example, intensions, or senses, are not well-defined entities—points that Quine, Kripke, and Putnam emphasize—so that we do not have criteria for determining when or whether two expressions have the same sense. It also requires that in a regimented language the existence of the putative referent must first be established before a proper name can be regarded as meaningful.

Russell's account, in contrast, does not. As I mentioned before, Russell's earliest account treats names as directly referential—they directly pick out an object without the intermediation of a description, or intension. But later he construes all grammatically proper names as abbreviations for descriptions. His earlier treatment has today been revived by Howard Wettstein, Marcus, Kripke, Kaplan, and Putnam, among others. They hold that proper names are directly referential. But they add an important qualification. Almost without exception, they hold that proper names are strictly meaningless. Their direct reference theory has some important advantages over Russell's. It can easily explain the difference between identity sentences that are necessary and those that are contingent without denying, as Russell did, that they are genuine identity sentences. Thus "Venus = Venus" is a necessary truth. Any object is necessarily identical with itself. In contrast, "Venus = the morning star" is contingent, since it is possible that in the distant future the object designated by "the morning star" may be something other than Venus. It merely happens to be the case now that Venus is the morning star.

The distinction between these two kinds of identity sentences thus turns on the distinction between proper names and descriptions. When the identity sign is flanked by proper names in a true sentence, the sentence in question is *necessarily* true. Marcus calls proper names "tags," and Kripke calls them "rigid designators." The theory can also distinguish between varieties of equivalence relations obtaining between the flanking expressions in identity sentences. That is, it can—as Marcus has shown—distinguish strict necessities such as "9 = 9" from other equivalence relationships, such as "9 = 4 + 5" and "9 = the number of planets." It can also extend the theory to certain kinds of common nouns, so-called natural kind terms such as "water" and "tiger." Its scope thus goes well beyond the analysis of proper names.

But it also has its difficulties. If "Venus" is not meaningful, then how can "Venus = Venus" be meaningful? And, furthermore, if it is not meaningful, how can it be regarded as a truth at all, let alone as a necessary truth? It also has a problem in analyzing the status of fictive names, like "Odysseus" and "Hamlet," because one cannot tag the nonexistent. Yet despite these problems, the direct reference theory has been widely accepted by philosophers of language today.

These differing approaches have generated a vast contemporary literature that extensively probes the merits and disadvantages of each account. We will not further discuss the direct reference theory here but will return to it in chapter 8, "Direct Reference Theories."

## Logical Atomism

In addition to contributing to the solution of specific traditional problems, symbolic logic was recognized to have broader conceptual significance.

Within a few decades it gave rise to a number of major philosophical movements: the logical atomism of Wittgenstein and Russell in the early 1920s, the logical positivism of the Vienna Circle that originated after World War I and continued as a major force for three decades, and Quine's naturalized epistemology, which began in the '50s and continues to be a vital presence. There is a clear stream of influence from the first of these to the third. Russell's logical investigations and Wittgenstein's *Tractatus* had a profound impact on the positivists, and their work in turn had a profound effect on Quine. We shall begin with logical atomism and discuss its successors in later chapters.

Logical atomism has a complicated history. The name stems from two of Russell's writings, a monograph, "The Philosophy of Logical Atomism," published in 1918, and an essay, "Logical Atomism," published in 1924. In "The Philosophy of Logical Atomism," but not in the later document, Russell gives credit to Wittgenstein for supplying "many of the theories" contained in it. By 1924 Wittgenstein's contributions were wholly assimilated into Russell's views and were developed in ways Wittgenstein would surely have disavowed. An interesting exegetical question is how much of Wittgenstein there is even in the earlier work. In it Russell mentions Wittgenstein four times (see Russell 1956:177, 187, 205, 226). In the preface, for example, he writes:

> The following is the text of a course of eight lectures delivered in [Gordon Square] London, in the first months of 1918, which are very largely concerned with explaining certain ideas which I learnt from my friend and former pupil Ludwig Wittgenstein. I have had no opportunity of knowing his views since August 1914, and I do not even know whether he is alive or dead. He has therefore no responsibility for what is said in these lectures beyond that of having originally supplied many of the theories contained in them. (p. 177)

In the text, on page 205, there is a virtual duplicate of this comment. There Russell says: "A very great deal of what I am saying in this course of lectures consists of ideas which I derived from my friend Wittgenstein. But I have had no opportunity of knowing how far his ideas have changed since August 1914, nor whether he is alive or dead, so I cannot make anyone but myself responsible for them."

When one compares Wittgenstein's *Tractatus* to "The Philosophy of Logical Atomism," one notes obvious similarities but also sharp divergencies. By 1918 Russell had developed an independent theory, and it is persuasive that his generous remarks about Wittgenstein's contributions to it emerged from his concerns about Wittgenstein's fate as a soldier. Born in Austria in 1889, Wittgenstein had come to Manchester in 1908 as a research student in aeronautical engineering but soon developed an interest in the foundations of mathematics. At Frege's suggestion he went to Cambridge, where Russell was then teaching, and for nearly two years studied with Russell. Russell was just finishing the third volume of *Principia* and was totally absorbed in the creation of the new logic. Wittgenstein joined in the quest and began to develop his own highly original ideas. When World War I was about to erupt, Wittgenstein left England and eventually joined the Austrian army. In her little essay entitled "My Brother Ludwig," written three decades after his death, his eldest sister, Hermine Wittgenstein, describes his army service in a moving passage:

> With the outbreak of war in 1914 he returned to Austria and insisted on enlisting the army, in spite of a double hernia which had already been operated on and as a result of which he had been exempted for military service. I know for certain that he was not motivated simply by the wish to defend his fatherland. He also had an intense desire to take something difficult upon himself and to do something other than purely intellectual work. At first he only succeeded in getting as far as a military repair depot in Galicia, but he kept on pressing to be sent to the front. Unfortunately I cannot now remember the comical misunderstanding which resulted from the fact that the military authorities with which he had to deal always assumed that he was trying to obtain an easier posting for himself when in fact what he wanted was to be given a more dangerous one. Finally his wish was granted. Then, after being awarded a number of medals for bravery and being wounded in an explosion, he completed a training course for officers in Olmutz and became, I believe, a lieutenant. (1984:3)

What Hermine Wittgenstein describes as a comical misunderstanding" had horrible consequences for Wittgenstein. In a letter in May 1916 he wrote: "The men of the unit hate me because I am a volunteer. So I am nearly always surrounded by people that hate me. And this is the one thing which I still do not know how to take. There are malicious and heartless people here. It is almost impossible to find a trace of humanity in them" (Rhees 1984:197).

Although he spent long periods at the front, he was able to work on an expansion of notes he had prepared in 1913 and that, after he had been captured by the Italians, he finished. This was published in English in 1922, after a complicated set of negotiations, with a title that Moore had suggested: *Tractatus Logico-Philosophicus*. The result was the outcome of nearly a decade's hard thinking about problems he had inherited from Frege and Russell. With the exception of a short paper, "Some Remarks on Logical Form," which appeared in the *Proceedings of the Aristotelian Society* in 1929, this was the only thing he was to publish in his lifetime. But he never stopped writing and produced an enormous amount of groundbreaking work, which is gradually being edited and released by the executors of his *Nachlass*. Since his death in 1951, about twenty-five books and monographs have been published.

The first sections of the *Tractatus* contain a logico-metaphysical doctrine that is frequently described as a variant of Russell's logical atomism. It had a substantive impact on logical positivism. Its later sections, however, express a quite different point of view, which was also to have an enduring influence on logical positivism and more generally on subsequent analytic philosophy. This part of the book advances the thesis that philosophy is a kind of therapy whose main function is not to create metaphysical visions but to dissolve the sorts of philosophical perplexities that such conceits invariably engender. I shall discuss the relation between Russell's version of logical atomism and that of the *Tractatus* in the next chapter, as well as describing the effect those works had on the Vienna Circle, whose founding members (Moritz Schlick, Otto Neurath, Hans Hahn, Herbert Feigl, et al.) developed the philosophy of logical positivism.

Still, even here it is worth mentioning certain similarities and differences. Both philosophers are concerned with the relationship between language and the world. Both argue that formal logic provides the best road to understanding this relationship, and both think that *Principia* is a paradigm of the kind of logical system one should espouse. But Russell thinks of *Principia* as providing an ideal language for analyzing specific philosophical difficulties, whereas Wittgenstein believes that it embodies the conditions that *any* language, to be a language at all, must satisfy. Some commentators, emphasizing this difference, have interpreted the early Wittgenstein as a neo-Kantian, as producing in effect a transcendental argument that specifies the conditions that any cognitively significant set of linguistic expressions must satisfy.

Because the differences between these two documents are substantial, I shall approach them individually, deferring my discussion of the *Tractatus* until the next chapter. The remainder of this chapter is devoted to Russell's version of logical atomism. According to Russell, the logical system he had created "implied"—though not in the strict logical sense of "imply"—a certain philosophical position, and it was this that he called "logical atomism." As he says in Lecture 1:

> As I have attempted to prove in *The Principles of Mathematics*, when we analyze mathematics we bring it all back to logic. It all comes back to logic in the strictest and most formal sense. In the present lectures, I shall try to set forth in a sort of outline, rather briefly and unsatisfactorily, a kind of logical doctrine which seems to me to result from the philosophy of mathematics—not exactly logically, but as what emerges as one reflects: a certain kind of logical doctrine, and on the basis of this a certain kind of metaphysic. The logic which I shall advocate is atomistic, as opposed to the monistic logic of the people who more or less follow Hegel. When I say that my logic is atomistic, I mean that I share the common-sense belief that there are many separate things: I do not regard the apparent multiplicity of the world as consisting merely in phases and unreal divisions of a single indivisible Reality. (p. 178)

As this passage reveals, the name "logical atomism" is misleading in a certain sense. It is certainly a philosophy that finds its sustenance in the new logic. But it is not "atomistic," in the familiar sense in which Democritus was an atomist or in which atomic theory is the basis of contemporary physics. Instead, Russell is using the term "atomism" in contrast to the forms of idealism advanced by such contemporary Hegelians as F. H. Bradley (1846–1924) and J. E. McTaggart (1866–1925). These were monistic in contending that reality constitutes a totality whose parts are internally and necessarily related to one another and therefore cannot be separated without distortion, even for descriptive purposes. One implication of this form of monism is that no single statement is either wholly true or wholly false; insofar as the notions of truth or falsity can be applied to individual pronouncements, they are at most partially true or partially false.

It was this idea that Russell refuses to accept. Instead, he argues that there are discrete facts composed of particular things. Such particular things are the "atoms" that form the basic units in his philosophy. The facts containing them could be individuated and described, and thus propositions about them are either true or false in a straightforward sense of those terms. G. E. Moore played an important role in Russell's philosophical development. He had earlier rejected the idealist position in favor of a commonsense realistic stance in which certain statements are wholly true or wholly false, depending on whether they do or do not correspond to particular discrete facts. Moore's philosophy, which I shall discuss in a later chapter, is in no way a form of logical atomism. Yet in holding that it is possible to isolate certain statements from a holistic linguistic background and in asserting that these can be wholly true or wholly false, Moore strongly influenced Russell.

As Russell makes plain, logical atomism is a metaphysical theory. Like many such systems, including those of the idealists, it seeks to give a synoptic account of reality. But unlike many metaphysical schemes, Russell's is carefully designed not to advance any theses that are inconsistent with the actual or potential findings of science. In the 1924 essay "Logical Atomism" there is a lengthy disquisition on the relationship between science and metaphysics (see Russell 1956:339–41). It is worth reading in its entirety, but I shall simply quote a segment of it:

> This brings me, however, to a question of method which I believe to be very important. . . . What shall we regard as having the greatest likelihood of being true, and what as proper to be rejected if it conflicts with other evidence? It seems to me that science has a much greater likelihood of being true in the main than any philosophy hitherto advanced (I do not, of course, except my own.). . . . We shall be wise to build our philosophy upon science, because the risk of error in philosophy is pretty sure to be greater than in science. . . . The business of philosophy, as I conceive it, is essentially that of logical analysis, followed by logical synthesis. . . . Philosophy should be comprehensive and should be bold in suggesting hypotheses as to the universe which science is not yet in a position to confirm or confute. But these should always be presented *as* hypotheses, not (as is too often done) as immutable certainties like the dogmas of religion.

It is clear from this passage that empirical questions must be left to the sciences; but if so, what remains to be done by philosophy in a constructive way—by logical synthesis? And what kinds of comprehensive hypotheses about the universe can philosophy formulate that are likely to be true yet not belong to the province of one or another of the special sciences? Russell's answer is that there are questions about certain fundamental features of the universe (e.g., whether there are *facts* and, if so, what they are) that fall into this category. In this respect Russell's aim is very traditional; one is reminded of the efforts by Aristotle and Kant to discover the basic categorial features in terms of which all events, processes, and objects can be described.

Such approaches are to be distinguished from those of Thales or Empedocles, say, who attempted to depict the fundamental *ingredients of reality*, such as water, earth, or air, rather than the basic categorical features under which all such ingredients can be subsumed. It is now clear that they were often advancing protoempirical hypotheses that science later showed to be mistaken. For Russell such a task should be left to science. In contrast, it is the fundamental structural features of the universe that the new logic uniquely can reveal, and this is something that the sciences will presuppose in their specific inquiries but do not and will not investigate.

The most interesting fact about the world that a logical investigation reveals is that such fundamental features are *obvious*. Russell says in Lecture 1, "I propose, therefore, always to begin any argument that I have to make by appealing to data which will be quite ludicrously obvious" (1956:181–82). A few sentences later he says: "The first truism to which I wish to draw your attention—and I hope you will agree with me that these things that I call truisms are so obvious that it is almost laughable to mention them—is that the world contains *facts*, which are what they are whatever we may choose to think about them, and that there are also *beliefs*, which have reference to facts, and by reference to facts are either true or false" (p. 182). In his "Defense of Common Sense," published in 1925, Moore would also speak about certain fundamental propositions ("The earth exists," and "The earth is very old") as "obvious truisms." It is worth noting in reflecting on Russell's remarks that some contemporary philosophers, self-styled "eliminative materialists," deny that scientific theory requires the existence of beliefs. So Russell's obvious truisms are for some modern philosophers neither obvious nor truistic.

For Russell it was patent that facts are part of the ultimate furniture of the world. But beliefs are not. If there were no cognitive beings, there would be no beliefs, and therefore no truth or falsity, but there would still be facts. Facts are complex features, such as a rock's being white or the moon's being a satellite of Earth. The existence of such features does not depend on any form of human cognition—for example, whether anyone believes or disbelieves that the moon is a satellite of Earth has nothing to do with whether that feature exists or not.

Russell thus begins his inquiry into "what there is" by drawing a distinction between an objective world of fact and the human capacity by means of language to describe and think about it. This distinction is classic and receives its canonical expression in the *Meditations* of Descartes. The "Cartesian model of the mind" distinguishes between mental sensations, which are subjective, private, hidden from others, and apprehensible by their proprietors without inference, and a presumed external, public, physical world, whose existence in no way depends on any form of sentience. It is believed that the "external world" is the source of some of these private sensations but also that such a belief can only be confirmed indirectly. The gap between these two domains leads to the fundamental question that Russell and Wittgenstein in the early parts of the *Tractatus* find so challenging, namely, what is the "hookup," or relationship, between thought and language on the one side and the external world on the other, such that it is possible to mean things by language, to get to know certain aspects of the world, and to communicate one's thoughts about the world to others? Russell's metaphysic is thus dualistic in contrast to the monisms of the idealists or contemporary eliminative materialists. Logical atomism is thus a theory about the objective world of fact and our human capacity, via language and thought, to access it.

What, specifically, does Russell mean by a fact?

> When I speak of a fact—I do not propose an exact definition, but an explanation so you will know what I am talking about—I mean the kind of thing that makes a proposition true or false. If I say 'It is raining,' what I say is true in a certain condition of weather and is false in other conditions of weather. The condition of weather that makes my statement true (or false as the case may be) is what I should call a 'fact.' (1956:182)

Facts are thus to be distinguished from particulars. The distinction is crucial to his metaphysics. The whole theory turns on this contrast; even the concept of an ideal language depends on it, since such a language will mirror the difference between these two features. The capacity of an ideal language to depict accurately the fundamental structural features of the universe by means of such an isomorphism is the ultimate justification for its use in resolving philosophical problems. Facts are complex and particulars are their constituents. Some particulars are simple: these are the ultimate atoms arrived at through logical analysis. They are "the building blocks" of the complex structures that are facts. The influence of modern atomic theory on Russell's conception is patent. Just as subatomic entities are the constituents of atoms, and atoms of molecules, and molecules of the macroscopic world, so simples are the ultimate ingredients from which more complex structures such as facts are composed.

Russell emphasizes that both facts and particulars belong to the external objective world and are to be distinguished from the beliefs and linguistic units that allow us to think and talk about them. Propositions describe facts and names denote particulars. But one must not confuse the linguistic or conceptual entities with those belonging to the external world. The connection between language and reality is thus via a double relationship: first, between propositions that correspond to facts and, when they do, give rise to truth; second, between names and the particulars such that if something really is a proper name, there must exist a corresponding individual thing that it denotes.

Russell's discussion in "The Philosophy of Logical Atomism" is thus to a great extent an exploration of the relationship between facts and particulars and how language mirrors these objective features. His starting point is that facts are never particulars and vice versa. As he says, "When I speak of a fact I do not mean a particular existing thing, such as Socrates, or the rain or the sun. Socrates by himself does not render any statement true or false" (1956:182). It is also important to emphasize that a fact itself is neither true nor false. Russell says that it is the sort of feature, such as "the condition of weather, that makes my statement true (or false as the case may be)" (p. 182). What are true or false are propositions (or perhaps beliefs) about facts. Propositions are true when there is a one-to-one correlation between the way its linguistic constituents are arranged and the particulars that "hang together" in the world, as Wittgenstein was later to put it.

Russell's categorization of facts in "The Philosophy of Logical Atomism" is extensive and complex; it is the main topic of four of the eight lectures. A major distinction he draws is between particular facts—"This is white"—and general facts—"All men are mortal." The word "particular" in this connection has nothing to do with its use to describe the atoms. The distinction is important because Russell argues that one cannot have a complete description of the universe without appealing to general facts. "Suppose," he writes, "you had succeeded in chronicling every single particular fact throughout the universe. . . . You will still not have a complete description of the universe unless you also added: 'These that I have chronicled are all the particular facts there are'" (1956:184).

There are also positive and negative facts and propositions that correspond to them. There are, moreover, atomic facts, which consist in the possession of a quality by some particular thing. A sentence like "This is white" is an "atomic sentence"; it describes an atomic fact. Russell denies that the world contains facts that correspond to molecular propositions, such as "This is white and that is black." There are thus no "molecular" facts, which raises a conceptual difficulty, namely, that the notion of an "atomic" fact seems to have no contrasting term. Most interestingly, Russell claims that you cannot name facts and that declarative sentences (propositions) are not names.

"You cannot name a fact. . . . The only thing you can do is to assert it, or deny it or desire it, or will it, or wish it, or question it, but all those are things involving the whole proposition" (1956:188). His view here is thus in sharp opposition to Frege's.

As with most of the assertions he makes about the difference between facts and particulars, Russell argues his case. The argument depends on accepting his view about the nature of an ideal language. In such a perfect language "the words in a proposition would correspond one by one with the components of the corresponding fact, with the exception of such words as 'or,' 'not,' 'if,' and 'then,' which have a different function" (1956:197). Starting from that assumption, he reasons as follows:

> It is very important to realize such things, for instance, as that *propositions are not names for facts.* It is quite obvious as soon as it is pointed out to you, but as a matter of fact I never had realized it until it was pointed out to me by a former pupil of mine, Wittgenstein. It is perfectly evident as soon as you think of it, that a proposition is not a name for a fact, from the mere circumstance that there are two propositions corresponding to each fact. Suppose it is a fact that Socrates is dead. You have two propositions: 'Socrates is dead,' and 'Socrates is not dead.' And those two propositions corresponding to the same fact, there is one fact in the world which makes one true and one false. That is not acci-

> dental, and illustrates how the relation of proposition to fact is a totally different one from the relation of name to the thing named. For each fact there are two propositions, one true and one false, and there is nothing in the nature of the symbol to show us which is the true one and which is the false one. . . . Both are equally essentially logical relationships which may subsist between the two, whereas in the case of a name, there is only one relation that it can have to what it names. A name can just name a particular, or, if it does not, it is not a name at all, it is a noise. It cannot be a name without having just that one particular relation of naming to a certain thing, whereas a proposition does not cease to be a proposition if it is false. (pp. 187–88)

In this passage Russell is reporting accurately when he states that he learned from Wittgenstein that propositions are not names for facts on the ground that for each fact there are two propositions, one true and one false. This is precisely what Wittgenstein says in the *Tractatus* (entry 4.0621; whenever scholars refer to the main works of Wittgenstein, they quote *entries* rather than page numbers because his philosophy is aphoristic and each entry is, in part, an aphorism). There Wittgenstein writes: "The propositions 'p' and '~p' have opposite senses, but to them corresponds one and the same reality." As we shall see in the next chapter, there are other remarkable parallels between their works. This brings us to the other key concept in the theory, the naming relationship. As Russell indicates, this is a one-one relationship between a proper name and a particular thing. It is, he points out, "the only kind of word that is theoretically capable of standing for a particular. Proper names = words for particulars. Df." (1956:200). In describing this relationship, he adds, "The whole matter of proper names is rather curious" (p. 200). But why should it be curious? It is curious because what are called "proper names" in ordinary speech are not really proper names as seen from the perspective of an ideal logical language. This is not merely because some proper names, such as "Odysseus" and "Hamlet," refer to fictive entities, or even because one living today cannot be acquainted with the defunct bearers of the names "Julius Caesar" and "Livy." It is more complicated; first of all, when one uses a grammatically proper name, one is not referring to a particular but to a system of classes; second, one cannot be acquainted with the referent of such a "name," that is, with any presently existing physical object, including existing persons. Here is the essence of this Pickwickian view:

> What pass for names in language, like 'Socrates,' 'Plato,' and so forth, were originally intended to fulfill this function of standing for particulars, and we do accept, in ordinary daily life, as particulars all sorts of things that really are not so. The names that we commonly use, like 'Socrates', are really abbreviations for descriptions; not only that, but what they describe are not particulars but complicated systems of classes or series. A name, in the narrow logical sense of a word whose meaning is a particular, can only be applied to a particular with which the speaker is acquainted, because you cannot name anything you are not acquainted with. . . . That makes it very difficult to get any instance of a name at all in the proper strict logical sense of the word. The only words one does use as names in the logical sense are words like 'this' or 'that.' One can use 'this' as a name to stand for a particular with which one is acquainted at the moment. We say 'This is white.' If you agree that 'This is white,' meaning the 'this' that you see, you are using 'this' as a proper name. But if you try to apprehend the proposition that I am expressing when I say 'This is white,' you cannot do it. If you mean this piece of chalk as a physical object, then you are not using a proper name. It is only when you use 'this' quite strictly, to stand for an actual object of sense, that it is really a proper name. (Russell 1956:200–201)

In this view names provide one of the two ways that language connects with the world. As Russell indicates, if N is a name, it "has got to name something or it is not a name." And what it names is a particular object and that object is its meaning. So language is tied to the world via a naming-meaning relationship and via combinations of names and predicates through the relationship of propositions to facts. This outline does not capture the full richness of Russell's position. Like Moore, he was an advocate of sense-data theory. As we shall see, this is itself a very complicated subject, but nearly every version of it distinguishes sense-data from physical objects. Russell (like Moore) contends that *what we are directly aware of* in any act of perception is a sense-datum and not a physical object. Thus for Russell the act of naming requires direct acquaintance with a sense-datum.

As he says, "A name, in the narrow logical sense of a word whose meaning is a particular, can only be applied to a particular with which the speaker is acquainted, because you cannot name anything you are not acquainted with." And he adds: "It is only when you use 'this' quite strictly, to stand for an actual object of sense, that it is really a proper name." This last addition about "an actual object of sense," is another way of describing a sense-datum. It follows from this position that the names we commonly use, like "Socrates," do not name sense-data. Accordingly, for Russell they are abbreviations for descriptions.

It is, of course, part and parcel of this view that descriptions are not names. Even if they mention particular persons, the persons in question are not the meanings of the descriptions. Indeed, descriptions have no meaning in isolation. They acquire meaning only in the context of a whole sentence, but even then they disappear from the analysans when such sentences are correctly analyzed. Thus Russell's theory of descriptions rejects what is the oldest and simplest notion about how the elements of language get their meanings, namely, that every locution is correlated with an element of the world and that element is its meaning. According to Russell, this intuitive view collapses in the face of negative existential sentences such as "Santa Claus does not exist," which is both meaningful and true, yet there is nothing in the actual world that "Santa Claus" denotes or picks out. Hence, "Santa Claus" cannot derive its meaning from a corresponding entity, because there is no such entity. Hence one would have to explain its meaning in some other way. The theory of descriptions is Russell's explanation. As we have just seen, according to that view, "Santa Claus" or "Julius Caesar" are not denoting terms (i.e., proper names) but abbreviated or covert descriptions.

But Russell (and Wittgenstein in the *Tractatus*) thought there was something right about the older theory—only what was right about it could not be generalized to language as a whole. But it was right about a special segment of language, namely, about its "atomic sentences." These are logically singular sentences of the form "Fa" whose English equivalents would be sentences in which a proper name replaces the logical constant "a." They are to be distinguished from molecular sentences, which are compound sentences that contain logical connectives. For example, two atomic sentences connected by "and" form a molecular sentence. Declarative sentences containing definite descriptions turn out to be complex general sentences that are molecular and not atomic when analyzed according to the theory of descriptions.

Russell believed the distinction between atomic and molecular sentences was crucial. He thought that when the uninterpreted logical symbols in atomic sentences were given a natural language interpretation, they had the capacity to be true or false. To make his point simpler, let us return to his earlier view that proper names denote physical objects. On that construal, "Fa" can be interpreted as "Smith is tall" and is true if Smith is tall and false otherwise. Likewise, a molecular general sentence in purely logical notation—such as (∃x) (Fx) when translated, for example, as "Some men are tall"—is also true or false. It is true if at least one human male is tall and false either if there is no such entity or if no existing human male is tall.

It is clear that no general sentence would be true unless a "value" of that sentence were true. By a value Russell meant a singular sentence. If (∃x) (Fx) is true, then at least one sentence having the logical form "Fa" must be true. Thus a general molecular sentence like "Some men are tall" is true if and only if at least one atomic sentence like "Smith is tall" is true.

Russell adhered throughout his career to the correspondence theory of truth. According to this view, as mentioned earlier, a sentence, p, is true if and only if there is some fact of the world that it accurately describes. "Smith is tall" is true if and only if Smith is indeed tall. A molecular sentence like "Smith is tall and Jones is short" is true because there are atomic sentences, such as "Smith is tall" and "Jones is short," that are true. And they are true because each accurately depicts an atomic fact. The correspondence theory is a theory of truth, but Russell saw that a variant of it—by means of the relationship between names and the particulars they denote—could be used as a theory of meaning.

In the ideal language of *Principia Mathematica* atomic sentences are key to the whole system of axioms and calculi. All theorems are molecular and are thus constructions from atomic sentences. Any molecular sentence can thus be reduced to a set of atomic sentences. It will mean nothing more or less than the combination of its atomic sentences. In turn, an interpreted atomic sentence, such as "Smith is tall," has meaning because there is a one-to-one correspondence between the names and predicates occurring in it and the entities they denote. The name "Smith" means the person Smith, and the word "tall" means the property *being tall.* In the case of "Smith," for example, the actual human being, Smith, is literally the meaning of the term.

Russell argues that it follows from this view that proper names have no meaning in an intensional sense, as Frege thought. For Frege a proper name like "Plato" could mean "the teacher of Aristotle," "the author of the *Republic*," or "the author of the *Meno*," and so forth. Each of these *Sinne* (senses) is expressible linguistically as a definite description. But if that is so, as the theory of descriptions claims, the sentences containing them are general sentences. But if all sentences were general, then there would be no direct way of hooking them up with the world of fact, and logic could not be said to be a discipline concerned with truth. That it is so concerned means that there must be singular sentences; if these are to be true, they must perforce be meaningful. In turn, they can be meaningful only if their denoting constituents are meaningful. Hence proper names are meaningful, but the only candidates left for them to mean are the objects they denote. Accordingly, the basic sentences of the ideal language are logically singular sentences whose subject terms denote actually existing objects.

Logical atomism is thus a metaphysical view that claims that mathematical logic mirrors the structure of reality. The theory of descriptions is a key component in the theory. When one translates a sentence of English into the perspicuous notation of *Principia*, one can identify its basic structure and through this translation or analysis (as Russell called it) its real meaning. For example, if a sentence contains a description, it will never be a singular sentence, and, if not, it will never be an identity sentence. Therefore if it does contain a description, it will never be a trivial truism in the way that each true identity sentence is. This is why, for Russell, "the author of *Waverley* is identical with the author of *Waverley*" is not an identity sentence.

Russell gives an independent argument from logical theory to support this conclusion. Any true identity sentence will contain proper names flanking the identity sign. Such a sentence can be represented symbolically as (Ia). It entails, by means of the law of existential generalization, [(∃x) (Fx)]. That is, from the fact that Smith is identical with Smith, it follows that there exists something that is identical with itself. But if we replaced "a" in the preceding formula by a descriptive phrase, for example, by "the greatest natural number," that would entail that the greatest natural number exists, which is false. So if we are allowed to replace logical constants (proper names) by descriptive phrases, we would turn into falsehoods logical laws that hold universally. Accordingly, no such substitution can be allowed. From these considerations it follows that no sentence containing a description will mirror those basic features of the world that Russell labels "atomic facts." Those facts are reflected only in the atomic sentences of the ideal language, and these are all singular sentences containing proper names. Logical atomism is thus a metaphysical construction concerning an isomorphic relationship between language, meaning, and the world of fact.

After its original powerful thrust logical atomism began to lose adherents and has virtually disappeared today. At least two factors were responsible for its eclipse. The earlier of these was logical positivism, another philosophy influenced by mathematical logic and the exciting developments in twentieth-century science. According to the logical positivists, metaphysics was nonsense, and because logical atomism was a form of metaphysics, it was rejected by proponents of this view. A different approach was pursued by P. F. Strawson in a celebrated paper, "On Referring," first published in 1950.

Strawson argues that Russell and the other logical atomists committed at least three errors: they confused what they called denoting with referring, failed to distinguish meaning from referring, and failed to discriminate the grammatical forms of linguistic units (such as names, phrases, and sentences) from their referential-, ascriptive-, and statement-making uses on particular occasions. It is persons who use language in its various forms to refer to or mention particular individuals or places or things, and it is a mistake to think that words or sentences per se have these properties. Meaning and statement making must be distinguished, for example. Meaning is a property of linguistic expressions. Thus "the present king of France is wise" has the same meaning in all contexts of its use. Its meaning is a function of the meaning of its lexical constituents. But it can be used on different occasions by speakers to refer to or mention different individuals.

When the individuals being referred to exist (say, when an Englishman in the seventeenth century used those words to refer to Louis XIV), that person was then making a statement that was either true or false. But the words, taken out of any context, are neither true nor false. Further, if they were to be used when no such person existed, certain statement-making presuppositions would have been violated, and, accordingly, no statement would have been made; in such a case the locution would be neither true nor false. Strawson's attack on Russell and on the presuppositions of logical atomism was generally accepted as correct and became one of the main factors leading to the demise of the earlier view.

Chapter Three

# Logical Positivism and the *Tractatus*

## Its Origin and Main Ideas

Despite Strawson's criticisms of logical atomism, Russell's general approach to philosophical problems was never to lose its influence. Russell described this approach as a "scientific philosophy, grounded in mathematical logic." As a guiding idea, it was enthusiastically accepted by the early Wittgenstein, by the positivists Moritz Schlick and Rudolf Carnap, and by such later writers as Quine, Marcus, Putnam, and Kripke. What Russell meant by "scientific philosophy" was essentially an empiricist epistemology, and it was this theory of knowledge that he felt should be grounded in mathematical logic. In chapter 2, I described some of the metaphysical consequences Russell drew from his work in formal logic. It remains to say a few words about his epistemological writings, since these also had a substantial impact on subsequent philosophy. But before turning to that topic, I shall begin with some comments about Russell himself.

Russell was born in 1872 and died in 1970. His life was unusual for a professional philosopher. Like Karl Marx, he was enormously influential both within philosophy and in the broader social community. Perhaps no other twentieth-century "intellectual" attracted more followers and opponents. He has been described as a "genius-saint" by his admirers and as "the greatest heretic and immoralist of our age" by detractors. During the World War I, he was an outspoken critic of England's involvement in the conflict. His views were both widely supported and vigorously attacked. In 1916 he was fined £100 and was dismissed from his lectureship at Trinity College, Cambridge. In 1918 he was jailed for six months for his public support of conscientious objection. Interestingly enough, incarceration did not affect his philosophical productivity. While in prison he wrote one of his most important books, *Introduction to Mathematical Philosophy*. After World War II, Russell, along with Albert Einstein and Linus Pauling, became a major spokesman for nuclear disarmament. The three Nobel laureates were focal points for the worldwide peace movement that erupted in opposition to the development and testing of nuclear weapons.

Russell wrote extensively not only on technical subjects in philosophy but also on a much broader range of issues. In such books as *Principles of Social Reconstruction*, 1916; *Roads to Freedom*, 1918; *The Practice and Theory of Bolshevism*, 1920; *Why I Am Not a Christian*, 1927; *Skeptical Essays*, 1928; *Marriage and Morals*, 1929; *Authority and the Individual*, 1949; and *New Hopes for a Changing World*, 1951, he discussed nearly all those "popular" matters that the "average man" encounters in daily life: the education of children, the role of religion, the relationships between the sexes, just versus unjust wars, freedom versus organization, and so forth. His attitude toward most of these topics ranged from the liberal to the radical and was coupled with a strong dose of skepticism about the integrity and intelligence of politicians. The strong effects his writings produced were the results of powerful rational argumentation, a brilliant and clear writing style, and a caustic wit. One might characterize him as a twentieth-century Voltaire.

A description of Russell's life would require a whole book, and indeed there exist numerous such biographies, for example, by Rupert Crawshay-Williams, G. H. Hardy, Alan Wood, and Ray Monk. Russell's own memoir—*The Autobiography of Bertrand Russell*—is a fascinating document. It was published in three volumes in 1968. He knew personally and/or corresponded with most of the famous people of his time—T. S. Eliot, Joseph Conrad, Katherine Mansfield, William E. Gladstone, Pearl Buck, and Harold Laski, inter alios. His grandfather, Lord John Russell, was prime minister of England on two occasions (1846–1852) and (1865–1866), and Russell himself, as 3d Earl Russell and Viscount Amberley, was in direct line of succession to the British throne.

His mother, father, and grandfather all died while he was a child, and he was brought up by his grandmother, Lady Russell. In a characteristically witty and ironical way he describes her as follows:

> My grandmother . . . was a Puritan, with the moral rigidity of the Covenanters, despising comfort, indifferent to food, hating wine, and

> regarding tobacco as sinful. Although she had lived her whole life in the great world until my grandfather's retirement in 1866, she was completely unworldly. She had that indifference to money which is only possible to those who have always had enough of it. (Russell 1963:5)

Russell married four times (Alys, Dora, Patricia, and Edith) and carried on long affairs with a number of women, among them Lady Ottoline Morell, Vivien Eliot (the wife of T. S. Eliot), and the actress Lady Constance ("Colette") Malleson. He was a lecturer at various American universities just before World War II erupted. One position to which he was appointed ended in a tremendous international flurry. In 1939 he resigned his professorship at the University of California at Los Angeles to accept a position at the City College of New York, and an enormous protest at his appointment broke out in New York. Here is how Russell describes the situation:

> The Government of New York City was virtually a satellite of the Vatican, but the professors at the City College strove ardently to keep up some semblance of academic freedom. . . . An Anglican bishop was incited to protest against me, and priests lectured the police, who were practically all Irish Catholics, on my responsibility for the local criminals. A Lady, whose daughter attended some section of the City College with which I should never be brought in contact, was induced to bring a suit, saying that my presence in that institution would be dangerous to her daughter's virtue. . . . The lawyer for the prosecution pronounced my works "lecherous, libidinous, lustful, venerous, erotomaniac, aphrodisiac, irreverent, narrow-minded, untruthful, and bereft of moral fiber." . . . A typical American witch-hunt was instituted against me and I became taboo throughout the whole of the United States.
> (Russell 1969:319–20)

The suit against Russell came before a judge ("an Irishman") who decided against him, leaving Russell without employment. Since he could not obtain funds from England because of the war, he was virtually destitute. He was temporarily saved by Dr. Albert Barnes, the inventor of the health tonic Argyrol, and the creator of the Barnes Foundation near Philadelphia. He arranged for a five-year appointment for Russell to teach at the foundation, but the eccentric Barnes tired of Russell and fired him on December 28, 1942. Fortunately, Russell was able to obtain a contract, with a substantial advance, from Simon and Schuster to publish his new book, *History of Western Philosophy*, which eventually became a best-seller and his major source of income for many years.

Russell was perhaps the most famous philosopher of his time. His literary output was incredible. He wrote seventy books, more than two thousand articles, and an estimated forty thousand letters. Ray Monk states that the quantity of writing that Russell produced in his lifetime "almost defies belief." There is now finally a complete bibliography of his work. It consists of three volumes. The authors, Kenneth Blackwell and Harry Ruja, spent thirty years gathering the data for it. The work contains more than four thousand entries. No similar compendium exists for the secondary literature about Russell. But no doubt, if and when it is compiled, it will be several magnitudes larger.

Now a few words about his epistemological views. During his long career as a philosopher Russell changed his mind on various points of doctrine. He began as an idealist but was converted to realism by G. E. Moore. He was a Platonist, and thus a kind of rationalist, in epistemology in his early years but later disavowed this view and supported a sophisticated form of empiricism. In the philosophy of perception his views ranged from forms of realism to phenomenalism, and his moral philosophy showed a similar vacillation. Yet, despite these changes, he never deviated from his general position that philosophy should be grounded in logic and be scientific.

As I mentioned earlier, Russell's writings covered a palette of subjects that included moral philosophy, education, political theory, and a wide gamut of popular themes. Nearly all these have skeptical overtones. It is impossible to deal with such a vast range here. We shall therefore restrict our discussion to his theory of knowledge. His major books in this area alone include *The Problems of Philosophy*, 1912; *Our Knowledge of the External World*, 1914; *Mysticism and Logic*, 1917; *The Analysis of Mind*, 1921; *The Analysis of Matter*, 1927; *An Outline of Philosophy*, 1927; *An Inquiry into Meaning and Truth*, 1940; *Human Knowledge: Its Scope and Limits*, 1948; *Logic and Knowledge*, 1956; and *My Philosophical Development*, 1959.

Russell's epistemology has two main influences: one historical, the other logical. The latter stems from an epistemological interpretation he gives to the theory of descriptions and turns on the distinction between knowledge by acquaintance and knowledge by description. The historical influences derive from the three British empiricists, John Locke, George Berkeley, and David Hume. Their most important effect on Russell was a commitment to sense-data theory, a modern version of the Lockean and Humean theories that what we are directly aware of are impressions and the ideas arising from them. This theory is an inheritance from Descartes, who held that we are directly aware of our own ideas and only indirectly aware of their sources in the external world. It is compatible with this sort of view that nothing might exist outside the circle of our own ideas. To hold such a view would be a radical form of skepticism. This is not Russell's position, as we shall see. Russell's empiricism gives rise to a weaker form of skepticism, namely, that even if we have some sort of access to the external world, it can never be direct and therefore can never give us certitude about what exists "outside of our minds." This is the nature of the problem that Russell confronts and with which his theories are designed to deal.

The problem arises on the basis of two plausible assumptions: first, that human beings have minds, and second, that there exist objects whose existence does not depend on being apprehended by any mind. Thus a distinction is drawn between such things as headaches, pains, feelings, and desires, which do not exist outside the mind, and things like tables, chairs, rocks, and the moon, which are believed to exist outside the mind. The "big" question is whether one is justified in believing in the existence of such putative external objects, given that the only evidence one has for their existence is the occurrence of mental sensations. It is always possible that one could have all the sensations one normally does yet that these might not correspond to anything external at all.

For theorists of perception, such as Russell, Moore, H. H. Price, and C. D. Broad, there have been historically only three "solutions" to the external world problem: direct realism, representative realism, or phenomenalism.

Direct realism is the view that *at least some of the time* we apprehend physical objects just as they are. In this view, when one sees a red tomato, one is directly apprehending a physical object. It is the real, independently existing red-colored object that one sees. It is agreed that there are hallucinations and other visual aberrations, but these are regarded as "abnormal." The theory is that under normal conditions, one sees an object like a tomato just as it really is. Representative realism, in contradistinction, holds that even in normal cases of perception one's apprehension of the object is always mediated by the sensations one has. Thus when one sees a tomato, what one sees is the product of a complex set of processes. Light bounces off the tomato, is reflected through the air, and is picked up by the human visual system. This processes the light through the eyes, the cones, the retina, the optic nerve, and finally to the brain. The brain "interprets" these data and "reproduces" an image of the object. It is not the object but the image that we see directly. We *infer* the nature of the object from the image. In such a view it is always possible that our perceptions may misrepresent the way the world is. This view is "realistic" in the sense that it posits the existence of external objects. Its problem is not to prove that such objects actually exist but rather how we can acquire knowledge of them. Representative realism is also called the causal, or copy, theory, because light bouncing off an object produces a causal sequence whose last event is called "seeing." Presumably, the sensation one has copies the external object.

Phenomenalism rejects both direct and representative realism. It holds that it is meaningless to speak of an existing external object. When we "see" something, all we are really aware of are various sensations. According to the phenomenalist, any form of realism goes beyond the empirical data in assuming the existence of external phenomena or events. Instead, such supposed external objects are simply identical with the sense experiences we have or might have. This is essentially Bishop Berkeley's theory. Thus what one means by a physical object is a set of actual and possible perceptions. To say that one sees a brown table, for example, is just to say that one is sensing a group of data that are brown, square, and have a certain sort of texture. There is no substratum or underlying material that has the properties of being brown, being square, and so forth. The external world problem is solved in this view by denying one condition that gives rise to the problem, namely, that there are objects that exist independently of our actual or possible perception of them.

Russell consistently rejected direct realism and throughout his career vacillated between representative realism and phenomenalism. Both theories give rise to skeptical challenges whose general validity Russell accepted. His philosophy of perception is to a great extent an attempt to accommodate such challenges while limiting their impact and scope. Both phenomenalism and representative realism start from a position that Russell felt to be beyond any sort of conceptual challenge. In this sense his starting point begins from something he holds to be certainly true, namely, that we are aware of certain kinds of basic data. These he calls "primitive data." They give rise to primitive knowledge, and such knowledge is to be distinguished from "derivative" knowledge, which is based upon the former. Thus when we have a certain sort of visual experience, for example, what common sense would call seeing a "dog," what we are directly aware of is a complex visual patch: a pattern of color, shape, texture, and size. Russell calls this "a canoid patch." In such a case we are certainly aware of something. But it is a matter of inference, and therefore derivative, to say that what we are seeing is a dog. Thus to see what we call a "dog" goes beyond what we are actually perceiving when we confront primitive data. Thus misrepresentation of the external object is always possible, and our "knowledge" of such an object can never be certain.

In a famous paper, "Knowledge by Acquaintance and Knowledge by Description," first published in 1912, Russell expands and refines the distinction between primitive and derivative knowledge. Now he provides an alternative account of this relationship. As the title of the paper indicates, there is first knowledge by acquaintance. This is the same kind of knowledge he has called "primitive," or "basic." There is also knowledge by description. This is roughly equivalent to derivative knowledge. Most knowledge is by description. In knowing today that Julius Caesar crossed the Rubicon, what we know derives from descriptions in books, or from statements made by teachers or others, about Caesar. But nobody alive today was ever acquainted with Caesar. Still, knowledge by description rests on certain facts that can be traced historically to the actual event of Caesar's crossing the Rubicon. Only an eyewitness to the crossing would have knowledge by acquaintance. But this sort of knowledge is the basis of later descriptions. In the end all knowledge by description ultimately depends on, or can be traced to, knowledge by acquaintance. As Russell puts it: "The fundamental epistemological principle in the analysis of propositions containing descriptions is this: *Every proposition which we can understand must be composed wholly of constituents with which we are acquainted.*"

This principle is a version of the reductive thesis that one finds in Locke and Hume. Its main idea is that all nonanalytic knowledge derives from experience, where "experience" in turn means "sense experience that involves the direct awareness of sense-data."

In adhering to this theory, Russell was rejecting any form of radical skepticism, since he contended that basic knowledge could not be mistaken. However, as soon as inference enters the picture, mistakes become possible, and this is where the skeptic's position must be taken seriously. In Russell's view we cannot have certainty about the physical world but only some degree of probability. According to this position, one must accept as a kind of practical knowledge the information that science generates. Such knowledge is never absolutely certain but is so well established and works so well in everyday life that one is justified in accepting it as true. Russell's skepticism is thus moderate and in the end represents his commitment to the validity of the information produced by the use of the scientific method.

Russell is a kind of Cartesian in terms of his starting point and in terms of wishing to discover a foundation for the whole edifice of knowledge that is beyond skeptical doubt. Like Descartes, he asks, "What can we know with absolute certainty?" and his answer is primitive data. But unlike Descartes, he does not think that from such primitive data we can arrive at certainty about the physical world, or God, or even about ourselves. We cannot even use the occurrence of thinking to infer that one exists. What is true is that thoughts and doubts exist, but it is a matter of inference that they should be *your* thoughts. To the question "How can there be thoughts you are aware of that are not yours?" he offers a theory derived from William James that he calls "neutral monism." This is too complicated to discuss in detail here, but according to neutral monism, basic data are neutral but can become mental or physical depending on the kind of causal sequences in which they exist. Thus they are originally nonmental and nonphysical and accordingly may exist as neutral events without belonging to any person. Whether this is an acceptable answer is open to question, but at least it offers the possibility that the cogito may not express basic or primitive knowledge after all. Still, whatever status basic knowledge has, it is the foundation from which all other, derivative knowledge, arises, including scientific knowledge. Russell's skepticism is thus a version of mitigated skepticism, namely, that some information is more reliable than other information but that none of it (except for primitive data) can be absolutely certain.

## Criticisms of Russell

Both Russell's representative realism and phenomenalism are open to criticism.

The representative realist holds that our mental representations copy or reproduce the external object when we are said to "see" such an object. But the view has a radical skeptical consequence, for it is impossible to compare such a mental representation with the actual object. That is, one cannot remove the mental representation and put it next to the external object to determine whether they are similar. Even worse, one cannot know but instead must *assume* that such an external object exists. The criticism thus has the consequence that each human being is aware only of his or her own mental sensations. Whether anything "external" exists or, if it does, what it is like cannot be known at all. Hence we are left with the original problem of the external world that a view like Russell's empiricism was designed to solve.

The phenomenalistic alternative does not fare much better. To insist that physical objects are just heaps of actual or possible sense-data is to say something that is intrinsically incredible. That is, to hold that a mountain or planet is simply a set of sensations is to produce a view that nobody of common sense could take seriously. For common sense the existence of such objects has nothing to do with their being perceived or thought of. Moreover, even if phenomenalism could be defended on philosophical grounds, it would still be subject to a serious rebuttal. In the phenomenalist analysis it is hard to see how perceptual error can occur and, accordingly, how such error could be objectively rectified and corrected. To say that one sees a table is ordinarily taken to imply that one might be right or one might be wrong. But if in any such case one experiences a heap of table-like sense-data, then the existence of error seems impossible, for there seems to be no way of distinguishing veridical from nonveridical perception. The critical riposte to Russell would insist that his phenomenalism has thus ruled out the possibility of error. Since any cogent theory of knowledge must acknowledge the possibility of error, Russell's view must be rejected. And further, to acknowledge the possibility of error is, of course, to admit that the skeptical challenge cannot be dismissed.

Still, despite these criticisms, Russell's idea that philosophy should take into account scientific and logical developments has never lost its grip on many philosophers, and as we shall now see, the adherents of logical positivism (like those of logical atomism before it) found the combination of science and symbolic logic to be a model their own inquiries should emulate. The emphasis upon science was especially important for logical positivism. The beginning of the twentieth century was one of the most spectacular periods in the history of science. It witnessed Einstein's special and general theories of relativity and the development of quantum mechanics. As a result of these creative successes, a new understanding of both the macroscopic and subatomic worlds was achieved. Such breakthroughs were felt by many humanists to have significant consequences for their particular disciplines. Logical positivism was notable in this respect. It was in fact a radical form of scientism, whose main thesis, derived from a careful though narrowly focused reading of the *Tractatus*, was that only the special sciences are able to make cognitively meaningful and true statements about the world. It found further support for this view in the deflationary empiricism of Hume's *Enquiry Concerning Human Understanding*. As Hume says at the end of that work: "If we take in our hand any volume; of divinity or school metaphysics, for instance; let us ask, *Does it contain any abstract reasoning concerning quantity or number?* No. *Does it contain any experimental reasoning concerning matter of fact and existence?* No. Commit then to the flames; for it can contain nothing but sophistry and illusion."

Wittgenstein does not restrict "the logical clarification of thoughts" (4.112) to science. He says: "The result of philosophy is not a number of 'philosophical propositions' but to make propositions clear. Philosophy should make clear and delimit sharply the thoughts which otherwise are, as it were, opaque and blurred" (4.112). So the purpose of philosophy, as construed by the positivists, is much narrower than the text of the *Tractatus* would justify. In their interpretation philosophy is a second-order discipline, describing and making articulate the essential principles and concepts—such as "theory," "probability," "law," and "cause"—of the first-order discipline, science. Logical positivism based its outlook on the new logic as providing an ideal language for the analysis of such notions. Thus the words "logical" and "positivism," which together form its name, also provide a compact description of its main tenets.

This outlook emerged from discussions held in Vienna by a group of intellectuals who named their association "The Vienna Circle" (*Der Wiener Kreis*). Its original members—Otto Neurath, Friedrich Waismann, Hans Hahn, Olga Hahn, Victor Kraft, Philipp Frank, Kurt Reidemeister, Herbert Feigl, and Schlick–were mainly scientists or mathematicians. Beginning in 1924, they met weekly to discuss issues raised by Einstein's special and general theories of relativity, Schlick's *Allgemeine Erkenntnislehre* (General Theory of Knowledge) of 1918, and the *Tractatus*.

Schlick, the founder of the circle and a trained physicist, was one of the first philosophers to analyze the methodological foundations of Einstein's theories and to point out their great significance for philosophy. The *Erkenntnislehre* was an important work that anticipated many ideas the circle would later espouse explicitly: the task of philosophy as an analysis of the foundations of scientific knowledge; a conception of meaning as determined by the rules of a language for the use of a sign; an emphasis on David Hilbert's formalistic method of introducing concepts through postulates (i.e., implicit definitions); a defense of the correspondence theory of truth; the thesis that the distinction between the physical and mental is not a distinction between two kinds of entities but merely a difference of two languages; and a compatibilist view of the relationship between freedom of the will and determinism.

As a result of frank and undogmatic discussions, they gradually arrived at a consensus in the mid to late 1920s about the nature of traditional philosophy and about the principles a scientifically oriented philosophy should espouse. Their views gradually became known to persons with similar interests, both within Austria (such as Karl Popper) and outside it, including Joergen Joergensen in Denmark, Arne Naess in Norway, C. W. Morris in the United States, and Alfred Tarski in Poland. The circle's enlarged membership eventually incorporated such eminent thinkers as Gustav Bergmann, Bela Juhos, Karl Menger, Richard von Mises, Edgar Zilsel, and Kurt Gödel. Carnap joined the circle in 1926 and was to become its most productive and authoritative spokesman. This chapter therefore concentrates on his achievements.

Logical positivism achieved international fame partly for its hardheaded, intellectually uncompromising philosophy, partly for political reasons, partly because of its distinguished journal, *Erkenntnis*, and partly as a result of a provocative and sensational book written by a young Englishman, Alfred J. Ayer (1910–1989). Though Ayer attended the circle's meetings for only two years (1932–1933), it was his *Language, Truth, and Logic*, published when he was only twenty-six, that introduced positivism to the broader Anglo-American philosophical community. Because of its brilliant literary style and forceful argumentation, it is still taught in many universities as the canonical statement of the doctrine. Though Ayer later made noteworthy contributions to a more relaxed form of positivism, especially in the area of perception, he was primarily a synthesizer and popularizer and a less original thinker than Carl Hempel, Carnap, Gödel, or Schlick.

But the political aspects were also important in its dissemination. Many positivists were Jews who emigrated from Europe because of the rise of Nazism; they were joined by some positivists who were not Jews, such as Carnap, who were repelled by aggressive forms of political irrationalisms. They eventually settled in the United States and England. Feigl was the first of this coterie. He immigrated to the United States in 1930, became a professor at the University of Iowa in 1931, and in 1940 was recruited by the University of Minnesota, where he spent the rest of his career. In the United States one of his early publications (with A. E. Blumberg), "Logical Positivism: A New Movement in European Philosophy" (Blumberg and Feigl 1931), created a flurry of interest. Others arrived in the United States or England via complicated and often dramatic routes. For example, Hans Reichenbach, who had close relationships with members of the circle and who was professor of the philosophy of physics in Berlin in the twenties, left Germany in 1933, made his way to Turkey, and taught in Istanbul until 1938 when he emigrated to Los Angeles and became a professor at UCLA. Popper, though not a formal member of the group, had a long-term relationship with it. He went to New Zealand in 1937, moved to England in 1945, and spent the rest of his career in the philosophy department at the London School of Economics. By 1940 a number of the most distinguished representatives of logical positivism, such as Philipp Frank, Carnap, and Feigl, were teaching on a permanent basis in the United States. Their writings had a profound impact on international philosophical activity, and one can observe resonances of it even today in the books and essays of such neopositivists as Nelson Goodman, Adolf Grunbaum, Patricia and Paul Churchland, Quine, and Putnam.

## The Influence of the *Tractatus*

In the mid-1920s Wittgenstein was living in Vienna, and some members of the circle—Schlick, Waismann, Carnap, and Feigl, especially—had long discussions with him, not only about the *Tractatus* but about a broad range of philosophical matters. Wittgenstein had not yet developed the views that have made his later philosophy so famous, but one can see from Carnap's descriptions of their conversations that these new ideas were already beginning to percolate. As Carnap points out, Wittgenstein now thought, as opposed to what he had said earlier in the *Tractatus*, that any attempt to resolve philosophical problems by an appeal to an ideal language was wholly misguided. In his "intellectual autobiography" Carnap describes Wittgenstein's attitude as follows:

> When we found in Wittgenstein's book statements about "the language," we interpreted them as referring to an ideal language; and this meant for us a formalized symbolic language. Later Wittgenstein explicitly rejected this view. He had a skeptical and sometimes even a negative view of the importance of a symbolic language for the clarification and correction of the confusions in ordinary language and also in the customary language of philosophers which, as he had shown himself, were often the cause of philosophical puzzles and pseudo-problems. (1963:29)

The positivist focus was on the *Tractatus*, the only thing Wittgenstein had then published and which all agreed was a work of genius. It is widely argued that many characteristic theses of positivism were derived from the *Tractatus*. I believe this assessment is correct and will explain why later. Yet it is also true that their reading of the book was highly selective. To illustrate the point, I shall mention three important features they overlooked.

1. They more or less ignored its beginning half, which is now generally regarded (and which they regarded) as a specimen of logical atomism and hence as a kind of metaphysical system. They downplayed its metaphysical aspects but accepted the thesis that an ideal (symbolic) language is necessary for philosophical analysis. Like Russell and Frege, Wittgenstein contends that because in ordinary language the same sign may apply to two different entities, it is necessary to develop an ideal language that avoids such errors. Here are some things he says in this connection:

> In the language of everyday life it very often happens that the same word signifies in two different ways—and therefore belongs to two different symbols—or that two words, which signify in different ways are apparently applied in the same way in the proposition. . . . Thus there easily arise the most fundamental confusions (of which the whole of philosophy is full). . . . In order to avoid these errors, we must employ a symbolism which excludes them, by not applying the same sign in different symbols and by not applying signs in the same way which signify in different ways. A symbolism, that is to say, which obeys the rules of *logical* grammar—of logical syntax. (3.323–25)

2. Like Russell, Wittgenstein thought that the ideal language of *Principia* depicts the structural features of the world and that these fall into two categories, facts and objects. As he wrote: "The world is the totality of facts, not of things" (1.1). "An atomic fact is a combination of objects (entities, things)" (2.01). "In the atomic facts objects hang one in another, like the links of a chain. . . . The way in which objects hang together in the atomic fact is the structure of the atomic fact. . . . The totality of existent atomic facts is the world" (2.03, 2.032, 2.04). Like Russell, he asserts that facts cannot be named (3.144) and that objects can only be named and cannot be asserted (3.221). He also sharply distinguishes between features of the objective world and the language used to describe these features. Only a proposition has sense and only a proposition is either true or false. Names have meaning (*Bedeutung*) but not sense (*Sinn*), and a name means (*bedeutet*) the object it names. In using the *Sinn/Bedeutung* distinction he is clearly thinking about Frege. Wittgenstein also echoes Russell's comment in the *Introduction to Mathematical Philosophy* that a name is a simple symbol that cannot be analyzed by any definition. As Wittgenstein says, "It is a primitive sign" (3.26).

That these remarks represent a version of logical atomism in Russell's use of that term is beyond doubt. It is true, of course, that Wittgenstein's account contains elements not found in Russell. One of these is the famous picture theory—the thesis that the way language "hooks up" with reality is through propositions that are pictures of facts. Its first expression appears in 4.01, where Wittgenstein asserts: "The proposition is a picture of reality." He amplifies this remark in the next entry: "At the first glance the proposition—say as it stands printed on paper—does not seem to be a picture of the reality of which it treats. But nor does the musical score appear at first sight to be a picture of a musical piece; nor does our phonetic spelling (letters) seem to be a picture of our spoken language. And yet these symbolisms prove to be pictures—even in the ordinary sense of the word—of what they represent" (4.011). And in 4.014 he adds: "The gramophone record, the musical thought, the score, the waves of sound, all stand to one another in that pictorial internal relation, which holds between language and the world. To all of them the logical structure is common."

In these passages we see clearly how he conceives of the relationship between language and the world. The linguistic-world relationship is twofold: propositions picture facts, and names by their denotative connection to objects give rise to meaning. "The logical propositions describe the scaffolding of the world. . . . They presuppose that names have meaning and that elementary propositions have sense. And this is their connexion with the world" (6.124). Language is thus conceived as a kind of map that stands in an isomorphic relationship to reality. The particular features a map depicts—cities, roads, rivers, and mountains—are like the objects that names in a proposition name. Such objects are related to one another—they "hang together" in the world and their interconnection is mirrored by the way names hang together in a proposition.

But when Wittgenstein speaks of "language," "propositions," and "names" in these passages, he is speaking of an ideal language. Not every proposition in everyday speech is a picture; only what he calls "elementary propositions," those that describe atomic facts, are pictures. As he affirms in 4.0311, "One name stands for one thing, and another for another thing, and they are connected together. And so the whole, like a living picture, presents the atomic fact." Thus not every name in ordinary speech denotes an existing object; only the genuine names that occur in elementary propositions denote an existing object. He is here thinking of a recursive logical calculus whose basic sentences stand in an isomorphic relationship to the facts that make up the world. As he states, "So, in some sense, one could say, that all propositions are generalizations of the elementary propositions" (4.52). Ordinary language, in contrast, may misrepresent reality. The influences of Frege and Russell are palpable in this part of the *Tractatus*. As we have seen, Frege says it is a defect of ordinary speech that it contains "names" such as "Odysseus" that lack a *Bedeutung*. Russell agrees. For him, "Odysseus" is not really a name but an abbreviated description. And this is Wittgenstein's outlook as well. As he says in 3.203, "The name means the object. The object is its meaning." As the quotation illustrates, if a putative name had no *Bedeutung*, it would lack significance and would simply be a meaningless noise. Accordingly, following his distinguished predecessors, Wittgenstein believes that to obtain an accurate picture of reality we must use a well-formed symbolic logic, such as that of *Principia*, that eliminates the defects found in everyday speech. Such a language is an accurate picture of the structural features of the world. It not only names existing objects but also depicts their structural relationships to one another. This vision of the correct way of doing philosophy occupies a substantial portion of the *Tractatus*. Any reading that ignores or minimizes it represents at best a partial interpretation and understanding of the book. It was regrettably true that the circle's construal gave short shrift to the metaphysical ingredients of the *Tractatus*.

3. The members of the circle also minimized or even failed to notice that embedded in the book is a kind of Kantian transcendental argument that describes the conditions that any significant utterance must satisfy. Even more important, much of the last section of the *Tractatus*, from entry 6.4 to the final sentence of the book, entry 7, is as metaphysical as anything in philosophy has ever been. As Carnap says in his "Intellectual Autobiography" (1963:27), the members of the circle gave little weight to these remarks. In these passages Wittgenstein speaks about ethics as transcendental, alludes to God and says that God does not reveal himself in the world, and in three passages (6.44, 6.45, 6.522) emphasizes the importance of the mystical (*das Mystische*): "There is indeed the inexpressible. This *shows* itself; it is the mystical" (6.522). As the quotation illustrates, the notion of the mystical is tied to a central theme—indeed for some commentators, *the* central theme of the *Tractatus*—namely, that what is philosophically important about the problems of life can only be shown but not said. Indeed, Wittgenstein's view is even more general than the quotation brings out. He holds "What *can* be shown *cannot* be said" (4.1212). Because all the propositions of science "can be said," he is suggesting that what is of ultimate philosophical significance is something that transcends the possibility of scientific investigation. In 6.52 Wittgenstein makes the point explicit: "If all possible scientific questions have been answered, the problems of life have not been touched at all." These utterances are a far cry from anything one could ever find in Carnap or in any of his colleagues in *Der Wiener Kreis*. Here are a few quotations from a larger set of similar remarks.

6.41. The sense of the world must lie outside of the world. . . . *In* it there is no value—and if there were, it would be of no value. If there is value, which is of value, it must lie outside all happening and being-so. For all happening and being-so is accidental. What makes it non-accidental cannot lie *in* the world for otherwise this would again be accidental. It must lie outside the world.

6.42. Hence also there can be no ethical propositions. Propositions cannot express anything higher.

6.421. It is clear that ethics cannot be expressed. Ethics is transcendental. (Ethics and aesthetics are one.)

6.4311 . . . If by eternity is understood not endless temporal duration but timelessness, then he lives eternally who lives in the present. Our life is endless in the way that our visual field is without limit.

6.4312 . . . Is this eternal life not as enigmatic as our present one? The solution of the riddle of life in space and time lies *outside* space and time. (It is not problems of natural science which have to be solved.)

6.432. How the world is, is completely indifferent for what is higher. God does not reveal himself *in* the world.

6.4321. The facts all belong only to the task and not to its performance. Not *how* the world is is the mystical, but *that* it is.

6.45. The contemplation of the world sub specie aeterni is its contemplation as a limited whole. The feeling of the world as a limited whole is the mystical feeling.

6.52. We feel that even if *all possible* scientific questions be answered, the problems of life have still not been touched at all. Of course there is then no question left, and just this is the answer.

6.521. The solution of the problem of life is seen in the vanishing of this problem. (Is not this the reason why men to whom after long doubting the sense of life became clear, could not then say wherein this sense consisted?)

6.522. There is indeed the inexpressible. This *shows* itself; it is the mystical.

Given these shortcomings in their interpretation, why do I say that the positivists were correct in thinking that their main, highly scientistically oriented viewpoint could be found prefigured in the *Tractatus*? The answer, I believe, is that because of its aphoristic and cryptic style, the *Tractatus* lends itself to different interpretations, and the positivists found substantial components in it that supported their form of scientism. I agree that those ingredients are unquestionably there. It is also persuasive that one can interpret the whole work as ultimately being antimetaphysical, despite all the citations I have just quoted. This, in my judgment, is how the positivists read it. I should qualify this last remark. It is an oddity in the history of positivism that none of the members of the circle produced a book that attempts to give an overall interpretation of the *Tractatus*, despite its seeming inconsistencies and obvious influence on their views.

When they spoke about it, they invariably referred to specific passages, ideas, or themes but never attempted to provide a synoptic reading of the whole book. Indeed, the first such account in English is by a nonpositivist, G. E. M. Anscombe, in her *Introduction to Wittgenstein's Tractatus*, published in 1959. The earliest positivistic document is Alexander Maslow's, *A Study in Wittgenstein's Tractatus*, published in 1961. By this late date, about forty years after the first appearance of the *Tractatus*, positivism had lost much of its original power and appeal so the impetus to give a wholesale interpretation of the *Tractatus* from that standpoint had also diminished. Nearly all later studies are not motivated by positivistic considerations. Therefore any attempt to write today, at the end of the century, about how the positivists actually read the *Tractatus* as a total work is bound to be conjectural. Still, given both what they did say, and what they failed to say, one can make a persuasive guess about how they might have read it.

I submit that, in effect, they believed that Wittgenstein had changed his mind during the long period in which the ideas that ultimately became the published document were gestating. According to this conjecture, they felt that under the influences of his teachers, Frege and Russell, he had espoused a form of logical atomism at the beginning of the *Tractatus*. And this was clearly a form of traditional metaphysics about the basic structure of the world. But as they explored the text, they could see that at some stage in it his attitude changed. He was now influenced by a growing scientism, according to which any form of metaphysics was nonsense. Only science can tell us about the basic structure of reality. At the end of the *Tractatus* he therefore boldly acknowledges that everything that he wrote earlier in that work was metaphysical and therefore was a form of nonsense. In contrast, he describes his new conception of the role of philosophy. This is one of the last three entries in the book:

> The right method of philosophy would be this. To say nothing except what can be said, i.e., the propositions of natural science, i.e., something that has nothing to do with philosophy: and then always, when someone else wished to say something metaphysical, to demonstrate to

> him that he had given no meaning to certain signs in his propositions. This method would be unsatisfying to the other—he would not have the feeling that we were teaching him philosophy—but it would be the only strictly correct method. (6.53)

This entry is followed by the most famous passage in the treatise:

> My propositions are elucidatory in this way: he who understands me finally recognizes them as senseless, when he has climbed out through them, on them, over them. (He must so to speak throw away the ladder, after he has climbed up on it). (6.54)

The remarks contained in these passages are light-years away from the metaphysics of logical atomism. But if so, an exegetical question remains, and the historian of ideas is challenged to explain how the positivists would have answered it. Why did Wittgenstein not write a wholly new book, given the presumed change in his philosophical views? One answer may be that something correct could be found in the early sections of the *Tractatus*, namely, the need for an ideal language in philosophy. But this could be purged of any of its metaphysical accretions and used in a neutral nonmetaphysical way. That is indeed the road that Carnap and many positivists were to follow. It is also the path that many neopositivists, such as Quine, were to pursue. Quine's naturalized epistemology is formalistic yet nonmetaphysical. We thus have a reasonable explanation of why Wittgenstein allowed the early sections to remain. In this interpretation he is urging us to accept a purified ideal language. It is simply its putative metaphysical implications that should be dropped. Support for this suggestion can be found in two places, first in the preface, obviously written after the text itself had been completed, and in 4.003. In the preface Wittgenstein says: "The book deals with the problems of philosophy and shows, as I believe, that the method of formulating these problems rests on the misunderstanding of the logic of our language." This compressed comment is greatly expanded in 4.003, which states:

> Most propositions and questions, that have been written about philosophical matters, are not false but senseless. We cannot, therefore, answer questions of this kind at all, but only state their senselessness.

> Most questions and propositions of the philosophers result from the fact that we do not understand the logic of our language. (They are of the same kind as the question whether the Good is more or less identical than the Beautiful). And so it is not to be wondered at that the deepest problems are really *no* problems.

These two passages seem to presuppose the need for an ideal language. They seem to imply (1) that scientism is true—namely, that the key to understanding the nature of the world is to be found only in science, and (2) that philosophy can and should be done via symbolic languages for purposes of explication. Both are principles the positivists would affirm explicitly. They clearly derive from the *Tractatus*, and their existence helps us explain its influence on the development of logical positivism and on later twentieth-century analytic philosophy.

Two other ideas that figure prominently in the *Tractatus* were imported into positivism and were to become fundamental elements in the doctrine. These were the notions that all so-called analytic sentences, including the theorems of mathematics, were tautologies and as such say nothing (5.43), and that "in order to be able to say 'p' is true or false, I must have determined under what conditions I call 'p' true, and I thereby determine the sense of the proposition" (4.063). A variant of this last comment is found in 4.024: "To understand a proposition means to know what is the case, if it is true." The positivists interpreted these last two entries, in particular, as an early statement of the principle of verification, the most celebrated of all the tenets of positivism.

## Three Main Tenets of Positivism

Let us now leave the *Tractatus* and focus on the central tenets of logical positivism itself. The doctrine rested on three principles: a sharp distinction between analytic and synthetic statements, in part derived from Hume and in part from Wittgenstein; the principle of verification, also thought to come from the *Tractatus*; and a reductive thesis about the role of observation in determining cognitive significance, whose origins can be traced to the classical empiricists, such as Locke and Hume. We shall consider each of these elements in turn.

*The Analytic-Synthetic Distinction*

Consider the following two propositions:

a. All wives are married.

b. All wives are mortal.

Let us agree that both propositions are true. Yet they differ in an important respect, namely, how we determine or ascertain them to be true. With (a) we do not have to investigate the world, conduct surveys of wives, or consult experience to know that it is true. Once we understand what the terms in the sentence mean, it is obvious that (a) is true. We can "see" this because it is part of the meaning of "wife," that every wife is married. By definition a wife is a married female. Hence (a) is tautologous; it states that every married female is married, and this is simply an application of the logical theorem that if p and q are true, then p is true (in logical notation: $p \wedge q \supset q$). But (b) is different. That a wife is mortal is not part of the definition of "wife." We think the proposition is true because past experience has shown that wives invariably die. But suppose through a medical advance some no longer die. In that case the proposition would not be true. The important point is that one can only establish the truth of (b) through observation and perhaps experiment, that is, by what the positivists called "sense experience."

Since the seventeenth century, a distinction has been drawn between these two categories of propositions. Depending on the philosopher, such as Leibniz, Hume, Locke, or Kant, the terminology for distinguishing the members of these two categories has taken different forms. Propositions that require some sort of empirical investigation for their confirmation were termed "synthetic" ("factual," "empirical," "contingent," or "a posteriori"), and those whose truth follows from the meaning of its constituent words were "analytic" ( "necessary," "tautological," or "a priori"). The positivists accepted this general contrast. Unlike Kant, the positivists interpreted the division as both exhaustive and exclusive—every cognitively significant proposition must be either analytic or synthetic and none can be both. Moreover, they concurred in the judgment that the theorems of symbolic logic and of arithmetic are analytic and not synthetic (a view that Mill rejected in his *System of Logic* of 1843 and that a century later Morton White, Quine, and Tarski were also to disavow). From these various assumptions they drew a powerful conclusion, namely, that analytic propositions do not give us any information about the world, that is, that they lack existential import. From the truism that all giants are tall it does not follow that there are any giants. As we have seen, this is an interpretation of logical truths that Wittgenstein developed in the *Tractatus*. Only synthetic propositions can be informative about reality, and they are true when what they assert corresponds to the facts.

According to the positivists, two important philosophical consequences followed from this analysis. First, it meant that a long rationalist tradition, refined and expanded by Plato and given further impulse by Descartes and Spinoza, culminating in the writings of Hegel and Bradley, could be rejected out of hand. These thinkers all believed that a symmetry existed between reason and reality, such that by consulting one's reason, one could discover facts about the real world. But if the positivists were right, namely, that all truths of reason were empty of factual content, the rationalist tradition was wholly misguided. In effect, this was a powerful defense of empiricism. The new position did not imply that reason—and the products of reason, such as logical truths—were not important. Such truths played roles in any deductive scheme, allowing for the derivation of truths from truths. But this facilitative role did not imply that they had any existential application to reality. Any discoveries about the nature of the real world thus had to be based on observational data, that is, upon sense experience.

The second important consequence that followed from this distinction is that all factual knowledge is probable only and never certain. Everything we learn about reality is based either on direct observation—having certain sorts of sense experiences at a given moment—or is based on past observations, recalled through memory. The difference may be explained as follows. Suppose I am now observing an instance of smoke in the distance and infer (though I cannot see any flames) that a building is on fire. My observation of smoke is direct; it is based on visual sensations I am presently having. But my belief that a fire is causing the smoke is indirect; it is not based on what I am now perceiving but on a set of past observations in which I have actually seen fire causing smoke. Thus whether fire gives rise to smoke is not determined a priori by reason but only by observations, past or present. Still, if this thesis is true, why does it follow from it that observational data are not strong enough to produce certainty?

There are two answers. The first applies to direct observation. It is always possible that any perceptual act is hallucinatory or could occur while I am dreaming. In either circumstance I could never know that what I am now perceiving is occurring in the real world. But if that is so, then there could never be a time that I can know with certainty that I am perceiving smoke. The second answer begins by pointing out that the proposition that fire çauses smoke is a generalization from past experience. But as Hume's analysis of the principle of induction shows, we cannot know either on the basis of reason or on the basis of past experience that the future will resemble the past. We have, according to this account, only two possible sources of knowledge about the world: reason and sense experience. But reason is empty of factual content, so it cannot assure us that the future will resemble the past. And if we assume that the past is a reliable guide to the future, we are arguing in a circle, assuming that which is at issue. Thus even if we have always found in the past that fire causes smoke, we cannot assume, without begging the question, that it will continue to do so. Hence no certainty about the future is possible.

Hume's analysis about the possibility of attaining certainty about the world was even more general than this particular result. It led to a general form of skepticism, namely, that no certainty about the world of fact is possible. He argued that insofar as we have certainty (via analytic truths), we know nothing about the world; insofar as we know anything about the world, based on observation, that knowledge cannot be certain. It is therefore impossible to have knowledge that is both about the world and is certain. The rejection of rationalism, which held that reason can give us certainty about the world, thus resulted in a type of skepticism. The positivists accepted this result. They were pleased to accept it, because it fit perfectly with what scientists would say about the possibility of certitude. The orthodox scientific position is that science deals only in probabilities and that no scientific principle is known to be true with absolute certainty. Thus it is probable given past evidence that the sun will rise tomorrow, that water will continue to boil at 100 degrees Celsius, and that ice will form when the water temperature drops to 0 degrees Celsius. But none of these beliefs is beyond revision in light of future experiment. Accordingly, if one takes skepticism to be the thesis that *certitude* about external reality is not possible, then science turns out to be a form of skepticism.

The analytic-synthetic distinction gives rise to a third difficulty. Metaphysicians affirm such things as "the universe has a first cause," and "God is infinitely wise." These locutions do not seem to be straightforwardly analytic or based on observational experience. They are also grammatically correct sentences. As such they seem to be meaningful and perhaps even true. From a positivist perspective how should they be analyzed? Are there types of truths and specimens of knowledge that are expressible neither as analytic sentences nor as synthetic sentences? If there are, that would mean that the positivist thesis that all significant propositions are either analytic or synthetic would be wrong. And if there are such "intermediate" propositions, isn't there a special domain of human activity, traditionally called "metaphysics," that is committed to the discovery and explanation of such truths? Therefore does metaphysics not give us a nonscientific knowledge of reality?

### *The Principle of Verification*

To this last question, and to the notion that there could be significant metaphysical propositions, the positivists firmly responded no. The justification for this answer derived from what they called the "principle of verification." It asserts, in its most simple form, that no sentence that refers to a "reality" transcending the limits of all possible sense-experience can have any cognitive significance. It follows, as Ayer puts it in *Language, Truth, and Logic*, "that the labours of those who have striven to describe such a reality have all been devoted to the production of nonsense" (1948:34). Note here the resonances of Wittgenstein's remark in the *Tractatus* that "when someone wished to say something metaphysical, demonstrate to him that he had given no meaning to certain signs in his proposition" (6.53).

Consider the sentence "The universe has a first cause." It must pass the test of being empirically verifiable if it is to be meaningful. That is, in order to understand what it means there must be a possible observation or set of observations that would allow one to determine whether it is true or false. But clearly no observer could have any observational data about the first cause of the universe. Therefore because no such observation is possible, even in principle, the sentence is, strictly speaking, nonsensical. Scientism is the further thesis that only the factual propositions of science are empirically verifiable and hence that only the propositions of science are cognitively meaningful. Scientism and the principle of verifiability were thus the main positivist grounds for rejecting traditional metaphysics, literature, theology, and the arts as capable of producing meaningful propositions. Virtually all the statements made in the humanistic disciplines were depicted in a wholesale fashion as being nonsensical.

The word "nonsensical" is important here; it did not mean absolutely deprived of any form of sense but rather was used in contrast to other uses that the term "meaning" might have. Thus nonscientific disciplines, such as literature, the arts, or traditional philosophy, might produce statements that could be described as having "poetical," or "emotive," or "pictorial," or "motivational" meaning, but none of these types of "meaning" was cognitive. For the positivists, to say that a locution was "nonsensical" thus meant that it lacked cognitive import, and this meant that it was neither empirically verifiable nor analytic.

Within the positivist movement itself there were different formulations of the principle of verification. In a celebrated paper entitled "Realism and Positivism," Schlick formulates the principle in at least five different ways. In *Language, Truth, and Logic* Ayer provides yet a slightly different characterization. According to him, a sentence will be factually significant to a given person if and only if that person knows how to verify the proposition that it purports to express. And to verify the proposition, Ayer states, is to know what observations would lead that individual to accept the proposition as true or reject it as false. There were all sorts of difficulties with all these formulations, many of which Ayer tried to address in the second edition of *Language, Truth, and Logic* (1948) but with only dubious success. One of these turned on the epithet "proposition." This was traditionally used in philosophy to mean something that was either true or false. However, to be true or false, that something had to be meaningful. Therefore to speak, as Ayer does, about the verification principle as dealing with propositions is already to speak of something that is meaningful prior to any form of verification. Hempel and others were later to show that there were even more serious difficulties than this.

Still, the key to Ayer's formulation—one that became widely accepted—was the term "observation." The point of the verifiability principle was that it must be possible to describe the observations that would allow one to determine whether the proposition is true or false. If an observation could be described that would be relevant in determining its truth or falsity, it would be a significant proposition; if not, it would be meaningless. Schlick invented an ingenious example to illustrate the principle. Suppose it were contended that the universe is shrinking uniformly, and by "uniformly" one meant that everything would shrink in exact proportion to everything else; all measuring rods would shrink proportionately, for example. In such a case there would no observation one could make that would reveal any change in the universe. Because "the universe" refers to everything that exists, no one—even in principle—could stand outside it to see its supposed shrinkage. The very meaning of "shrinkage" entails that something is growing smaller—but smaller relative to something that remains unchanged. If everything is presumably "shrinking" uniformly, then nothing would remain unchanged. The "claim" that the universe is shrinking uniformly is thus not empirically verifiable and hence is a species of nonsense.

The positivists also drew a distinction between "verified" and "verifiable." They did not mean that a proposition must be verified to be meaningful, only that it must be *verifiable*. The difference is important. The proposition "There is human life in outer space" is, given present technical limitations, unverified. But it is verifiable in principle and hence meaningful. One now knows what kind of observations would have to be made to determine whether the proposition is true or not; that is sufficient to show it to be meaningful. But what kind of observations would show the proposition "God is infinitely wise" to be true or false? According to the positivists, no such observations are possible and hence that collection of words is not cognitively significant.

### *The Reductive Thesis and the Role of Observation*

The positivists also differed in their interpretations of what was meant by "observation." Following such earlier empiricists as Locke and Hume, and Russell in "Knowledge by Description and Knowledge by Acquaintance," some of them (notably, Carnap in *Der logische Aufbau der Welt* [1928], and Ayer in *The Foundations of Empirical Knowledge*, 1940) held that an observation consists in the direct apprehension of visual sense-data and thus gave the theory a phenomenalistic cast. Later, especially because of pressure from Neurath, the observed (the "given") was taken to be physical objects. This was the so-called physicalistic interpretation of positivism. Later, in *The Logical Syntax of Language* (1937), Carnap advanced what he called "the principle of tolerance," which affirmed that either observational base could be used for analytic purposes. Thus whether one adopted a phenomenalistic or a physicalistic language was a matter of convenience. But in either case, he emphasized, the reductive thesis holds that all factual knowledge can be reduced to observable data. And for him this was the essential point, because observation is, whatever its content, the heart of the scientific method. Hence for Carnap and most of the positivists the reductive thesis and the analytic-synthetic distinction were necessary components of any form of empirical philosophy. But in 1950 Quine challenged this particular interpretation of empiricism. He rejected both principles, calling them "two dogmas of empiricism." Quine was thus opting for a characterization of empiricism that, in his opinion, should strictly reflect scientific practice. Such an account required neither the reductive thesis nor the analytic-synthetic distinction. In effect, Quine was drawing a distinction between "empiricism" and "logical empiricism." Quine baptized his new view "naturalized epistemology"; it is essentially empiricism minus the two dogmas. But Carnap never abandoned either of the so-called dogmas, and, as we shall see shortly, for the rest of his life he and Quine, who were close friends, were to engage in a spirited debate about the status of these principles.

## Rudolf Carnap

The single most important theoretical achievement of any member of the Vienna Circle was Kurt Gödel's incompleteness theorem (see chapter 2). It is widely regarded as the most significant contribution to logical theory in the twentieth century and an outstanding contribution to mathematics in general. But, with one or two exceptions, Gödel restricted his published writings to logic. Carnap's work was of wider scope and thus had the greater influence in the broader philosophical community. From his analysis of metaphysics to his development of a nonfrequency theory of probability, everything he published was of high intellectual quality. Carnap, who was born in 1891 in Rondsdorf, Germany, spent most of his career in the groves of academe and, unlike Russell, was not well known outside such circles. Despite this somewhat cloistered existence, his "Intellectual Autobiography" in *The Philosophy of Rudolf Carnap* (1963) is a fascinating document. He there presents a detailed picture of the discussions and personalities within *Der Wiener Kreis*, depicts his extensive interactions with Frege, Schlick, Tarski, and Wittgenstein, and describes meetings he had with Einstein and Russell. His sketches thus provide some of the most perceptive accounts we have of these personalities and the diverse influences they had on his philosophical development.

### *Biography*

Carnap was basically an Enlightenment figure. Brought up in a deeply pious family, he gradually abandoned his religious convictions and, even before his university days, arrived at the view that man and society could be explained in wholly naturalistic terms. As he writes in his "Intellectual Autobiography":

> Together with the belief in a personal God, I abandoned also the belief in immortality as the survival of a personal, conscious soul. The main factor in this development was a strong impression of the continuity in the scientific view of the world. Man has gradually developed from lower forms of organisms without sudden changes. All mental processes are intimately connected with the brain; how can they continue when the body disintegrates? Thus I arrived gradually at a clear naturalistic conception: everything that happens is part of nature, man is a higher form of organism and dies like all other organisms. . . .
>
> The transformation and final abandonment of my religious convictions led at no time to a nihilistic attitude toward moral questions. My moral valuations were afterwards essentially the same as before. It is not easy to characterize these valuations in a few words, since they are not based on explicitly formulated principles, but constitute rather an implicit lasting attitude. The following should therefore be understood as merely a rough and brief indication of certain basic features. The main task of an individual seems to me the development of his personality and the creation of fruitful and healthy relations among human beings. This aim implies the task of co-operation in the development of society and ultimately of the whole of mankind towards a community in which every individual has the possibility of leading a satisfying life and of participating in cultural goods. The fact that everybody knows that he will eventually die need not make his life meaningless or aimless. He himself gives meaning to his life if he sets tasks for himself, struggles to fulfill them to the best of his ability, and regards all the specific tasks of all individuals as parts of the great task of humanity, whose aim goes far beyond the limited span of each individual life. (1963:8–9)

The first of his perceptive personality sketches involves Gottlob Frege (1848–1925). Between 1910 and 1914 Carnap was a student at the University of Jena and attended various courses given by Frege. At that time, although Frege was already past sixty, he was only an associate professor (*Professor Extraordinarius*). His work was unknown in Germany, either to philosophers or mathematicians. Carnap states that it was obvious that Frege was bitter about this "dead silence." No publishing house was willing to bring out his treatise, *Grundgesetze der Arithmetik* (Fundamental Laws of Arithmetic), and he had it printed at his own expense in 1903. He was also upset about Russell's discovery of a contradiction in his system (i.e., Russell's famous paradox of the class of all classes that are not members of themselves), though Carnap states that he cannot remember that Frege actually discussed the difficulty in any of his lectures. Carnap describes Frege in the following words:

> In the fall of 1910, I attended Frege's course "Begriffschrift," (conceptual notation, ideography), out of curiosity, not knowing anything either of the man or the subject, except for a friend's remark that somebody had found it interesting. We found a very small number of other students there. Frege looked old beyond his years. He was of small stature, rather shy, extremely introverted. He seldom looked at the audience. Ordinarily we saw only his back, while he drew the strange diagrams of his symbolism on the blackboard and explained them. Never did a student ask a question or make a remark, whether during the lecture or afterwards. The possibility of a discussion seemed to be out of the question. (1963:5)

Carnap says that the three great influences on his philosophy derived from Frege, Russell, and Wittgenstein. But he states that it was only much later, after World War I, when he read Frege's and Russell's books with greater attention, that he recognized the value of Frege's work not only for the foundations of mathematics but for philosophy in general. Indeed, Frege was hardly known to philosophers (Russell excepted, of course) until Carnap's *Meaning and Necessity* was published in 1947. The semantic theory in that monograph, which uses Frege's distinction between *Sinn* and *Bedeutung*, awakened all those interested in the philosophy of language to the importance of Frege's writings. One can say retrospectively that Carnap's book was the work that made Frege famous.

Carnap was a socialist, though he sedulously kept his political views separate from what he called his "scientific philosophy." He does not mention Frege's political outlook in the "Intellectual Autobiography," and one can assume that Frege did not discuss politics in his courses in logic. Carnap, who greatly admired Frege, might have been appalled had he known about Frege's sympathies with the extreme right in Germany after the First World War. From March 10 to May 9, 1924, Frege kept a diary that was not published during his lifetime. Three entries, dated March 23 to March 25, appeared in "*Nachgelassene Schriften* (Posthumous Writings)," but the major parts of the diary, which consists of reflections on the political developments of the period, were first published in German in 1994. An English translation of the whole diary, with a commentary by Richard L. Mendelsohn, can be found in the journal *Inquiry* (1996). It is an extraordinary document.

In the introduction to *Frege: Philosophy of Language*, Michael Dummett writes this about it:

> There is some irony for me in the fact that the man about whose philosophical views I have devoted, over years, a great deal of time to thinking, was, at least at the end of his life, a virulent racist, specifically an anti-semite. This fact is revealed by a fragment of a diary which survives among Frege's Nachlass, but which was not published with the rest by Professor Hans Hermes in *Frege's nachgelassene Schriften*. The diary shows Frege to have been a man of extreme right-wing opinions, bitterly opposed to the parliamentary system, democrats, liberals, Catholics, the French, and above all, Jews, who he thought ought to be deprived of political rights, and preferably, expelled from Germany. When I first read that diary, many years ago, I was deeply shocked because I had revered Frege as an absolutely rational man, if, perhaps, a not very likeable one. I regret that the editors of Frege's Nachlass chose to suppress that particular item.

In the twenty-five years that followed Dummett's revelation about the existence of the diary, no published comments appeared in English about Frege's political attitudes except for some brief remarks made by Hans Sluga in *Heidegger's Crisis: Philosophy and Politics in Nazi Germany* (1993). Sluga says:

> Frege confided in his diary in 1924 that he had once thought of himself as a liberal and was an admirer of Bismarck, but his heroes now were General Ludendorff and Adolf Hitler. This was after the two had tried to topple the elected democratic government in a coup in November 1923. In his diary Frege also used all his analytic skills to devise plans for expelling the Jews from Germany and for suppressing the Social Democrats. (p. 99)

Mendelsohn disagrees with Sluga, calling this description of the diary "quite misleading." Mendelsohn states: "The diary sustains Sluga's claim that Frege admired Ludendorff, but not that he admired Hitler; and certainly not as a result of the 1923 putsch, which Sluga's second sentence seems to imply, for Frege disapproved of Ludendorff's involvement; Sluga's final sentence presents a gross distortion of the content of the diary" (1996:304).

I think Mendelsohn is correct in asserting that the diary does not contain any comments specifically stating that Frege admired Hitler. But all commentators agree that the diary contains explicit anti-Semitic remarks. Here are several, some of which I have shortened because of space constraints:

> What a misfortune that Jews had such influence in the National Liberal party, very much an after-effect of the earlier period of reaction, which Bismarck had been unable to obliterate. (1996:325)

> I have only in the last years really learned to comprehend antisemitism. If one wants to make laws against the Jews, one must be able to specify a distinguishing mark (*Kennzeichen*) by which one can recognize a Jew for certain. I have always seen this as a problem. (pp. 330–31)

> One can acknowledge that there are Jews of the highest respectability, and yet regard it as a misfortune that there are so many Jews in Germany, and that they have complete equality of political rights with citizens of Aryan descent; but how little is achieved by the wish that the Jews in Germany should lose their political rights or better yet vanish from Germany. If one wanted laws passed to remedy these evils, the first question to be answered would be: How can one distinguish Jews from non-Jews for certain? That may have been relatively easy sixty years ago. Now, it appears to me to be quite difficult. Perhaps one must be satisfied with fighting the ways of thinking (*Gesinnung*) which show up in the activities of the Jews and are so harmful, and to punish exactly these activities with the loss of civil rights and to make the achievement of civil rights more difficult. (p. 336)

As Mendelsohn points out in a footnote, a defining distinction between Jews and non-Jews was established eleven years later, in 1935 during the Nazi dictatorship. In excluding all Jews from citizenship, it was stipulated that "he is a Jew who is descended from at least three grandparents who are purely of Jewish race." Though Mendelsohn is correct in saying that the diary contains no explicit statement in which Frege says that Hitler is one of his heroes, something close to admiration is implied in one of the last entries, dated May 5, 1924: "Adolf Hitler writes correctly in the April issue of *Deutschlands Erneuerung*, that Germany no longer had a clear political goal after the departure of Bismarck" (pp. 338–39).

An interesting historical question is why Frege abandoned the liberalism he says he espoused in earlier years for such a racist and reactionary perspective. Could it have been the profound disappointments, late in life, about the lack of recognition in Germany for his work? Carnap gives us a portrait of an embittered human being, and it is not unreasonable to infer that such discontent may well have led to the changes in his political views. No doubt, Carnap would have been horrified had he known of Frege's political opinions. But I suspect, given his rational approach to life, Carnap would have distinguished those convictions from Frege's abilities as a logician and, accordingly, that his professed admiration for him, at least in that respect, would not have altered.

One of the most interesting sections of the "Intellectual Autobiography" treats Carnap's interrelationships with Wittgenstein. Here is a case of a rational, highly gifted college professor who encounters a mystical genius. That these two minds could never function on the same plane of communication is not unexpected. Carnap, in particular, never understood why Wittgenstein finally cut off all communication with him. It is ironical that rational understanding failed in this case. Although he wrote his autobiography about forty years after he first met Wittgenstein, Carnap continued to say that "Wittgenstein was perhaps the philosopher who, besides Russell and Frege, had the greatest influence on my thinking." Let us look at Wittgenstein in 1927 through Carnap's eyes:

> Before the first meeting, Schlick admonished us urgently not to start a discussion of the kind to which we were accustomed in the Circle, because Wittgenstein did not want such a thing under any circumstances. We should even be cautious in asking questions, because Wittgenstein was very sensitive and easily disturbed by a direct question The best approach, Schlick said, would be to let Wittgenstein talk and then ask only very cautiously for the necessary elucidations.
>
> When I met Wittgenstein, I saw that Schlick's warnings were fully justified. But his behavior was not caused by any arrogance. In general, he was of a sympathetic temperament and very kind; but he was hypersensitive and easily irritated. Whatever he said was always interesting

and stimulating, and the way in which he expressed it was often fascinating. His point of view and his attitude toward people and problems, even theoretical problems, were much more similar to those of a creative artist than to a scientist; one might almost say, similar to those of a religious prophet or seer. When he started to formulate his view on some specific problem, we often felt the internal struggle that occurred in him at that very moment, a struggle by which he tried to penetrate from darkness to light under an intensive and painful strain, which was even visible on his most expressive face. When finally, sometimes after a prolonged arduous effort, his answer came forth, his statement stood before us like a newly created piece of art or a divine revelation. . . . The impression he made on us was as if insight came to him as through a divine inspiration, so that we could not help feeling that any sober rational comment or analysis of it would be a profanation.

Thus, there was a striking difference between Wittgenstein's attitude toward philosophical problems and that of Schlick and myself. Our attitude toward philosophical problems was not very different from that which scientists have toward their problems. For us the discussion of doubts and objections of others seemed the best way of testing a new idea in the field of philosophy just as much as in the fields of science; Wittgenstein, on the other hand, tolerated no critical examination by others, once the insight had been gained by an act of inspiration. . . . Earlier when we were reading Wittgenstein's book in the Circle, I had erroneously believed that his attitude toward metaphysics was similar to ours. I had not paid sufficient attention to the statements in his book about the mystical, because his feelings and thoughts in this area were too divergent from mine. . . . Even at the times when the contrast in *Weltanschauung* and basic personal attitude became apparent, I found the association with him most interesting, exciting, and rewarding. Therefore, I regretted it when he broke off the contact. From the beginning of 1929 on, Wittgenstein wished to meet only with Schlick and Waismann, no longer with me and Feigl, who had also become acquainted with him in the meantime, let alone with the Circle. Although the difference in our attitudes and personalities expressed itself only on certain occasions, I understood very well that Wittgenstein felt it all the time and, unlike me, was disturbed by it. He said to Schlick that he could talk only with somebody who "holds his hand."

(1963:25–28)

In reflecting on his conversations with Wittgenstein and in rethinking the *Tractatus* in the light of them, Carnap decided that their views differed in three fundamental respects. First, he and the members of the circle had a "lively interest" in science and mathematics, whereas Wittgenstein, according to Carnap, looked on these fields with an attitude of indifference and even contempt. The histories of British and American philosophies in the post–World War II world reflect these divergencies: the Americans were, generally speaking, more influenced by Carnap than by Wittgenstein, and the converse was true in England. Second, Wittgenstein and Carnap differed over the relevance of constructed language systems. For Carnap they were indispensable for the analysis of philosophical problems, whereas Wittgenstein thought just the opposite. Again, the majority of British philosophers were to share Wittgenstein's position and the Americans that of Carnap. Third, in the *Tractatus* Wittgenstein claims that the relationship between a sentence and a fact shows itself but cannot be said. Carnap, accepting Tarski's views about the difference between a metalanguage and an object language, argues that it is possible to construct a theory about language in which the properties of language could be both shown and said. This idea was to lead him later to a theory that he called "the logical syntax" of language. For the later Wittgenstein, because the problem arose only for an ideal language and because he regarded such languages as irrelevant to the solution of philosophical problems, the issue was moot. His followers in England were of a similar persuasion.

Shortly after their last contact, Wittgenstein left Vienna for Cambridge, where he began to work out his "new method," a philosophical conception of great originality and widespread influence. It has had an enormous impact both within philosophy and in broader intellectual circles, in psychology, anthropology, linguistics, sociology, and literature. We shall discuss these post-Tractarian ideas in chapter 5. Carnap remained in Europe, teaching at Prague University from 1931 to 1935, until the rise of Nazism in the Sudeten impelled him to come to the United States, where he spent the rest of his professional life. With the exception of his contributions to probability theory, his later career consisted less in inventing new ways of thinking about philosophical problems than in deepening and expanding the conceptions that he and the other members of the circle had developed earlier. These ideas were extremely fruitful and, as I have noted, much of subsequent American philosophy has been carried out in their spirit.

*Carnap's Philosophy*

Carnap's writings are so extensive that I cannot possibly hope to discuss even a fraction of them. Instead, because of their philosophical significance, I shall pick out two of his books for brief discussions.

His earliest major work, published in 1928, was *Der logische Aufbau der Welt* (The Logical Construction of the World). Here a theme he was never to abandon first appears. He calls it "rational reconstruction." We recall that the positivists were basically scientistically minded philosophers who held that only science can give us genuine knowledge about the world. But the question then arises: what is left for philosophy to do? We saw that, following Wittgenstein, they said that philosophy could play a role, namely, that of explicating the main concepts of science and thus of achieving a more perspicuous view of the nature of human knowledge. What Carnap calls rational reconstruction is a variant of the task of explication. The two words, "rational" and "reconstruction," are important here. "Rational" in this context means giving a second-order account of the nature of scientific knowledge that is wholly justified. It begins with data that are certain and from them gradually builds up a picture of the macroscopic world that scientific laws describe. The logical order—and "logical" and "rational" have much the same meaning for Carnap—of our scientific knowledge is not the actual order that humans follow in arriving at such knowledge. We normally and preanalytically begin by noting certain phenomena in human experience and then, by means of the sophisticated techniques of science, arrive at principles that provide a deeper and more thorough explanation of these phenomena. The scientific order of discovery is thus the opposite of the natural prescientific order. Scientific principles allow us to explain, for example, why the same natural laws cover such diverse phenomena as the tides, apples falling from trees, and the revolution of the moon about the Earth. But it is these phenomena we notice before we develop a scientific explanation of them. A "reconstruction" is thus different from a "construction." The reconstruction in fact reverses the natural order of discovery. It starts from the most certain data and on that basis gives a rational picture that explains how scientific knowledge is possible.

The reconstructive methodology of the *Aufbau* is reductionist. It begins by laying out a series of definitions that reduces a field of data to a limited set of concepts called "the basis," a process that is carried out by a logical system based on *Principia Mathematica*. We immediately see Carnap's emphasis upon the importance of an ideal language for philosophical purposes. Carnap calls such a language a "constitution system." It is a structure of exact definitions and theorems. In this particular case its application is to epistemology. According to Carnap, all known objects fall into four categories: sociocultural entities, other minds, physical objects, and one's private sensations. In reconstructing our system of knowledge, the *Aufbau* starts from private sensations: they are certain in a way in which the other classes of objects are not. Its key concept is a single primitive asymmetrical relationship, *remembrance of similarity*, (probably derived from Russell's *Our Knowledge of the External World* of 1914 and the calculus of relations in *Principia Mathematica*). Carnap is able to define such notions as "class of qualities," "similarity of qualities," "sense class," "sensation," "neighboring colors," and certain concepts of temporal succession. This allows for a construction of the space-time world whose sensible qualities could be assigned to its points. He is then able to define "visual objects" and "my own body." This done, he carries the construction further, to be able to characterize the world of perception, the biological world, and, finally, human cultural objects. The result is a rational picture of the knowledge that science, and to some extent social science, has of various objects and phenomena.

In the final section of the *Aufbau* Carnap discusses the relevance of constitution theory for philosophy. His main concern is the relationship between the mental and the physical, a problem that is central to the Cartesian tradition. He distinguishes empirical questions about the relationship from philosophical questions. The relationship between the events in one's brain and one's felt experiences is a scientific question, as distinct from any interpretation placed on this interaction, such as whether the mental is immaterial. The latter he declares to be metaphysical and not susceptible to cognitive resolution. This distinction, which he emphasized in his later publications, leads to a view he never abandoned, namely, that a discrimination should be drawn between hypotheses that are verifiable in principle, and hence cognitively meaningful, and those that are not. All metaphysical views are relegated to the latter category.

Ideas that first surfaced in the *Aufbau* were to generate two interesting consequences in his later philosophy. The first was that the construction actually followed in the *Aufbau* that used sense-data as a basis was not necessary. A physical object basis could be used for a construction as well, and Carnap later showed how such a construction could be carried out. The choice was essentially arbitrary and a matter of preference. He eventually formulated this notion as his "principle of tolerance." It made no philosophical or ontological difference how one started any such constitutional system. The second important consequence concerned the analytic-synthetic distinction, which Quine was to reject vehemently as necessary to any form of empirical philosophy. Carnap argues that empirical questions (i.e., scientific questions) are sharply to be distinguished from questions about the basis from which a constitutional system should start. Thus a question like "Was the Trojan War an historical event or merely a product of Homer's imagination?" was an empirical question, whereas in contrast "Is there a world external to our sensations?" was a metaphysical question and could not be incorporated into a constitutional system. This led him eventually to distinguish between "framework" questions about wholesale constitutional systems, or theories, and the "internal questions" that arise in such systems. The former are analytic, the latter synthetic. The analytic-synthetic distinction was thus transformed, in his later writings, into the distinction between external and internal statements. Quine was never to accept even this reinterpretation of the analytic-synthetic.

I turn now to Carnap's *Meaning and Necessity* of 1947, a major study in semantic theory. In his writings before he came to America, such as *Logische Syntax der Sprache*, published in 1934, and *Philosophy and Logical Syntax*, published in 1935, Carnap maintained that philosophical problems are primarily syntactical in character. But under the influence of Tarski's semantic analyses, such as his formulation of a semantic conception of truth, Carnap decided that logical analysis must transcend syntax, which is the study of the structural relationships between linguistic expressions without regard to their meaning. His view, after arriving in the United States, was that logical analysis must be extended to semantics, that is, to those notions that involve meaning and truth. In rapid order he published a series of books and papers showing how semantics could be treated via an ideal language. *Meaning and Necessity* culminated this series. It is an attempt to develop a regimented metalanguage that could be used for various philosophical purposes. Carnap indeed applies the language to the explication of certain modal terms, such as "possible," and "necessary," which have played important roles in the history of philosophy, where their use is vague. His explication gives them precise meaning. He also shows how his system can solve the famous problem of the paradox of analysis. Because analysis is what most English and American philosophers had engaged in since the beginning of the century, the paradox presented a genuine problem for them. It can be stated as follows. If we call a term to be analyzed, say, "brother," the *analysandum*, and the locution "male sibling," which purports to capture its exact meaning, the *analysans*, and we call the product of this process the *analysis*, we face the following difficulty. If the analysans is synonymous with the analysandum, the analysis is trivial and nothing has been learned by the process. But if the analysans is not synonymous with the analysandum, then the analysis is false. But either the analysans is or is not synonymous with the analysandum, so all analysis is either trivial or false. Because most analytic philosophers have presupposed that their explications of various concepts, including those of science, give us new information and a new understanding of the meaning of those notions, the paradox presented them with a profound problem. One of the results that Carnap attempts to achieve in *Meaning and Necessity* is a solution to the paradox. It falls out as a special case of the general semantic theory he develops there.

Carnap begins by showing how an ideal semantic metalanguage can be construed. The method applies to expressions of a system he calls "S." Such expressions he labels "designators." The class of designators includes declarative sentences, individual expressions (i.e., individual constants or descriptions), and predicators (predicate constants, compound predicate expressions, including abstract expressions). The metalanguage S is constructed by means of four types of rules: rules of designation, rules of truth, rules of transformation, and rules of ranges. Rules of designation, for instance, will connect a designator in the metalanguage, such as "s," with a particular individual, Scott, and "w" with the book *Waverley*. Other rules govern designation for predicates. "Hx" is thus translated as "x is human." Rules of truth are complicated. Carnap gives a rule of truth for atomic sentences (which he has previously defined). It reads: An atomic sentence, Si (containing a predicate and individual constant), is true if and only if the individual to which the constant refers has the property to which the predicate refers. Thus the symbolic sentence "Bs" is true if and only if Scott is a biped. Rules of truth for all the connectives are given. The rule of truth for "or" is: A sentence (Gi v Gj) is true in Si if and only if at least one of its two components is true.

Various terms used in older philosophical texts—such as "analytic," "synthetic," "self-contradiction," "logically equivalent," "factual"—are given precise explications in terms of these rules. The basic concept, which allows for the explication of these notions, is that of a "state-description." Carnap defines it as a class of sentences that contains for every atomic sentence either this sentence or its negation but not both and no other sentences. A range is the class of all those state-descriptions in which a given sentence, Gi, holds. Thus "analytic" is replaced by "L-true" in Si. "L-true" means "logically true," so a sentence, Gi, is L-true if and only if it holds in every state-description in Si. "Self-contradiction" is replaced by "L-false," which is defined as ~Gi is L-True, and "logically equivalent" is defined as Gi L-implies Gj in Si if and only if Gi ⊃ Gj is L-true. A distinction is drawn between extensional and nonextensional contexts (e.g., a belief sentence such as "Jones believes that Alameda is in California" is nonextensional), and inferences are then drawn as to which kinds of expressions can replace others in these different contexts while preserving synonymity and/or truth.

Carnap develops a new notion, "intensional isomorphism," which allows him to solve the paradox of analysis. According to his theory, the analysans and the analysandum can be intensionally isomorphic, and thus synonymous, without being trivial. The correctness of this account has been questioned by various writers, such as Benson Mates and Leonard Linsky, but the issues are too complicated to be explored further here.

A profound criticism of Carnap's entire approach to philosophy is to be found in a review by Gilbert Ryle entitled "Discussion of Rudolf Carnap: *Meaning and Necessity*," first published in *Philosophy* in 1949. I quote two passages that capture the tone of the review:

> He still likes to construct artificial 'languages' (which are not languages but codes), and he still interlards his formulae with unhandy because, for English speakers, unsaying Gothic letters. But the expository importance of these encoded formulae seems to be dwindling. Indeed I cannot satisfy myself that they have more than a ritual value. They do not function as a sieve against vagueness, ambiguity or sheer confusion, and they are not used for the abbreviation or formalization of proofs. Calculi without calculations seem to be gratuitous algebra. (1971:225)

> My chief impression of this book is that it is an astonishing blend of technical sophistication with philosophical naiveté. Its theories belong to the age that waxed with Mill and began to wane soon after the *Principles of Mathematics*. The muddled terminology of extension and

> intension which belonged to the muddled and obsolete doctrine of terms is disinterred in order to help construct a two-dimensional relational theory of meaning, at a time when it ought to be notorious that relational theories of meaning will not do. Carnap's influence on philosophers and logicians is very strong. The importance of semantic problems in philosophy and logic cannot be over-estimated. It is because I fear that the solutions of these problems may be impeded by the dissemination of his mistakes that I have reviewed so scoldingly the treatise of a thinker whose views are beginning to be regarded as authoritative. (235)

Despite such criticisms, Carnap's work was widely accepted, especially in the United States. It was also, for complicated reasons, gradually disassociated from the kinds of objections philosophers were to make of canonical forms of positivism. Orthodox positivism rested on the verification principle, the analytic-synthetic distinction, and a special form of reductionism that emphasized the role of observation in any empirical philosophy. All three tenets were to be challenged vigorously in the years to come.

### *Criticisms of Positivism*

Such challenges were generally regarded as successful, which may help explain why logical positivism (at least in its canonical form) has disappeared from the contemporary stage. Let us explore some objections to the principle of verification here and reserve a discussion of problems about the analytic-synthetic distinction and the reductive thesis until the chapter 7, which is devoted to Quine. First, the positivists could never overcome several "internal" criticisms. These concerned the status of the principle of verification itself. If it were cognitively significant, then, according to the theory, it must be either analytic or synthetic. If the former, it was empty of factual content. If the latter, it had to be verifiable. But how would one go about verifying it? What kind of observations would show that it is either true or false?

Unfortunately, nobody could make a convincing case that it was susceptible to observation at all, and thus, by its own criterion, it was cognitively meaningless. Some positivists suggested that it could be interpreted as a heuristic principle—namely, that it was a useful guide for separating nonsense from cognitive sense. But this simply begged the question. Others argued that it represents a linguistic proposal that provides a reasonably close analysis of the explicandum "cognitively meaningful locution"—and that this claim implies an empirical assertion. Those following Carnap suggested that such an explication achieves a "rational reconstruction" of the explicandum. But proposals and rational reconstructions are neither true nor false, so strictly speaking even these suggestions did not save the principle. It thus became clear that the principle of verification was part of the disease the theory was designed to cure.

A second difficulty arose from attempts to express the principle precisely. I mentioned earlier that in the second edition of *Language, Truth, and Logic* (1948) Ayer proposes various formulations designed to avoid vagueness and certain counterexamples. His final version states, in effect, that a sentence, S, has empirical import if from S, in conjunction with suitable subsidiary hypotheses, it is possible to derive observation sentences that are not derivable from the subsidiary hypothesis alone. In a paper published two years later, "Problems and Changes in the Empiricist Criterion of Meaning," Carl G. Hempel shows that such a formulation could not accommodate counterinstances. According to Hempel, Ayer's criterion allows empirical import to any sentence whatever. Thus let us assume that the sentence, S, namely, "The absolute is perfect," is meaningless by the principle of verification. We can then form a new sentence, R, a subsidiary hypothesis in Ayer's terms, "If the absolute is perfect, then this apple is red." S and R together entail the observation sentence "This apple is red," which does not follow from either S or R taken singly. This shows that any meaningless sentence can be used as a subsidiary hypothesis in a well-constructed formula to entail any observation sentence. Hence Ayer's criterion is too liberal. In none of the subsequent literature has any successful formulation been achieved.

A third objection derived from J. L. Austin's speech act theory. Austin identified a group of sentences, "performatives," which play special roles in everyday speech. These locutions look like statements, but they do not make assertions or claims and, accordingly, are neither true nor false. According to Austin, they have the characteristic that in saying something, one is doing something. Two examples: In the marriage ceremony a minister may utter the sentence "I now pronounce you husband and wife." His saying those words in that particular circumstance is a way of marrying persons. A woman who breaks a bottle of champagne on the prow of ship as it is being launched while saying "I name you *Elizabeth II*" is naming the vessel. It would be nonsense to claim that the utterances of the minister and of the woman are either true or false. The notions of truth and falsity do not apply to such speech acts. Nevertheless they are perfectly meaningful and are understood by all those participating in such ceremonies. The verification principle would rule them out as meaningless. But clearly they are not, so the verification principle is to be rejected as a criterion of meaningfulness.

Apart from this problem, the attitude that science and science alone can provide significant information about reality did not convince or appeal to some philosophers. They believed that they could make assertions about the real world that were not only meaningful but true—and that these were not propositions of science. A major philosopher who espoused this point of view was G. E. Moore. Moore is one of the initiators of an informalist way of doing philosophy and is probably the source of twentieth-century philosophical analysis. His commonsense outlook and his patient and meticulous scrutinizing of the meaning of certain assertions were to have a profound influence on his contemporaries and successors. In particular, they showed there were alternatives to logical positivism and indeed to any form of scientism. It is one of the curiosities of the history of twentieth-century philosophy that Moore seems wholly oblivious to Carnap's writings. Carnap was a younger contemporary of Moore's and their periods of greatest creativity overlapped. They both did work of high visibility from the mid-1920s to the mid-1940s. Both were influenced by Russell and Wittgenstein, yet Moore was not only not moved by Carnap's achievements: he does not even seem to be aware of them. Perhaps his distrust of doing philosophy in a formalist way is the reason for his silence. But whatever the reason, Carnap's philosophy plays no significant role in Moore's thought.

Chapter Four

# G. E. Moore: A Ton of Bricks

## Biography

George Edward Moore was born in 1873 in Upper Norwood, a suburb of London, and died in Cambridge in 1958. Beginning with a famous book, *Principia Ethica*, and an equally celebrated article, "Refutation of Idealism," both published in 1903, he continued throughout his long career to make fundamental contributions to philosophy. Any list of the most illustrious British philosophers of the twentieth century would surely include Moore as a prominent member. Like Russell and Wittgenstein, he had his admirers and critics. In an obituary that appeared in the *Manchester Guardian* of October 25, 1958, one of his champions, C. D. Broad, wrote:

> It is doubtful whether any philosopher known to history has excelled or even equalled Moore in sheer power of analysing problems, detecting and exposing fallacies and ambiguities, and formulating and working out alternative possibilities. He knew his own limitations, and within the field of absolutely fundamental problems to which he confined himself, he illuminated and transformed every subject which he treated.

J. L. Austin was once asked what he thought of Wittgenstein. He replied, "Moore is my man." But despite these accolades, Moore had his detractors. Rudolf Metz complained:

> Though we may call Moore the greatest, acutest, and most skilful questioner of modern philosophy, we must add that he is an extremely weak and unsatisfying answerer. When questioning is excessively luxuriant, answering must naturally be scanty. Solutions and results are hardly to

> be expected from Moore, and if they occasionally appear, they are only like crumbs that fall from the master's table. (Stebbing 1968:521)

In an essay originally published in the *New Statesman* in 1963 and reprinted the first volume of *Gilbert Ryle: Collected Papers* in 1971, Ryle, who greatly admired Moore, reluctantly concurred with Metz's assessment:

> Like Socrates, Moore was apt to suppose that his analytic operations would terminate, if ever successful, in some analyses or definitions of composite concepts. But, like Socrates, he produced very few such analyses. Nor does what we have learned from him consist in a repertoire of such analyses. He taught us to try to assess and how to assess the forces of the expressions on which philosophical issues hinge. It is a not very important accident that he, with many of his critics and champions, did not fully realize that, before these forces have been assessed, definitions can do no good, and after they have been assessed, there is no more good for them to do, save the little good that mnemonics do. In his "Autobiography" (p. 33) Moore announces gladly and unenviously the drastic reorientation that Wittgenstein was giving to philosophical enquiries and methods. He realized, without any resentment, that the tide of interest was ebbing from the estuaries in which he had so pertinaciously dredged. He does not mention, and probably never mentioned to himself, how much Wittgenstein's sails needed the keel and the ballast that Moore provided. (1971:270)

Despite these reservations, Ryle was expansive in praising the example Moore set for young philosophers like him. In a wonderful passage he describes Moore as reminding him, "in quick succession, of a Duns Scotus, a ton of bricks, and one's farmer uncle on a holiday."

> Himself free from both vanity and humility, he saw no reason, and he taught us to see no reason, why matters of personal prestige or sensitiveness should be considered at all. He never pulled his punches, but he never bullied; he tore to pieces our bad arguments, but he never sneered at us. Sometimes he applauded and availed himself of our valid points; but he never complimented us. He never tried to score. He never cheated. He had no philosophical gospel to broadcast and no philosophical party to campaign for. His own darling philosophical cruces were not very numerous, and their cardinal teasers often seemed

> to us factitious. We came across few theses which we could cite as Moore's doctrines, and we felt no special tug to accept those that we could cite. None the less we left for home feeling full of fight, but also feeling firmly resolved to put better edges on our arguments next time. He reminded one, in quick succession, of a Duns Scotus, a ton of bricks, and one's farmer uncle on a holiday. (1971:271)

Perhaps the greatest tribute to Moore was indirect. In the last year and a half of his life Wittgenstein labored over some earlier famous papers of Moore's. Wittgenstein's collection, posthumously published in 1969 under the title of *On Certainty*, consists of 676 entries, most of them dealing explicitly with such matters as Moore's proof of an external world and his claim to know a number of propositions with certainty. The last seven entries were written just two days before Wittgenstein died. There is no doubt that Wittgenstein thought Moore's contributions were of major importance or he would not have spent what he knew to be his last days reflecting on them. But apart from what people said or thought about Moore, what he actually did in philosophy was very impressive.

The notion of philosophical paradox first appears in his writings, and a distinction he draws in his 1912 book, *Ethics*, between asserting and expressing is perhaps the earliest source of speech act theory. His discovery of what is called "Moore's paradox," exhibited by a sentence like "Smith left the room but I don't believe it," is the genesis of presupposition theory. The sentence is not formally self-contradictory yet embodies a tension between what one asserts in saying "Smith left the room" and what one asserts in saying "I don't believe it." The paradox arises from conflicting presuppositions rather than from any formal incompatibility between the two propositions. According to Wittgenstein, this was an important finding. It showed, as he said in a letter to Moore, that "logic isn't as simple as logicians think." Beyond these achievements, Moore's defense of common sense, and his emphasis on the importance of analysis, were both extremely influential.

How shall we characterize his approach to philosophy? Like the positivists, he disavowed any form of idealism, or pure rationalism, or any form of speculative metaphysics, but he cannot be classified as an "empiricist." He rejected some of their key doctrines: that contingent propositions are never certain and that science and science alone is the key to reality. He is perhaps better described as inheriting and developing the commonsense tradition of Thomas Reid, though even this characterization would ultimately have to be qualified in view of Moore's adherence to sense-data theory, which is anything but commonsensical. For example, in his last paper, "Visual Sense-Data," published a year before he died, Moore defended a sophisticated form of the representative realism found in Locke.

Moore's personal life was uneventful, spent mainly in academic circles. In 1911 he became university lecturer in moral science and in 1925 professor of philosophy at Cambridge University, a post he held until his retirement in 1939. He replaced G. F. Stout as editor of *Mind* in 1921 and served in that capacity for more than twenty years. In 1951 he received the Order of Merit. Moore was forty-three when he married. As he engagingly remarks in his autobiography, "At the end of the year 1916 I had the great good fortune to be married to Miss D. M. Ely, a young lady with whom I had become acquainted when she attended my lectures in the academic year 1915–1916." Moore, as Norman Malcolm, Ryle, and Broad tell us, was a man of simple character, completely devoid of affectation, pose, and pretense. He enjoyed the pleasures of eating, drinking, walking, gardening, and talking with his friends. He is described bv his contemporaries as an "exceptional and lovable personality."

Moore's approach to problems was piecemeal and critical and almost entirely directed to issues in epistemology and ethics. Despite this restricted focus, his writings and his jargon-free literary style exercised considerable influence on philosophers and nonphilosophers alike, setting high standards for making sharp distinctions, for talking in straightforward ordinary discourse, and for advancing lucid arguments. As Tom Regan has pointed out in his 1986 *Bloomsbury's Prophet*, the Bloomsbury group—Virginia Woolf, Lytton Strachey, J. M. Keynes, and others—saw in Moore's *Principia* a philosophy that emphasized the liberation of the individual and the rejection of a life led in conformity with the rules of conventional morality. Apart from these literati, Moore affected such eminent philosophers as John T. Wisdom, O. K. Bouwsma, Russell, Wittgenstein, Malcolm, and a host of younger thinkers, many of whom are still writing today. Russell, for example, swayed by Moore's arguments, eventually abandoned a deep commitment to idealism. As he states in *My Mental Development*, "He [Moore] took the lead in rebellion, and I followed, with a sense of emancipation."

The best accounts of Moore's life (as distinct from commentaries on his philosophical views) are to be found in his charming autobiography in *The*

*Philosophy of G. E. Moore* (1968), in Leonard Woolf's *Sowing* (1960), and in Ray Monk's *Ludwig Wittgenstein: The Duty of Genius* (1990). In the autobiography Moore describes his schoolboy days, his family background, and the intellectual ferment he encountered in Cambridge as an undergraduate. His assessments of such persons as Russell ("I have certainty been more influenced by him than by any other single philosopher"), Frank Ramsey, Henry Sidgwick, James Ward, J. M. E. McTaggart, Henry Jackson, Broad, Stout, and Wittgenstein make compelling reading. Of Wittgenstein he says:

> When I did get to know him, I soon came to feel that he was much cleverer at philosophy than I was and not only cleverer, but also much more profound, and with a much better insight into the sort of inquiry which was really important and best worth pursuing, and into the best method of pursuing such inquiries. . . . How far he has influenced positively anything that I have written, I cannot tell; but he certainly has had the effect of making me very distrustful about many things which, but for him, I should have been inclined to assert positively. He has made me think that what is required for the solution of philosophical problems which baffle me, is a method which he himself uses successfully, but which I have never been able to understand clearly enough to use it myself. (1968:33)

Moore first met Wittgenstein in 1912 when the latter attended his lectures and got to know him very well over the next two years. Moore does not mention in his autobiography that he and Wittgenstein had a falling out that lasted fifteen years. In that period they had absolutely no communication with one another. The fault seems to have been Wittgenstein's. The episode is related in Monk's *Wittgenstein* (1990:103). In 1914 Wittgenstein sent a letter to Moore from Norway, asking whether some material he (Wittgenstein) was then working on might serve as his bachelor's thesis at Cambridge. Moore inquired and was told by Wittgenstein's tutor at Trinity (W. M. Fletcher) that the work would not be eligible as it then stood. Upon hearing this, Wittgenstein wrote the following letter to Moore:

> Dear Moore:
> Your letter annoyed me. *When I wrote Logik I didn't consult the Regulations*, and therefore I think it would only be fair if you gave me my degree without consulting them so much either! As to a Preface and

> Notes; I think my examiners will easily see how much I have cribbed from [Bernard] Bosanquet—If I am not worth you making an exception for me *even in some* STUPID *details* then I may as well go to HELL directly; and if I *am* worth it and you don't do it then—by God—you might go there. The whole business is too stupid and too beastly to go on writing about it so—

Moore was greatly offended by this missive and severed all relations with Wittgenstein until Wittgenstein returned to Cambridge as a doctoral degree candidate in 1929. Despite his annoyance with Wittgenstein, Moore agreed to serve on his dissertation committee, and he and Russell were appointed examiners. Wittgenstein submitted the *Tractatus Logico-Philosophicus*, published seven years previously, as his thesis. In his report Moore wrote: "It is my personal opinion that Mr. Wittgenstein's thesis is a work of genius; but, be that as it may, it is certainly well up to the standard required for the Cambridge degree of 'Doctor of Philosophy.' " In his autobiography Moore does mention that when he retired as professor he was "glad to think" that Wittgenstein was his successor.

As colleagues at Cambridge, Russell and Moore not only had careers that overlapped but each greatly influenced the thought of the other. Moore wrote extensively about the theory of descriptions and about Russell's epistemological views (e.g., in "Four Forms of Skepticism"). Russell, in turn, commented on Moore's work and its effect on him. Even as early as 1898, he says: "I came to disbelieve [F. H.] Bradley's arguments against relations, and to distrust the logical bases of monism. I disliked the subjectivity of the 'Transcendental Aesthetic.' But these motives would have operated more slowly than they did but for the influence of G. E. Moore."

In his wonderful sketch of Moore in *Sowing*, Leonard Woolf describes the kind of discussions that took place between Russell and Moore and why the latter often greatly influenced the former. The year is 1902; Moore is twenty-nine and Russell thirty:

> Russell used to come to Moore's rooms sometimes in order to discuss some difficult problem that was holding him up. The contrast between the two men and the two minds was astonishing and fascinating. Russell has the quickest mind of anyone I have ever known; like the greatest of chess players he sees in a flash six moves ahead of the ordinary player and one move ahead of all the other Grand Masters. However.

> serious he may be, his conversation scintillates with wit and a kind of puckish humour flickers through his thought. Like most people who possess this kind of mental brilliance, in an argument a slower and duller opponent may ruefully find that Russell is not always entirely scrupulous in taking advantage of his superior skill in the use of weapons. Moore was the exact opposite, and to listen to an argument between the two was like watching a race between the hare and the tortoise. Quite often the tortoise won—and that, of course, was why Russell's thought had been so deeply influenced by Moore and why he still came to Moore's rooms to discuss difficult problems. (p. 134)

Woolf's assessment of these two powerful intellects is interesting. Russell is facile and brilliant. But Moore, in Woolf's opinion, is of a different order:

> I think . . . that George Moore was a great man, the only great man whom I have ever met or known in the world of ordinary, real life. There was in him an element which can, I think, be accurately called greatness, a combination of mind and character and behavior, of thought and feeling which made him qualitatively different from anyone else I have ever known. I recognize it in only one or two of the many famous dead men whom Ecclesiasticus and others enjoin us to praise for one reason or another. (p. 150)

## Moore's Early Philosophy

From a conceptual point of view, 1903 was one of the nodal moments of the century. That year saw the publication of Moore's *Principia Ethica* and "The Refutation of Idealism," as well as Russell's *The Principles of Mathematics*. These three works, each dealing with a different subject matter, revolutionized twentieth-century philosophy. Russell's book was his first major study in the foundations of mathematics and began a process of research that led to *Principia Mathematica* and to the development of symbolic logic. Inasmuch as we have already discussed Russell's accomplishments in this domain, we shall turn our attention to Moore. Our focus will be on his epistemological writings. These took two forms: a defense of certainty via an appeal to common sense and a defense of a form of realism in the theory of perception that rested on sense-data theory. But to set the stage we shall begin with his two great achievements in 1903, starting with *Principia Ethica*.

### *Ethics*

In a synoptic account of the twentieth-century history of moral philosophy, "Toward Fin de Siècle Ethics," that appeared in the *Philosophical Review* in 1992, coauthors Stephen Darwall, Allan Gibbard, and Peter Railton say: "The *Philosophical Review* is a century old; so too—near enough—is a certain controversy in moral philosophy, a controversy initiated by G. E. Moore's *Principia Ethica*. Both centenarians are still full of life" (p. 115).

These authors rightly see Moore as of central importance in twentieth-century ethics. Moore defended a view, now called "moral realism," whose most famous classical exponent was Plato. This is the doctrine that moral judgments can be either true or false. In this view the world contains facts of various types, some of which are "moral," and when moral pronouncements correspond to these, they are true. But in defending such a thesis, Moore developed a devastating argument against any form of reductionism in ethics. This argument he called the "naturalistic fallacy." The fallacy consists in trying to give a definition of a moral concept, goodness, in nonmoral terms—that is, by defining the good in terms of happiness, or desire, or pleasure, and so forth. According to Moore, every true "naturalistic" proposition about the nature of goodness, such as "pleasure is good," will be synthetic. Thus one can always conceive of a case where something is pleasant but not good; accordingly, the two concepts do not mean the same thing. The analysis applies to any naturalistic property, such as preference, utility, and the like. Thus the argument demonstrates that goodness is a simple property and hence is indefinable. This result means that no reductive (or scientific) account of goodness is possible. Here, then, was an example of how philosophy could make factual discoveries about the world that were nonscientific in character. That this is so is one of the major differences between Moore and the positivists.

This view created an enormous literature in response, both supporting and criticizing Moore. The logical positivists developed one of the main criticisms, which received its most powerful statement in chapter 6 of Ayer's *Language, Truth, and Logic*. Ayer holds that moral judgments are neither true nor false because they are not cognitively significant. They are utterances that evoke emotions and feelings, and speakers use them to elicit similar emotions from auditors. This view, which Ayer called "the emotive theory of ethics," was widely accepted, especially in the sophisticated form given to it by Charles L. Stevenson in his *Ethics and Language* (1945). In various forms it is still alive today; indeed, Allan Gibbard, one of the authors of the *Philosophical Review* essay mentioned earlier, is an eminent proponent of a roughly emotivist; noncognitivist point of view. Moore later acknowledged these criticisms as having force and stated that his original arguments were full of mistakes. But he never abandoned the view completely. He said, wittily, in *The Philosophy of G. E. Moore* (Schilpp 1968:545) that he was inclined to accept the emotive theory of ethics, and also inclined to reject it, and did not know which way he was inclined most strongly.

*Moore's Attack on Idealism*

The 1903 paper, "The Refutation of Idealism," had an equally powerful impact. Before this paper appeared, the prevailing mode of philosophy, both on the Continent and in the English-speaking world, was idealism. It took many different forms, some post-Kantian, some post-Hegelian, and some post-Berkeleyan, but all had in common the notion that reality was ultimately mental. McTaggart, Bradley, T. H. Green, and Bosanquet were prominent representations of the idealist tradition in England around the turn of the century. Moore's refutation was of Bishop Berkeley's so-called subjective idealism, a doctrine encapsulated in the formula, *esse* is *percipi*. (Berkeley's formulation is peculiar; it always uses two italicized Latin words connected by the English word "is" in roman type. Why he did not use "*est*" is very strange). What this view meant was that whatever was perceived was mind dependent. Thus the existence of tables, people, planets, and so on depends upon their being perceived by some mind. Moore thought this proposition to be "monstrous" and developed a series of arguments against it. The main argument rests upon a distinction between the act of perceiving and the object perceived. The act, he argues, is clearly mind dependent, but the entity perceived (say, a blue patch) is not. There is no good reason to believe that the existence of the blue patch has the same status as the existence of the act of perceiving. Indeed, he contends, there is good reason to believe the opposite. As a result of Moore's critique, Berkeleyan idealism has more or less vanished from the Western philosophical scene. It has been replaced by various forms of realism, the doctrine that there exist mind-independent entities. Moore called these "material," or "physical," objects. He would consistently defend a form of this doctrine in his epistemological writings.

## Moore's Later Philosophy

After the publication of *Ethics* in 1912, Moore's writings on moral philosophy dwindled to a trickle. He had a short paper in a 1932 symposium, "Is Goodness a Quality?" and a long discussion on ethical theory (about ninety pages) in his "Reply to My Critics" in *The Philosophy of G. E. Moore* (Schilpp 1968). Otherwise, for the rest of his career he concentrated on metaphysics and epistemology. The remainder of the chapter will thus be devoted to these topics. As I said earlier, Moore's later writings fall into two categories that are closely connected but that should be separated for expository purposes. The first of these was his defense of certainty. His opponents in this category were skeptics, whether mitigated or radical, because both hold, though for different reasons, that knowledge and certitude are impossible. The second was a defense of realism. Here the idealists were his antagonists. Idealism, whether of the subjectivist or absolutist variety, maintains that the basic "stuff" of reality is mental. It thus denies that there are any physical or material objects if such objects are supposed to be composed of nonspiritual stuff. In such a view objects that seem to be material, such as rocks and chairs, are analyzed as composites of sense-data. Accordingly, idealism maintains that none of the objects with which human beings are or could be acquainted are mind *independent*.

Realism, in contrast, holds that there are mind-independent objects. Realism is thus a metaphysics. It claims that the world contains ingredients whose existence does not depend either logically or causally upon any form of cognition or perception. Metaphysical realism, however, has an epistemological component, which is divided into two main categories: direct (or naive) realism and representative (or causal) realism. Metaphysical realism is both logically and historically prior to epistemological realism. The metaphysician attempts to describe the fundamental ingredients of the world, and the epistemologist is interested in whether and how human beings can achieve cognitive awareness of those ingredients.

Putting the matter somewhat differently, we can say that epistemology as a philosophical enterprise raises questions about the possibility, nature, and extent of the knowledge humans have of mind-independent objects. The notion of "mind independent" in this context is taken by the tradition to be a synonym for "external," and both are key terms in the theory of knowledge. The main differences between between the two forms of epistemological realism do not turn on disagreements about the existence of our "internal states"—about our sensations, ideas, and beliefs, since it seems obvious that they do exist and that we have direct knowledge of them—but about "external objects." These have a different status. It is not obvious that we are directly aware of their existence in the way we are of our mental states, sensations, and ideas. There is thus a huge divergence among realists about whether the knowledge we have of "external objects" is direct or inferential.

In Moore's time (as distinct from present-day theories in cognitive science) such intermediaries were called "sensa" or "sense-data." Exactly what sense-data are, and how they function, were the main subjects of the theory of perception in the first three decades of the century. Defenders of direct realism agreed there are aberrant visual experiences, such as illusions, hallucinations, and even delusions and that what one is seeing in those cases cannot be real existents. But realists contended that "in normal cases" of perception, no images, sense-data, or any sort of visual intermediaries are present. One just sees physical objects directly. Representative realists argued that such intermediaries are always present. A barrage of arguments, some based on the science of optics, were adduced to bolster their case. Some of these appealed to the causal sequence of events that begins when light is reflected off an object and is finally picked up by the human visual system. A typical argument of this sort claimed that we could not *now* be seeing a star directly because it takes years for light to arrive on Earth and in that time the star may have ceased to exist. Other arguments, such as the argument from synthetic incompatibility and the argument from illusion, supported this position. They attempted to demonstrate that we never directly see the surface of any physical object.

Here is a brief formulation of the argument from synthetic incompatibility. Suppose we are looking at a penny. We know that it is made of copper and, accordingly, that it has certain real properties, for example, that it has a certain size, weight, and shape We also know that unless something very unusual is happening, the size, weight, and shape of the coin do not change while we are looking at it. In particular, its shape normally remains approximately circular while the act of perception is taking place. The coin has two surfaces, an upper and a lower surface, separated by an edge. As we look at the coin from directly above, its upper surface looks circular. But as we move away from it, what exists in our visual field at a certain point is no longer circular but elliptical. Moore says that at that moment we are directly seeing an elliptical X, and this he calls a "sense-datum." But because the surface of the coin is circular and what we are directly seeing is elliptical, it follows that what we are directly seeing cannot be the surface of the coin. This follows on the premise that the same object cannot be both elliptical and circular at the same time. The argument gets its name from the incompatibility of the original circular image and the elliptical image. The argument calls attention to one of the most puzzling features of perception: the oddity that the elliptical sense-datum seems to fit the circular surface of the coin exactly. There is no overlap and the coin does not project behind the elliptical sensum. So, then, where is the sense-datum, if it is not exactly where the surface of the coin is? This is the heart of the conundrum. More generally, all these arguments purport to show that the perception of any physical object is always *indirect*.

In the history of modern epistemology Moore is very unusual in at least two respects. First, he holds that there is a distinction between an "external object" and a "physical object." By saying something is external, he means that it exists outside of any *human* mind. Physical objects, such as chairs and rocks, are external in this sense. But the pains of animals exist outside of *human* minds and thus are "external," yet like all pains they are not physical objects. Accordingly, the two concepts must be distinguished. Most of the philosophical tradition has identified these notions, as I mentioned a moment ago, so Moore's approach is idiosyncratic with respect to the tradition. Second, he does not hold that sense-data are always mental entities. Though he consistently argued that there were sense-data, he differed from his coevals, H. H. Price, Russell, Broad, and Ayer, in refusing to define them as mental states. This is because he initially tried to defend a theory of direct perception. He did this by considering the possibility that when one looked at an opaque physical object, say, an apple, one was directly seeing something (a sense-datum) but that it was just the facing part of the object's surface. Part of the surface was thus a physical entity and at the same time it was a sense-datum.

Thus, though one was not seeing all of the object, one was still seeing (at least part of) the object itself. As a metaphysical realist, Moore believed in the independent existence of physical objects, and as a potential naive realist he wished to establish that we see physical objects directly. But he also held a third view, namely, that in every act of perception we see a sense-datum directly. The two latter views seem prima facie incompatible since nobody has ever held that sense-data and physical objects are identical. But Moore tried to homogenize them by the clever suggestion that the sense-datum was just part of the surface of the perceived object. So there is a sense in which it could plausibly be said that we see both a sense-datum and some part of a physical object directly. In "A Defense of Common Sense," published in 1925, he was forced to acknowledge that the latter two views could not exist side by side. In that essay and in his final paper, "Visual Sense-Data," published in 1957, he was unable to counter the argument from synthetic incompatibility and concluded that some form of representative realism must be correct.

Once one is committed to the existence of sense-data, a host of epistemological problems arise, the most famous of which is the problem of our knowledge of the external world. Every epistemologist from Descartes through Moore and into the contemporary scene has grappled with the issue. In *Skeptical Essays* (1981) Benson Mates gives a lucid formulation of the problem: "Ultimately the only basis I can have for a claim to know that there exists something other than my own perceptions is the nature of those very perceptions. But they could be just as they are even if there did not exist anything else. Ergo, I have no basis for the knowledge-claim in question" (p. 104).

It is easy to see from Mates's description how the twin devils that Moore ceaselessly tried to exorcise—idealism and skepticism—were justifiable responses to the problem. If one holds that the only evidence we have about the existence of anything is our own perceptions, then it is short step to idealism. All we are aware of are our own ideas; supposititious physical objects like tables and chairs are nothing but congeries of sense impressions. We are therefore never justified in believing that any nonmental entities exist. This was the conclusion arrived at by Bishop Berkeley. Or, one could say, because we never get outside the circle of our own percepts, we are justified in doubting that anything "external" to our percepts exists. Hence we arrive at Hume's radical form of skepticism, entitled "Of Skepticism with Regard to the Senses," in Part IV of the *Treatise*. Moore could never accept idealism or skepticism. Defending realism while avoiding these twin perils set the agenda for the remainder of his career. Two of his four famous late essays, "Certainty" and "Four Forms of Skepticism," first published in 1942 and 1944, respectively, are wholly devoted to attacking skepticism. A third, "Proof of an External World," published in 1939, confronts idealism and gives a proof that material objects exist. It is one of the most widely discussed articles in twentieth-century philosophy. Wittgenstein devotes more than half of *On Certainty* to it. The fourth essay, "A Defense of Common Sense," published in 1925, discusses both skepticism and idealism. It also deals with the concept of analysis and with sense-data theory. It is a very complicated study, which intertwines these four themes in intricate ways. Because it is generally acknowledged to be Moore's finest paper, I shall devote the rest of the chapter to it.

## "A Defense of Common Sense"

Given the complexity of the essay, it is probably sensible to begin by summarizing it so that the reader may more easily understand the detailed discussion of Part I that follows. All page references are to Moore's *Philosophical Papers* (1959). The article is divided into five parts. In Part I, Moore's targets are skepticism and idealism. With respect to the former he argues that he and many other human beings know many propositions to be true and to be true with certainty. Moore gives examples of such propositions and describes them as "obvious truisms." His point is that anyone can see that they are true and are known by many persons to be so. Because the skeptic denies that knowledge and certainty are attainable by humans, skepticism can thus be rejected. Idealism also falls by the wayside since many of these truisms imply the existence of material (physical) objects and the reality of space and time. Moore's purpose in articulating these truisms is to describe what he calls "the common sense view of the world." The fundamental thrust of the essay is to defend the commonsense view against doctrines, such as idealism and skepticism, that run counter to it. Moore's position is that the commonsense view is wholly true and that any doctrine inconsistent with it can be dismissed in a wholesale fashion.

In Part II, Moore holds that there is no good reason to suppose that every physical fact is either logically or causally dependent on some mental fact. He gives various definitions of "physical," "mental," "fact," "logically dependent," and "causally dependent" (pp. 45–51). This part is wholly devoted to refuting idealism and extends the argument in Part I to that effect. In Part III, Moore argues that there is no good reason to suppose that all material things have been created by God. Moore also holds that there is no good reason to suppose that there is a God or that we shall continue to exist and be conscious after the death of our bodies. Moore's main point here is not to question the truth or even the meaningfulness of religious maxims but simply to argue that no religious proposition is part of the commonsense view of the world, that is to say, is an obvious truism. Part IV is convoluted and difficult to abridge. Moore draws a distinction between propositions he knows with certainty (as in Part I) and what he calls their "correct analysis." He does not explain what he means by "analysis." How they are to be analyzed depends on how propositions of a simpler type are to be analyzed (p. 53). Thus the statement "material objects exist" depends on the analysis of "I see a hand" and this in turn on a still simpler proposition, "this is a hand," and the latter on "I am perceiving this." The analysis of these simpler propositions, he states, is very difficult, but two things are certain: the proposition is always about a sense-datum, and what I know or judge to be true is not that the sense-datum itself *is* a hand, a dog, the sun, and so on. He is thus drawing a distinction between a *whole* physical object, like a hand, and a sense-datum. The ground for the distinction is that we never see a whole hand *directly* (i.e., we do not see its obverse and reverse sides and its inside at the same time and hence do not see all of it *directly*). Thus when we say we see a hand, an inference is involved. But in any veridical act of perception there is an object in our visual field, and this we see directly. This is what Moore means by a sense-datum. He gives an elaborate explanation on page 54 of how to identify a sense-datum when one looks at one's hand. Given this definition, he asserts that it is *certain* that he does not *directly* perceive his (whole) hand (p. 55) but directly perceives something related to it, and this is, of course, a sense-datum. He claims that no philosopher has given a correct account of the relationship between the directly perceived entity (i.e., the sense-datum) and the corresponding physical object. Such an account would be an analysis of the proposition "this is a hand."

He believes that there are only three possible views as to this relationship. These are direct realism, the doctrine that the sense-datum is identical with part of the surface of the physical object; representative realism, the thesis that the sense-datum is different from any part of the surface but representative of the physical object; or phenomenalism, that a physical object is simply a heap of actual and possible sense-data. He finds all these views to have fundamental objections and cannot decide between them.

In Part V he concludes by saying that he is in no doubt about the *truth* of such propositions as "this is a hand" or "this is a table" but has "the gravest doubt" about their correct analysis. Many philosophers, he indicates, have assumed that there is little or no doubt about the correct analysis of such propositions, and many have held that the propositions are not true. These positions, he says, are exactly the reverse of his.

Because part I is generally considered to be the most important section of the essay, I shall focus on it in what follows. But afterward I will say a few words about the concept of analysis that plays such a major role in Part IV and more generally in twentieth-century analytic philosophy.

### *Part I*

Moore's "Defense of Common Sense" exploded on the philosophical scene, and most of its shocking power comes from Part I. The essay starts out innocuously enough. Moore says that "in what follows, I have merely tried to state, one by one, some of the most important points in which my philosophical position differs from positions which have been taken up by *some* other philosophers" (p. 32).

He follows this modest opening with two points. In stating the first, under the heading (1), he says he will enunciate a long list of propositions, each of which *he knows, with certainty, to be true*. He adds that, under the heading (2), he then will assert a single proposition he also knows, with certainty, to be true. He characterizes as "obvious truisms" all the propositions in (1) and the single proposition (2).

Moore divides the large list of propositions in (1) into two categories. Let us call them A and B, respectively. The difference between the two groups is that the majority of propositions in A are about "his body," whereas most of those in B are about "his mind" ("the self"). Here are specimens of the propositions in A:

> There exists at present a living human body, which is *my* body. This body was born at a certain time in the past, and has existed continuously ever since, though not without undergoing changes; it was, for instance, much smaller when it was born, and for some time afterwards, than it is now. Ever since it was born, it has been either in contact with or not far from the surface of the earth. . . . and there have, at every moment since its birth, been large numbers of other living

> human beings. . . . But the earth had existed also for many years before my body was born; and for many of these years also, large numbers of human bodies had, at every moment, been alive upon it; and many of these bodies had died and ceased to exist before it was born. (p. 33)

Here are some examples of the propositions in B:

> I am a human being, and I have, at different times since my body was born, had many different experiences, of each of many different kinds, e.g., I have often perceived both my own body and other things which formed part of its environment, including other human bodies. . . . I have had expectations with regard to the future, and many beliefs of other kinds, both true and false; I have thought of imaginary things and persons and incidents, in the reality of which I did not believe; I have had dreams; and I have had feelings of many different kinds. (pp. 33–34)

In contrast to the long list of assertions in (1), (2) consists of a single proposition. Moore's statement of this contains 176 words. I will simplify it. In essence, (2) is the proposition that "each of us" has frequently known with respect to himself or herself propositions about his or her own body and self that correspond to each assertion in (1) that Moore claims to know about himself. That is, (2) states that each of us knows that he or she has a body, that his or her body was at one time smaller than it is now, that each of us has had many experiences, such as dreams, and so forth. Moore says of (2) that it is an obvious truism, and he also states that he, Moore, knows (2) to be true with certainty. He is thus saying that he knows with certainty that others have known with certainty propositions about themselves analogous to those in (1). Proposition (2) is key to the argument against idealism and skepticism that follows in Part I. It expresses what Moore means by the common sense view of the world. His contention is that there is a *common* store of knowledge that many human beings possess. Virtually everyone knows that the earth exists, that it is very old, that other human beings have lived and died during the period in which each of us has lived, and that each of us has had various kinds of psychological experiences, which resemble those that others have had. The arguments against idealism and skepticism consist in the implications Moore draws from the fact that there is such a commonsense view. The boldness and power of these conclusions shook the philosophical world.

We can divide his arguments into those that refute idealism and those that refute skepticism. Broadly speaking, he will claim that idealism is false but not self-contradictory and that skepticism is self-contradictory. Before producing the arguments, Moore describes two features of the commonsense view. First, he says that all the propositions in (1) and the single proposition, (2), are *wholly* true. He is here contravening absolute idealism, the view that there can only be one proposition that is wholly true and that applies only to the Absolute, the totality of what exists. For idealists any individual proposition, for example, that this pen is green, is only partially true because it is logically tied to a host of other propositions, such as the pen is not white, and the pen is not yellow, and so forth. The total set of properties that define the pen is thus inexhaustible; accordingly, any single assertion about it cannot be wholly true. Moore acknowledges that a given statement can be partially true, but he asserts that each proposition he has enunciated is wholly true. The notion that there are complete truths about particular facts is one that he held for many years. As we have seen, it influenced Russell's development of logical atomism. Accordingly, he will be using the word "true" in such a way that if a statement is only partially true, it is not "true" in his sense. This is an important thesis because he contends that the commonsense view of the world is true and, accordingly, that any proposition inconsistent with it, even if partially true, is therefore not true.

Second, he asserts that in the propositions in (1), and in (2) itself, he is using words with their ordinary meanings. This is one of the places where Moore's approach earned him the sobriquet of "ordinary language philosopher." Then comes a shocker, the first of many. One of the most disconcerting things ordinary folk discover in talking to a philosopher is hearing that individual say, "It all depends on what you mean." So if the ordinary person asks a simple question, for example, "Do you still live in California?" a philosopher's response is likely to be: "Well, it all depends on what you mean by 'still,' or by 'live,' or by 'in.'" This kind of fancy dancing infuriated Moore. In one of the most devastatingly critical passages in the history of Western philosophy of philosophical practice, he blistered:

> In what I have just said, I have assumed that there is some meaning which is *the* ordinary or popular meaning of such expressions as 'The

> earth has existed for many years past.' And this, I am afraid, is an assumption which some philosophers are capable of disputing. They seem to think that the question 'Do you believe that the earth has existed for many years past?' is not a plain question, such as should be met either by a plain 'Yes' or 'No,' or by a plain 'I can't make up my mind,' but is the sort of question which can properly be met by: 'It all depends on what you mean by "the earth" and "exists" and "years": if you mean so and so, and so and so, and so and so, then I do; but if you mean so and so, and so and so, and so and so, or so and so, and so and so, and so and so, or so and so, and so and so, and so and so, then I don't, or at least I think it is extremely doubtful.' It seems to me that such a view is as profoundly mistaken as any view can be. Such an expression as 'The earth has existed for many years past,' is the very type of unambiguous expression, the meaning of which we all understand. (pp. 36–37)

One can appreciate why "A Defense of Common Sense" created such a furor.

Moore followed this denunciation by distinguishing the question of whether we understand the meaning of a proposition like "the earth has existed for many years past," which he says we all do, with a different question: what is its correct analysis? The latter he says is "a profoundly difficult question, and one to which, as I shall presently urge, no one knows the answer." But giving an analysis, he points out, is an entirely different thing from whether we understand an expression. He says that we cannot even raise the question of how the proposition is to be analyzed unless we do understand it. He adds, "So soon, therefore, as we know that a person who uses such an expression is using it in its ordinary sense, we understanding his meaning." We shall hear more from him about this later.

The argument against idealism draws specific inferences from the truth of (2). This proposition, it will be recalled, states that many others have known propositions analogous to those that Moore states he knows in (1). Since the idealist denies that any single proposition can be (wholly) true, it follows from that view, according to Moore, that (2) is not true. But (2) speaks about "us." Therefore, if (2) is not true, then "us" has no application, which means that no humans now exist or have ever existed. If that is so, then no philosopher has ever existed, and, accordingly, none could have held that no proposition belonging to the commonsense view is true.

Moore says he is more certain that some philosophers have existed than he is about the truth of that theory. In effect, he is asking the reader to consider which option is the more likely: that other human beings, including philosophers, have existed or that idealism is true. Moore concludes by saying that because idealism contradicts the commonsense view that time and space are real, and that external objects and human selves exist, it can be dismissed without examining its specific arguments in detail.

To appreciate the force of Moore's style I will briefly quote part of the preceding argument. He writes:

> For when I speak of 'philosophers' I mean, of course (as we all do), exclusively philosophers who have been human beings, with human bodies that have lived upon the earth, and who have at different times had many different experiences. If, therefore, there have been any philosophers, there have been human beings of this class; and if there have been human beings of this class, all the rest of what is asserted in (1) is certainly true too. Any view, therefore, incompatible with the proposition that many propositions corresponding to each of the propositions in (1) are true, can only be true, on the hypothesis that no philosopher has ever held such a view. It follows, therefore, that, in considering whether this proposition is true, I cannot consistently regard the fact that many philosophers, whom I respect, have, to the best of my belief, held views incompatible with it, as having any weight at all against it. (p. 40)

Idealism is given a different status from skepticism. Idealism is simply false. Moore says there is nothing logically inconsistent about holding that time and space are not real or that there are no other selves besides one's own. It might have been the case that space is not real or that time is not real. But, in fact, they are, so idealism is mistaken. But the skeptic's problems are more profound. His view is that skepticism is self-contradictory and can be discarded on that ground.

Skepticism, Moore reminds us, holds that none of us knows for certain any propositions that assert the existence of material things, or the existence of selves, other than myself, or that such selves have also had experiences similar to mine. Moore holds that the skeptic is speaking not only about himself but about other human beings as well when he says, "No human being has ever known of the existence of other human beings." But in making this assertion the skeptic is implying that he knows (and knows with certainty) that many other human beings have existed and that none of them has ever known anything with certainty. But this statement is self-contradictory. As Moore says, such a philosopher is asserting that he knows with certainty the very thing—that others exist—which he is declaring that no human being has ever known with certainty. Here is how Moore describes the skeptic:

> If he says: 'These beliefs are beliefs of Common Sense, but they are not matters of *knowledge*, he is saying: 'There have been many other human beings beside myself, who have shared these beliefs, but neither I nor any of the rest has ever known them to be true.' In other words, he asserts with confidence that these beliefs *are* beliefs of Common Sense, and seems often to fail to notice that, *if* they are, they must be true since the proposition that they are beliefs of Common Sense is one which logically entails . . . the proposition that many human beings, besides the philosopher himself, have had human bodies, which lived upon the earth, and have had various experiences, including beliefs of this kind. This is why this position . . . seems to me to be self-contradictory. It . . . is making a proposition about *human knowledge* in general, and therefore is actually asserting the existence of many human beings. . . . They regard the proposition that those beliefs are beliefs of Common Sense, or the proposition that they themselves are not the only members of the human race, as not merely true, but *certainly* true; and *certainly* true it cannot be, unless one member, at least of the human race, namely themselves, has *known* the very things which that member is declaring that no human being has ever known. (p. 43)

Moore is thus claiming that it is self-contradictory to maintain that *we* know such beliefs to be features in the commonsense view and yet are not certainly true, since to say that *we know this* presupposes that they are certainly true. Accordingly, skepticism is hoist upon its own petard. Moore concludes Part I by saying: "And there are, of course, enormous numbers of other features in 'the Common Sense view of the world' which, if these are true, are quite certainly true too: e.g. that there have lived upon the surface of the earth not only human beings, but also many different species of plants and animals, etc. etc." (p. 45).

Moore's account in Part I thus defends a view that any person of common sense would hold: that there is an external world that is peopled by other humans and that these individuals have had many experiences like those that the ordinary person knows with certainty that he or she has had. One can thus say good-bye to any philosophical theory that contradicts such a commonsense outlook.

## The Concept of Analysis

As I said, Moore does not tell us in "A Defense of Common Sense" what he means by "analysis." In his "Reply to My Critics" in *The Philosophy of G. E. Moore,* published seventeen years later, we find his first explicit discussion of this matter. First, he denies that he ever said anywhere that philosophy consists in analysis. He states in responding to John Wisdom: "But it is not true that I have ever either said or thought or implied that analysis is the only proper business of philosophy! By practicing analysis I may have implied that it is *one* of the proper businesses of philosophy. But I certainly cannot have implied more than that. And, in fact, analysis is by no means the only thing I have tried to do" (Schilpp 1968:676).

Second, he stresses that, as he has used the term, "an analysis" is never of verbal expressions. Instead it is always of concepts or propositions, even though, in order to give an analysis, one must use verbal expressions. He says:

> In my usage, both *analysandum* and *analysans* must be concepts or propositions, *not* mere verbal expressions. But, of course, in order to *give* an analysis, you muse *use* verbal expressions. What will be the proper way of *expressing* what I should call an analysis? I can give several. Suppose I say: "The concept 'being a brother' is identical with the concept 'being a male sibling.'" I should say that, in making this assertion, I am "giving an analysis" of the concept "being a brother;" and, if my assertion is true, then I am giving a *correct* analysis of this concept. But I might also give the same analysis of the same concept by saying: "The propositional function 'x is a brother' is identical with the propositional function 'x is a male sibling.'" And I might also give the same analysis by saying: "To say that a person is a brother is the same thing as to say that person is a male sibling." (p. 664)

## Criticisms of Moore

Moore's bold defense of common sense, his proof of an external world, and his commitment to sense-data theory have been widely criticized. Because of space considerations I shall restrict my discussion to four criticisms.

1. It has been held that "A Defense of Common Sense" begs the question against skepticism. The criticism claims that Moore simply assumes that the commonsense view is true but never justifies this claim. He never explains how he knows such propositions as "the earth has existed for many years past." He asserts that he obviously does not know this proposition directly but only on the basis of other things that were evidence for it. He says that this seems to him to be no good reason for doubting that he does know it. He states: "We are all, I think, in this strange position that we do *know* many things . . . and yet we do not know *how* we know them, i.e., we do not know what the evidence was" (1959:44).

Two skeptical objections arise in response to these remarks. Both skeptics and dogmatists agree that to affirm that A knows that p logically implies that p is true, A cannot be mistaken about p, and that A has "good" grounds for his belief in p. Their disagreement is not about the meaning of "know" but about whether any cases satisfy the definition. Let us designate "the earth has existed for many years past" as the proposition "p." Because Moore's presumed knowledge of p is admittedly inferential and not direct, then there is a gap between the evidence and p. But if so, a mistake is always possible in concluding that p is true, and if that is so, then, given the definition of "know," Moore cannot know p with certainty.

Second, if one does not even know what the evidence is, then the assertion that one knows that p has no evidential support whatsoever. It is just a dogmatic affirmation and cannot establish that one really knows that p is true. People often make dogmatic assertions, for example, that the world will come to an end on such and such a date or that the speaker is God. Yet dogmatic assertion does not entail truth. Wittgenstein puts this point precisely when he states in *On Certainty* (entry 521): "Moore's mistake lies in this—countering the assertion that one cannot know that, by saying 'I do know it.'" Wittgenstein's point is that Moore's inability to answer the skeptical question "How do you know?" without adducing supporting grounds is not a legitimate move in the ordinary process of human communication. Moore's procedure is thus question begging. It asserts as obvious exactly that which requires justification. He *claims* to know, but claiming is not the same thing as knowing. One must be able to explain *how* one knows; if one cannot do so, then the claim cannot be accepted as a genuine case of knowledge. His refutation of skepticism is thus abortive.

2. A second criticism comes from the idealist camp. As I mentioned, in "Proof of an External World" Moore claims he can prove there are external objects. He does so by holding up his hands and saying: "Here is one hand, and here is another. Therefore, there are two material objects." Everyone, including the idealist, agrees that if there are any material objects, then there are external objects, since material objects are prototypes of the kinds of things that would be mind independent. But the idealist denies that there are any such things. He holds that what Moore is calling "a hand" is not a material object at all but simply a collection of actual and possible sensations. Because all sensations are "ideas," and because all ideas are mental entities, hands are not mind independent. Accordingly, to show that two hands exist does not show that the external world exists. The criticism is to the effect that once again Moore has begged the question. He has assumed that hands are external objects, but whether they are is just the point at issue. Though Wittgenstein rejects idealism (but for different reasons), he agrees with the idealist that Moore's proof will not do. Moore, from a Wittgensteinian perspective, does not understand that the issue between him and the idealist is not an empirical issue, namely, whether there are really two hands in front of him, and whether he is really holding them up, but a deeper philosophical issue about the basic constituents of the world: whether those constituents, including hands, are really mental or not. And that is not an issue that can be decided simply by holding up one's hands. It requires a different kind of approach to show how and why the idealist is wrong.

3. As Moore admitted, he was *never* able to give a satisfactory answer to the question of how sense-data give us knowledge of physical objects. In the case of an elliptical sense-datum, how can it allow us to infer that a penny is really round? Moore's failure to respond to this question raised suspicions among some philosophers that something was factitious or even spurious about the way he had formulated the problem of perception. Moore's description of the problem assumes that sense-data are real objects and on that assumption asks how (say) an elliptical object is related to the surface of a circular coin. But these critics, among them, G. A. Paul,

W. H. F. Barnes, and Austin, denied that the description of the perceptual situation given by Moore, Price, Broad, and Russell is correct.

They asserted that it is misleading, and indeed positively wrong, to say that we do not see the surface of a coin directly as we walk around it. It is more correct to say that the coin *appears* to be elliptical from such and such a point of view rather than to say there is an elliptical object that exists in one's visual field, as Moore attempted to demonstrate. That things look different from one perspective than from another does not justify the inference that we are perceiving different sorts of visual entities in such cases. There is thus no problem, they contend, about trying to explain the relationship between two different kinds of entities (a sense-datum and a physical object). There are no entities over and above the physical object in such a perceptual situation, and therefore there is no special entity that has to be related to the perceived physical object.

The so-called argument from synthetic incompatibility is thus not a compelling line of reasoning at all and arises only from a set of false assumptions. Reject those and the argument loses its force. This view was termed "the theory of appearing." It did not deny that there are visual illusions, mirages, and other perceptual oddities. But even granting that these exist, it does not follow that any anomalous perceptual situation is best characterized by positing a class of entities called "sense-data." Epistemologists have widely accepted this account, and sense-data theory today is virtually nonexistent. In saying this, however, I should emphasize that the theory of representative perception takes new forms in cognitive science and in modern philosophy of perception. In these later views the mental representations that give us knowledge of external objects are not the sorts of entities Moore labeled "sense-data." Modern representative forms of realism (sometimes called "causal theories") thus deny that one sees physical objects directly while also denying that representations, or "intermediaries," are sense-data. What they are is a complicated matter that we shall defer to a later chapter. What is worthy of note, however, is that the direct-indirect distinction is still a fundamental point of contrast in contemporary theories of perception.

4. A fourth criticism of Moore's whole approach to philosophy was mounted by Wittgenstein in *On Certainty*, and as the previous remarks about Moore's not understanding the nature of idealism suggest, it is a profound one. We shall speak about it in more detail in the next chapter. But the criticism can be encapsulated by a comment Wittgenstein makes in

that work: "Instead of 'I know. . . . ,' couldn't Moore have said: 'It stands fast for me that . . . '? And further: 'It stands fast for me and many others'" (1969:116).

Wittgenstein thinks that Moore's defense of the commonsense view is important and that there is something right about it. But he also thinks that there is something wrong—and fundamentally wrong—about it. What is right is that there are such things as knowledge and certainty and Moore is to be commended for defending that point of view. But what is wrong about it is that it conflates knowing and certitude. Moore thinks that the examples he gives of the commonsense view—that the earth is very old, that there are other human beings, that he (Moore) is a human being—are the sorts of things that can be said to be *known*. But this is a serious misdescription of how the concepts of knowledge and certainty apply in ordinary life. Where knowledge claims are appropriately advanced, then justification is necessary. But the examples he gives do not need justification. They are certain, and no mistake about them is possible. As Wittgenstein pointedly remarks to Malcolm: "Certain propositions belong to my 'frame of reference.' If I had to give *them* up, I shouldn't be able to judge *anything*. Take the example of the earth's having existed many years before I was born. What evidence against it could there be? A document?" (Malcolm 1984:75).

Hence certitude has a completely different status. That which is certain (that which "stands fast for me and for many others") is beyond justification, truth, the adducing of evidence, or knowledge. *On Certainty* is Wittgenstein's last book, and it attempts to show where Moore goes wrong and what the correct account of the difference between knowledge and certainty is. It salutes Moore as a great explorer yet admonishes him for finding the wrong continent.

Chapter Five

# Wittgenstein's Later Philosophy: "The Stream of Life"

No single sentence can summarize Wittgenstein's later philosophy. But the aphorism "words have meaning only in the stream of life" expresses one pervasive theme. This remark represents an enormous change from his views in the *Tractatus*. It is deeply connected to a "new method" he had discovered in the early 1930s for analyzing and resolving philosophical problems. The method rejects the notion that an ideal language contributes to philosophical understanding by enhancing ordinary speech and instead emphasizes the importance of accurately describing the complex ways in which people use language in the course of their daily activities. Such activities are what he means by "the stream of life." It is in the stream of life that the elements of discourse acquire their meanings and their points or purposes. In an alternative formulation he also calls such everyday activities "language games."

I will describe his new approach in some detail here. Its extraordinary influence and capacity to illuminate a vast range of conceptual issues has made Wittgenstein the most celebrated philosopher of the century. Indeed, since his death in 1951 he has become a cult figure within and outside philosophy: in psychology, art, sociology, anthropology, linguistics, political science, and literature. Previously known only to a coterie of specialists, he has become the subject of biographies, plays, novels, movies, and a virtually inexhaustible and continuing stream of interpretive essays and books. At the personal level he was austere, intensely self-critical, and driven by a relentless pursuit of truth and understanding. His commanding presence elicited reverence, awe, and often fear in students, colleagues, and friends. Bertrand Russell said he was "perhaps the most perfect example I have ever known of genius as traditionally conceived, passionate, profound, intense, and dominating. He had a kind of purity which I have never known equalled except by G. E. Moore."

As further evidence of this kind of purity, one can cite Wittgenstein's decision on his arrival home after World War I to dispose of his entire estate. His father, Karl, an industrialist, had been one of the wealthiest men in Europe. Through his financial astuteness in transferring his wealth into foreign, principally United States, equities, Karl left an enormous sum at his death to his children, including Ludwig. By any standards Ludwig was rich. To the concern of his family and the family accountant, he insisted that his entire inheritance should be transferred to his sisters Helene and Hermine and his brother Paul. He arranged with the accountant to make sure that no money would belong to him in any shape or form. The accountant reluctantly helped Wittgenstein commit what he labeled "financial suicide." From 1919 on, his life was simple and austere. Frank Ramsey visited him at Puchberg in 1923 and gave this description of Wittgenstein's living conditions: "He is very poor, at least he lives very economically. He has one tiny room whitewashed, containing a bed, washstand, small table and one hard chair and that is all there is room for. His evening meal which I shared last night is rather unpleasant coarse bread, butter and cocoa."

Norman Malcolm's *A Memoir* and G. H. von Wright's *Biographical Sketch* create an unforgettable picture of Wittgenstein, in which (though the comparison is never mentioned) the resemblance to Socrates is overwhelming. During his lifetime Socrates published nothing, and during his lifetime Wittgenstein published only *The Tractatus Logico-Philosophicus* in 1922 and a short paper, "Some Remarks on Logical Form," in 1929. His international status rests mostly upon a legacy of posthumously discovered writings. As we move into the twenty-first century, about twenty-five such works have been issued. The entire corpus, not all of it philosophical, is estimated to consist of ninety-five volumes. The editorial process is projected to continue until all the manuscripts have been disseminated.

The first work to be promulgated was *Philosophical Investigations*, which according to scholars who have surveyed the remaining documents, is probably his chef d'oeuvre. It was published in 1953 and created a sensation. But other studies of importance have subsequently appeared, among them, *Last Writings on the Philosophy of Psychology* (vols. 1 and 2), *Culture and Value*, *Zettel*, *Lectures on the Foundations of Mathematics*, *Remarks on Colour*, and *On Certainty*. Each of these monographs has generated a scholarly and interpretative literature in its own right, though not comparable to the vast outpouring of articles, monographs, collections of essays, and commentaries devoted to the *Investigations*.

Why Wittgenstein's reputation in recent years has spilled beyond the bounds of philosophy confounds most experts since his philosophy is deep and difficult to understand and, because of its nonsystematic aphoristic character, even more difficult to explain. No doubt it is in part because of his charismatic personality, but that factor by itself does not account for its impact. Von Wright articulates the elements of the puzzle as follows:

> It is fairly certain that both the work and personality of Wittgenstein will provoke varying comments and different interpretations in the future. The author of the sentences 'The riddle does not exist' and 'Everything that can be said can be said clearly' was himself an enigma, and his sentences have a content that often lies deep beneath the surface of the language. In Wittgenstein many contrasts meet. It has been said that he was at once a logician and a mystic. *Neither* term is appropriate, but each hints at something true. Those who approach Wittgenstein's work will sometimes look for its essence in a rational, matter-of-fact dimension, and sometimes more in a supra-empirical, metaphysical one. In the existing literature on Wittgenstein there are examples of both conceptions. Such 'interpretations' have little significance. They must appear as falsifications to anyone who tries to understand Wittgenstein in all his rich complexity. They are interesting only as showing in how many directions his influence extends. I have sometimes thought that what makes a man's work *classic* is often just this multiplicity, which invites and at the same time resists our craving for clear understanding.(1984:20)

## Biography

Wittgenstein's philosophical career is generally seen as falling into two parts, the first beginning before World War I when, following Frege's advice, he went to Cambridge to study with Russell. This period culminated with the publication of the *Tractatus*. As mentioned in chapter 3, Wittgenstein felt that in the *Tractatus* he had solved all philosophical problems and in the next decade turned his attention to nonphilosophical matters. For six years (1920–1926) he taught elementary school in Lower Austria, in the hamlets of Trattenbach and Otterthal, but eventually abandoned this task. Whether he left voluntarily is an interesting question. Like many teachers of the period he practiced corporal punishment. In

April 1926 he struck a young boy several times on the head. The child collapsed, and his father, in a rage, brought charges against Wittgenstein. A trial, or, better yet, a hearing, ensued and Wittgenstein was cleared of misconduct. Nevertheless the event devastated him, in particular because in defending himself against the charge of brutality he lied about the extent of physical punishment he had administered to his students. The sense of guilt he felt haunted him for years.

Fania Pascal, in "Wittgenstein: A Personal Memoir," describes a confession he made to her in 1937. She says: "I can remember two 'crimes' to which he confessed: the first had to do with his being Jewish in origin, the second with a wrong he committed when he was a teacher in a village school in Austria . . . when he denied he had done it. On this occasion he did tell a lie, burdening his conscience for ever."

In the mid-1920s, devastated by the events in Otterthal, he returned to Vienna. While there he assisted the architect Paul Engelmann in designing a house in Vienna for his sister Margarete Wittgenstein Stonborough. Wittgenstein personally supervised the construction and designed many of its details—windows, doors, window locks, and radiators. The structure was characteristically simple, reminiscent of the Bauhaus style. It still exists and is the site of the Cultural Department of the Bulgarian Embassy in Vienna. Evidently, its interior is now greatly altered and those who have seen it agree that Wittgenstein would have been appalled at its changes. Earlier, I commented on the contacts he had with members of the Vienna Circle during this period—especially with Moritz Schlick, Friedrich Waismann, Rudolf Carnap, and Herbert Feigl—interactions that did not impel him to resume his philosophical career. But in 1928 Wittgenstein heard a lecture by the famous Dutch intuionistic logician L. E. J. Brouwer that rekindled his interest in the foundations of logic and mathematics. These were matters that, while teaching in Lower Austria, Wittgenstein had already explored in discussions with the brilliant Cambridge mathematician Frank Plumpton Ramsey, who died in 1930 at the age of twenty-six.

In 1929 Wittgenstein decided to return to Cambridge and submitted the *Tractatus* as his doctoral dissertation to a committee consisting of Moore and Russell. The examination seems to have been something of a farce. According to one of his sisters, Hermine Wittgenstein, it "consisted of the professors asking Ludwig to explain to them passages from his book." When Moore retired, Wittgenstein replaced him in 1939 as professor at Cambridge. Before he could begin teaching, war broke out. As he had done in 1914 (see chapter 2), Wittgenstein immediately left the groves of academe and volunteered his assistance but this time to the English war effort. Too old to be a soldier, he served for a time as a porter at Guy's Hospital in London and then later as a laboratory assistant in Newcastle. As von Wright mentions, Wittgenstein at various times in his life was strongly attracted to the medical profession and in the 1930s even seriously considered leaving philosophy and becoming a doctor. In 1944, as the European phase of World War II was coming to an end, he returned to Cambridge. But he was never happy as a professor and resigned his chair in 1947 in order to pursue his research. That Wittgenstein was already a legend in his time is confirmed by his having been granted such a prestigious position without any publications other than the two works mentioned earlier.

From 1929 until his death Wittgenstein's main residence was in Cambridge, though he spent much time in Austria and Norway as well. This period is considered the second phase of his career, and his writings are generally described as "the later philosophy of Wittgenstein" in contrast to his pre-*Tractatus* notebooks and the *Tractatus* itself. Some scholars also divide the "later philosophy" into two parts, the earlier one a "transitional" period of about four years while he was developing his new method, which is first exemplified in the *Blue and Brown Books*, published in 1933–1934. His life was extraordinarily interesting. Since his death a large and varied number of works about him have appeared. These range from an eponymous film (1994) to a novel (*The World as I Found It*, by Bruce Duffy, 1987) to several collections of memoirs (e.g., *Wittgenstein in Norway*, edited K. J. Johannessen, Rolf Larsen, and K. O. Amas, 1994). There are also a number of biographies. The three most interesting are W. W. Bartley III's *Wittgenstein* (1973); Brian McGuinness's *Wittgenstein: A Life—Young Ludwig, 1889–1921* (1988); and Ray Monk's *Ludwig Wittgenstein: The Duty of Genius* (1990).

The latter works are excellent studies, balanced and judicious in their descriptions of Wittgenstein's personality, his human interactions, and psychological anxieties. Both give brief accounts of his philosophy, but because the McGuinness biography ends in 1921, its discussion is confined to the *Tractatus*. Bartley's monograph is a stunning piece of investigative scholarship. Though, like Monk's book, it discusses the early and late phases of Wittgenstein's philosophy, its concentration is on the period from 1920 to 1929, most of which Wittgenstein spent in Austria. In the late 1960s and early '70s, Bartley went to the villages where Wittgenstein lived and taught and met (to his surprise) some of the inhabitants who had been Wittgenstein's pupils forty-five years earlier and who remembered him well. Bartley's firsthand interviews with these individuals are fascinating and have become the accepted bases of the subsequent scholarship on Wittgenstein's teaching career. But the book had one other feature that made it a cause célèbre. It contained a description, based on personal interviews, that revealed Wittgenstein to have been a promiscuous and guilt-ridden homosexual. I quote some of it now:

> By walking for ten minutes to the east, down Marxergasse and over the Sophienbrücke (now called the Rotundenbrücke) he could quickly reach the parkland meadows of the Prater, where rough young men were ready to cater to him sexually. Once he had discovered this place, Wittgenstein found to his horror that he could scarcely keep away from it. Several nights each week he would break away from his rooms and make the quick walk to the Prater, possessed, as he put it to friends, by a demon he could barely control. Wittgenstein found he much preferred the sort of rough blunt homosexual youth that he could find strolling in the paths and alleys of the Prater to those ostensibly more refined young men who frequented the Sirk Ecke in the Kartnerstrasse and the neighboring bars at the edge of the inner city. And it was to this particular spot—still used for the same purpose at night, and still about as dangerous—that Wittgenstein was to hie almost as long as he lived in or visited Vienna. Similarly, in later years in England he was from time to time to flee the fashionable and intellectual young men who were ready to place themselves at his disposal in Cambridge, in favor of the company of tough boys in London pubs. (Bartley 1973:47)

This book caused a huge uproar, especially since Bartley refused on the ground of confidentiality to name the sources of his information. The condemnations ranged from statements by psychiatrists that they knew Wittgenstein was not a homosexual to personal attacks on the author. Defenders of Bartley suggested a coverup, especially by the executors of Wittgenstein's *Nachlass*. Supporting this idea was a statement by Professor Elizabeth Anscombe, one of the three executors, in a letter to Paul Engelmann: "If by pressing a button it could have been secured that people would not concern themselves with his personal life I should have pressed the button." Furthermore, it is curious that McGuinness, a close associate of Anscombe's, never mentions Wittgenstein's sexuality in his biography. Why there might have been a supposed coverup is almost impossible to explain, because Wittgenstein's sexual orientation occasioned gossip long before Bartley's study was published. In her "Wittgenstein: A Personal Memoir," Pascal describes her extensive acquaintance with Wittgenstein in the 1930s—she taught him Russian—and mentions that she and her husband wondered whether Wittgenstein was homosexual. Their judgment was that he was not. Here is her account:

> He became the freeest of men, certainly with full freedom of choice where to live, and with whom to consort. Yet he had to do his work unremittingly, and for this he depended on a small select band of pupils and disciples: this was the only tie that bound him and this he accepted. If it should be asked, was that tie in any form of manner a homosexual one (a question much in fashion nowadays), I can only say that to my husband and myself, and as far as I know to all others who knew him, Wittgenstein always appeared a person of unforced chastity. There was in fact something of *noli me tangere* about him, so that one cannot imagine anyone who would ever dare as much as to pat him on the back, nor can one imagine him in need of the normal physical expressions of affection. In him everything was sublimated to an extraordinary degree. (1984:48)

In contrast to McGuinness, Ray Monk expressly addresses the issue of homosexuality in the final chapter of his book. In a measured and fair-minded way he discusses Bartley's contentions and various attempts (e.g., by Rush Rhees and J. J. Stonborough) to refute them. In Monk's opinion these attempted refutations are unsuccessful. But he also says that because Bartley refused to reveal the sources of his information, the question remains open about Wittgenstein's promiscuity in the Prater. As I read him, Monk seems to concede that Wittgenstein did have sexual relationships with David Pinsent, Francis Skinner, and Ben Richards—as Monk indicates, "over a period of thirty years or so." Monk's chief concern is therefore to deny the allegations about Wittgenstein's promiscuity rather than those about his homosexuality. From Monk's perspective Wittgenstein is faithful to a small number of young men and not promiscuous. Most commentators agree that the issue of Wittgenstein's sexual orientation is of no importance in understanding Wittgenstein's philosophy. I concur. In the major texts, such as *Philosophical Investigations*, the *Tracta-*

*tus*, and *On Certainty*, there is no talk about homosexuality or indeed sexuality at all. So whether Wittgenstein was or was not homosexual is not generally considered to be of any assistance whatever in understanding his deepest thought. The issues he was considering, as we shall see, are entirely of a different order.

A recent controversy has also arisen about his attitude toward the Jews. A number of scholars have argued that Wittgenstein was an anti-Semite. Monk, for example, claims that Wittgenstein was a "ranting anti-Semite" when he was writing parts of *Culture and Value* between 1929 and 1931. Concerning some of Wittgenstein's comments, Monk states: "Were they not written by Wittgenstein, many of his pronouncements on the nature of Jews would be understood as nothing more than the rantings of a fascist anti-Semite" (1990:314). Monk further suggests that Wittgenstein is echoing Hitler's comments that the Jew is a parasite and that Jewish cultural contributions are entirely derivative and reproductive. Gerhard D. Wasserman, in "Wittgenstein on Jews: Some Counter-Examples" (1990), makes similar allegations. He says that "Wittgenstein absorbed like a sponge, and re-emitted, anti-Semitic lies, past and present," and that he "accepted uncritically, and propounded dogmatically, as if true, anti-Semitic views that were already widely current in Germany and Austria in the 1920's" (p. 361). In a recent paper, "Was Wittgenstein an Anti-Semite? The Significance of Anti-Semitism for Wittgenstein's Philosophy," Professor Béla Szabados carefully examines these charges and the textual evidence for them. He contends that they are groundless and are based on a misreading and misunderstanding of Wittgenstein's remarks. His argument is persuasive and I agree with him. As I mentioned earlier, the main evidence is to be found in *Culture and Value*, a collection of snippets written between 1914 and 1951. This text has twelve passages about Jews (see 1980:1, 5, 12, 13, 16, 18, 19, 20, 21, 22, and 23), most of which are straightforwardly commendatory about Jews (e.g., "The Jew is a desert region, but underneath its thin layer of rock lies the molten lava of spirit and intellect"). In a passage written in 1931, long before his discussion in 1937 with Fania Pascal about his guilt, Wittgenstein openly acknowledges he is a Jew. He writes on page 18, "Amongst Jews 'genius' is found only in the holy man. Even the greatest of Jewish thinkers is no more than talented (Myself for instance)."

The question of his Jewish heritage has also been controversial. Ludwig was baptized as a Catholic and died as a Catholic. He was not a religious person in any conventional sense. But as Pascal's memoir indicates, Wittgenstein's lie about the degree of his Jewish heritage bothered him. He told Pascal that most people who knew him, including his friends, took him to be three-quarters Aryan and one-quarter Jewish. In fact, he knew that the proportion was the reverse and had done nothing to prevent this misapprehension She suggests that the rise of Nazism in Germany may well have been the source of his guilt.

The question of his ancestry is complicated, but Bartley's careful investigations have confirmed that Wittgenstein was three-quarters Jewish. There is a full discussion of the controversy on pages 184 to 186 of Bartley's book. Bartley concludes:

> Another family tree, however, prepared in Jerusalem since the war, reports that Hermann Christian Wittgenstein was the son of Moses Meier Wittgenstein, Jew of Korbach, and the grandson of Moses Meier, Jew of Laasphe and Korbach. Although the records of the Jewish community in Korbach were destroyed when the SS burned the Korbach synagogue in November 1938, family tradition, comments in the diary of Hermine Wittgenstein, and significant facts—such as that the Wittgenstein family in Vienna possess portraits of Moses Meier and his wife Brendel Simon—suggest that this line of descent is correct. If so, Ludwig Wittgenstein was indeed three-quarters Jewish, the family name having been changed from Meier to Wittgenstein in 1808 when Napoleonic decrees required that Jews adopt a surname.

Those close to Wittgenstein knew that he was much impressed with Otto Weininger, who had become a cult figure in Vienna by writing a lurid book, *Sex and Character*, and then committing suicide at the age of twenty-three. Weininger, a Jew, saw civilization as decaying and identified as Jewish those aspects of modern civilization that he most disliked. As the title of his book indicates, he also saw the social trends of the period as arising from the sexual polarity of the masculine and feminine. Monk describe's Weininger's book as containing an "obsessive, lunatic" theory justifying misogyny and anti-Semitism. Wittgenstein was both attracted to some of Weininger's ideas and repelled by them. Weininger is thus a frequent topic in Wittgenstein's correspondence. But these themes are virtually absent from his major writings. For example, although Wittgenstein wrote about religion in *Lectures and Conversations on Aesthetics, Psychol-*

*ogy, and Religious Belief*, there is no evidence that his concerns were sectarian. Exegetes generally agree that his worries about his Jewish heritage had virtually no influence on his philosophical outlook. Béla Szabados's essay lends strong support to this judgment. What that outlook is—and it is complex—is a matter we shall turn to now.

## The Later Philosophy

One of the most vigorously debated issues in Wittgenstein scholarship is whether, or at least to what degree, there is a continuity between Wittgenstein's earlier and later philosophy. Almost all commentators concur that though the *Tractatus* begins with an affirmation of a species of logical atomism, that is, with a metaphysical doctrine, it ends on a therapeutic note that rejects metaphysics as nonsense and is central to the later books. Those who stress the continuity thesis thus emphasize this facet of the *Tractatus*. But a majority of exegetes favor the position that the later philosophy embeds a wholly different approach to philosophy. First, it is therapeutic in a more sophisticated sense than the *Tractatus*; second, it recognizes a kind of depth and insight in traditional approaches; and third, it identifies and recommends a positive nontherapeutic role for philosophy. All these features are functions of what Wittgenstein called a "new method" he discovered after his return to Cambridge. The majority view thus sees a radical difference between the two phases of his career. Von Wright's assessment expresses the majority point of view.

> The young Wittgenstein had learned from Frege and Russell. His problems were in part theirs. The later Wittgenstein, in my view, has no ancestors in the history of thought. His work signals a radical departure from previously existing paths of philosophy. But his problems grew to a great extent out of the *Tractatus*. This, I think, is the reason why Wittgenstein wanted the work which embodied his new philosophy to be printed together with the work of his youth. . . . The *Tractatus* belongs in a definite tradition in European philosophy, extending back beyond Frege and Russell at least to Leibniz. Wittgenstein's so-called 'later philosophy', as I see it, is quite different. Its *spirit* is unlike anything I know in Western thought and [is] in many ways opposed to aims and methods in traditional philosophy. (1984:14, n. 17)

We shall follow von Wright's interpretation here. A major difference between the two periods in support of this reading concerns Wittgenstein's treatment of meaning. In the *Tractatus* Wittgenstein put forth the notion that language pictures facts and does so in part because names mean their bearers (a thesis that Gilbert Ryle was later to dub the "Fido-Fido theory of meaning"). The isomorphisms between names and objects, and sentences and facts, give rise to meaning. In this view language is static in just the way that a picture or a map is. But in the later philosophy Wittgenstein says: "Don't ask for the meaning, ask for the use." Words thus have meaning only in the stream of life. With this emphasis he sees language as an essential feature of human action, as a kind of doing rather than a kind of picturing. The significance of this shift can only be appreciated by understanding his new method, to which we shall now turn.

## The *Philosophical Investigations and the Birth of a New Method*

Shortly after he arrived in Cambridge, Wittgenstein began a three-year course of lectures that Moore faithfully attended. Moore's detailed notes, entitled "Wittgenstein's Lectures in 1930–1933," are of monograph length and are reprinted in his *Philosophical Papers*. They provide the best account of Wittgenstein's thinking in this period. According to Moore, Wittgenstein said that what he was doing was a "new subject" and not merely a stage in a "continuous development of human thought," and that it was comparable to that what occurred when Galileo and his contemporaries invented dynamics. Wittgenstein said that a "new method" had been discovered, as had happened when "chemistry developed out of alchemy," and that for the first time there could be "skillful" philosophers, though of course in the past there had been "great" philosophers.

Wittgenstein went on to say that though philosophy was now "reduced to a matter of skill," this skill, like other skills, is very difficult to acquire. One difficulty is that it requires a "sort of thinking" to which "we" are not accustomed and for which we have not been trained—a sort of thinking very different from what the sciences require. That it is different from scientific thinking is one of the essential features of the later writings and amounts to a defense of the autonomy of philosophy. Wittgenstein averred that the required skill could not be acquired merely by hearing lectures: discussion was essential. With respect to his own work, he said that it did not matter whether his results were true or not; what mattered was that "a method had been found."

What, then, is this method? Unfortunately, Wittgenstein never gives a meta-account of it. The reader must pick it up from his actual practice. In the preface to the *Investigations* he says that it will issue in "sketches of landscapes," and he thus seems to be implying that it will not take a discursive literary form or involve explicit argumentation that engenders the kinds of definitive "results" traditional philosophy has expected. The method rests on two presuppositions that Wittgenstein articulates in entries 89 to 133 in the *Investigations*. The first is that philosophical problems arise in complex labyrinthian forms and represent a tangle of assumptions, principles, and theses, usually united by a conceptual model, or vision, that organizes the world for the philosopher who wishes to explore reality at its deepest levels. Because of this network of concepts, philosophical problems resist theoretical simplification, easy explanations, and generalized solutions.

They cannot be dealt with properly in discursive forms of argumentation. The method of coping with them must reflect and be sensitive to this complexity. As a result, it consists of a criss-cross pattern of comments, remarks, and apothegms that expose the underlying sets of assumptions and theses from various points of view. From a stylistic standpoint, the method takes an aphoristic literary form; in my *Moore and Wittgenstein on Certainty* (1994), I dubbed it "the broken text." It is marked by the quasi-Socratic device of posing questions and often leaving them hanging and unanswered. These questions are sometimes addressed to an unnamed auditor or reader, sometimes to himself, and sometimes it would seem to no one at all. He discusses the same topics obsessively, examining and reexamining them from numerous different perspectives. This kaleidoscopic process is never brought to closure. Thus for the reader there is seldom, if ever, a summary of earlier sections or a signpost to mark where the inquiry stands at that moment or any indication that these aphoristic remarks are gradually unraveling the threads of a submerged argument. The method seems to imply that there can never be a final solution to a serious philosophical problem. The resemblance to the "methods" of the Socrates of the early *Dialogues* is indeed striking. Each of those dialogues—*Charmides, Euthyphro, Laches,* and *Lysis*—is open ended; none of them comes to any definite conclusion. Yet the exploration itself is of intense interest.

The second presupposition of the method is that philosophy takes two forms. One of these is what might be called "traditional philosophy." The other is Wittgenstein's proposal about how philosophy should be done. It derives from his "new method." Traditional philosophy, for Wittgenstein, is a conceptual activity that attempts in nonscientific, nonfactual, or nonempirical ways to understand the nature of the world, including its human inhabitants. The new conception of philosophy rejects theorizing and "explanation." It replaces explanation by description (see Wittgenstein 1958:109). It attempts to give a true picture of things by describing the resemblance and difference between "cases" or scenarios, including intermediate cases (*Zwischengliedern*).

Let us look at both conceptions, beginning with traditional philosophy. It attempts to provide an explanation of whatever topic is under investigation by finding coherent patterns in what seems to be a confusing flux of events, phenomena, and processes that impinge upon the human psyche. These patterns are not to be found in surface features—if they were, anyone could discern them. Instead, they are benthic and thus hidden from the naked eye. Wittgenstein depicts traditional philosophy as committed to the quest to uncover the hidden, the essences of things, the covert principles that allow one to make sense of the world. "We feel as if we had to *penetrate* phenomena," he writes and adds that "the essence is hidden from us" (1958:92).

Traditional philosophy for him is not to be dismissed, as the positivists would have it. It must be taken seriously, for it is profound in its attempt to discover the basic principles of reality. In its effort to discover the ultimate principles behind the phenomenal world, traditional philosophy models itself on science. Newton's great achievement is envisaged as the paradigm to be followed. His theory explains a vast array of seemingly unconnected phenomena: why apples fall to the earth, why the moon continues to circle the earth without falling into it, and why there are tides on the earth. It does so via a single simple principle, the law of universal gravitation. The philosopher wishes to discover a similar key to reality. But, according to Wittgenstein, philosophy is not a fact-finding activity. On the contrary, it does not so much discover patterns in reality as impose a conceptual model upon them. This imposition leads to misunderstanding, misdescription, and paradox.

Consider the deep philosophical insight that human beings are nothing but machines. As Hobbes said, "What is the heart but a spring and what are the nerves but so many strings?" Eliminative materialists in cognitive science take a similar view. According to them, there are no such things as beliefs or thoughts: there is simply brain activity, and the brain is nothing but a very complex, parallel-processing computer. According to Wittgenstein, a traditional philosopher is "captured by a picture." This "picture," or "conceptual model," allows one in the grip of it to see deeply into things, making connections that the ordinary person would miss. Thus to arrive at the conception that organisms that seem radically different from machines are nothing but complicated mechanico-chemico-electric devices is a profound insight. It allows the physical sciences to accommodate and explain the mystery of the mind. Yet despite this insight, the view is ultimately paradoxical. In homogenizing diverse phenomena under one rubric, that of a machine, it does not provide an accurate picture of reality. The reality is that living things must be distinguished from artifacts; accordingly, any theory that attempts to blur such a distinction is profoundly misleading.

Wittgenstein's alternative to this mode of philosophizing emerges from his new method. According to that method, philosophy is not a fact-finding discipline, but its function is to change one's orientation to and understanding of reality. It does this by calling attention to facts one has known all along but that are so obvious as to be ignored or dismissed as unimportant. The new philosophy will be a corrective to this orientation. As he says: "Philosophy simply puts everything before us, and neither explains nor deduces anything. . . . One might give the name 'philosophy' to what is possible *before* all new discoveries and inventions. The work of the philosopher consists in assembling reminders for a particular purpose." (1958:126, 127). In these passages Wittgenstein is describing how, following his method, philosophy should be done. The key entry in the *Investigations* with respect to this point is 109: "We must do away with all *explanation*, and description alone must take its place."

In order to grasp the power of his approach, we should consider a specific example. In the *Investigations* (p. 89) and in the *Brown Book* (pp. 107–108), Wittgenstein discusses a passage from Augustine's *Confessions*. In Book II, chapters 14 to 16, Augustine states that he finds the concept of time puzzling. As he puts it,

> What is time? Who can easily and briefly explain this? Who can comprehend this even in thought, so as to express it in a word? Yet what do we discuss more familiarly and knowingly in conversation than time? Surely we understand it when we talk about it, and also understand it when we hear others talk about it. What, then, is time? If no one asks me, I know; if I want to explain it to someone who does ask me, I do not know. (1960:287)

Wittgenstein concentrates upon two features of this passage. When Augustine thinks about time and tries to form a general conception of it, he cannot articulate what it is. Yet in his ordinary everyday conversation he finds no difficulties. At that level he says one understands it; yet when he tries to explain what it is to someone else, he cannot do so. Why can he not do so? As Wittgenstein says in the *Investigations* (p. 89), "We want to *understand* something that is already in plain view. For *this* is what we seem in some sense not to understand." Wittgenstein points out in the same passage that this could not be said about a question of natural science ("What is the specific gravity of hydrogen? for instance"). Something that we know when no one asks us but no longer know when we are supposed to give an account of it is "something that we need to *remind* ourselves of. (And it is something of which for some reason it is difficult to remind oneself)." This is why the work of the philosopher using the new method, he says, consists in assembling reminders for a particular purpose.

Augustine goes on to say that time seems to him to flow past an observer, and when it does, it can be measured. But what puzzles him, as he reflects on this concept, is how the past can be, since it no longer exists, and how the future can exist when it is not yet present. And compounding the puzzle is a difficulty about how long the present is. If it is a period between past and future, then it cannot have any real duration, because the past immediately impinges upon the future. Moreover, if the observer of the flow of time is motionless, that means he is outside of time, but clearly that is not possible. So how can there be any such thing as time?

Wittgenstein asks whether Augustine lacks some fact or set of facts about the nature of time. Clearly, some questions that are factual in character cannot be decided because one lacks the appropriate sort of information. Is the Ebola virus transmitted from monkeys to humans? The answer is not known, but the question is clearly factual. Perhaps it will eventually be answered. But what kinds of facts would solve Augustine's dilemma? Wittgenstein says that Augustine's problem is not that kind of problem. It is a traditional philosophical question and therefore must be dealt with in a different way.

Augustine admits that he is not at a loss when it comes to the use of temporal terms in his everyday life. It is when he theorizes about the nature of time that it seems incredibly puzzling to him. But why should this be so? Wittgenstein's diagnosis in the *Brown Book* (p. 108) is that Augustine is imposing a certain conception or "picture" upon his everyday experience in trying to understand what time is. That "picture" seems to be that time is a kind of river, flowing past a fixed observer (as Augustine says, "As long as time is passing by, it can be perceived and measured"). This vision carries with it certain implications: just as the river is extended in space, so time, it would seem, is extended in space, having forward and backward parts. This picture is intuitively plausible and, moreover, seems to fit the facts of experience, for it does seem as if time flows, moving inexorably, as it were, past a fixed percipient.

But this picture of time is perplexing in the way that the conception of a river is not. A real river is extended in space, has parts that have not arrived at a place where an observer stands, and has parts that have passed the observer. Both parts still exist. But if one holds that neither the past nor the future now exists, then the river model does not help one understand the nature of the past and the future. So it is the river model that has distorted Augustine's understanding of time. That Augustine not only has an understanding of time but indeed a mastery of it is revealed by his comment that "surely we understand it when we talk about it, and also understand it when we hear others talk about it." What he fails to understand is that his everyday use of the concept of time *is* a mastery. And he fails to understand that because that is so, there are no residual problems about time to be solved. Thus Wittgenstein emphasizes that Augustine's problems are of his own making. He wishes to impose a model that will simplify and order a seemingly chaotic set of uses of the concept of time. But this is both unnecessary and confusing. As Bishop Berkeley was later to say of philosophers, "We first cast up a dust and then complain we cannot see." What is driving Augustine is thus a search for the real meaning or essence of time, something hidden behind the everyday idioms that he can deploy so easily and successfully.

But for Wittgenstein there is nothing to be discovered by this process. No real facts about the nature of time are at issue; no facts are missing and nothing is left to be explained. Wittgenstein is urging us to see that there is no theoretically adequate description of time because "time" is used in many ad hoc ways. What is true of the concept of time is true of *all* the concepts philosophers have traditionally found puzzling: knowledge, truth, certainty, name, object, and so forth. It will be a function of the new philosophy to *remind* traditional philosophers that in every case they possess such knowledge. One can do this by "bringing words back from their metaphysical to their everyday use" (Wittgenstein 1958:116).

Wittgenstein generalizes from the case of Augustine. All powerful philosophical insights will issue in pictures or conceptual models of this sort. These are unremitting in their hold on the reflective person. We say of the world, "This is how it has to be." It is in this powerful co-optive sense that Wittgenstein says that "a picture held us captive. And we could not get outside of it, for it lay in our language and language seemed to repeat it to us inexorably." For Wittgenstein these pictures force themselves upon us. They seem unavoidable and to be great intellectual discoveries. They help us make sense of our ambience by illuminating it like flashlights that cast spears of light into the dark. Yet each such model will inevitably issue in paradox, that is, in a constricted and distorted picture of the world. One cannot continue to do philosophy in that way. An alternative to it is needed, and this is what Wittgenstein's new method is designed to provide.

There is thus a second conception of philosophy in Wittgenstein's later works that is designed to give us a more accurate understanding of the world than traditional philosophy. In particular, it is designed to avoid paradox. According to Wittgenstein, it consists in replacing explanation by description. But what does he mean by "description" here? And what is it that is to be described? By "description" he means an accurate nontheoretical depiction of some situation or group of situations in which language is used in an ordinary everyday way. These situations and the linguistic uses they embody are the elements of the world to be described. For this everyday world—its practices, institutions, and linguistic uses—he uses various appellations: "the stream of life," "a form of life," or "the language game." The new philosophy thus turns on three features: an appeal to everyday language, an appeal to a gamut of cases and the contexts in which they occur, and an appeal to human practices. We can illustrate these as follows.

We have seen that for Wittgenstein, Augustine in effect is misusing the word "time." He is attempting to employ it in a way that is not found in daily speech. We have many idioms in which this term is used—"I will be there on time," "I have time on my hands," "There is plenty of time to do it," and so forth. The word "time" is part of a ramified, ordinary vocabulary that uses a range of related expressions, such as "early," "late," "at this moment," and so forth. One who can use this vocabulary correctly—where "correctly" means in accordance with the patterns followed by native speakers—has a mastery of the *concept* of time. Consider the word "now." For Augustine this is puzzling: how can an extended present exist between a past and a future that are contiguous, that run together in such a way that no extended period can occur between them? Yet clearly the present exists. Moreover, its scope is not puzzling, as we can see from the enormous number of different uses that the word "now" has in ordinary speech.

These allow for a range of temporal possibilities: "The games will begin now" might mean sometime this morning or within a few minutes or exactly when a whistle is blown. No mysterious hidden essence lies behind this array of idioms. One who understands them understands what "now" means and thus has a partial understanding of what time is. When one understands the uses of all such temporal idioms, one understands what time is. That is all there is to it. And, of course, every native speaker understands this range of expressions. The new philosophy *reminds* the reflective person of this fact. It asks such individuals to change their orientation so as to recognize the mastery they have: a mastery they have had all along but that, because they are "bewitched by language," they ignore or simply do not recognize. The bringing of words back from their "metaphysical use to their ordinary use" is an instance of such a reminder. It is an example of the technique Wittgenstein uses to solve (or resolve) various classical problems.

A second feature of the method is its appeal to a gamut of cases. This feature is used in contrast to the approach of the traditional method, which looks for one key model that will probe beneath surface phenomena. What Wittgenstein means by a "case" is a *description* of an activity, phenomenon, object, or event in a particular context in ordinary life. He urges that a range of cases be compared and contrasted with one another. This procedure will allow one to understand how some key concept, say that of "know" or "believe," is in fact being used. The method of cases is frequently tied to the appeal to ordinary language in his writings, but the two techniques are distinguishable. Here's an example from *On Certainty* in which ordinary language plays a critical role:

> I go to the doctor, shew him my hand and say "This is a hand, not . . . ; I've injured it, etc., etc." Am I only giving him a piece of superfluous information? For example, mightn't one say: supposing the words "This is a hand" *were* a piece of information—how could you bank on his understanding this information? Indeed, if it is open to doubt "whether that is a hand," why isn't it also open to doubt whether I am a human being who is informing the doctor of this? But on the other hand one can imagine cases—even if they are very rare ones—where this declaration is not superfluous, or is only superfluous but not absurd. (1969: 460)

In this passage Wittgenstein explicitly uses the term "cases." He is comparing and contrasting a set of situations that might occur in ordinary life. He does not fully describe what might be called the standard case as such, though in effect he alludes to it with the words "I've injured it, etc., etc." The standard case would be one where, if you injured your hand, you would go to a physician, show him the hand, and say, "I've injured myself here, etc., etc." In saying this, you would *presuppose* that the doctor was not in doubt that you are a human being, that what you are showing him is a hand and not an artifact. This case is to be contrasted with the situation Wittgenstein explicitly mentions. Suppose you went to the physician and said, "This is a hand . . ." In normal circumstances this would be a peculiar remark. Obviously, the physician knows it is a hand, so why do you begin this way? The suggestion is that if you did begin this way, you would be implying that something is odd about the object or about the circumstances: does the hand not look like a hand, or does the patient think that the physician is unable to see the object before him? and so forth. If no unusual circumstances obtain, then how is the remark to be understood?

Does it purport to be a piece of information? If so, its use presupposes that the background conditions are not standard, as mentioned previously. But, as Wittgenstein says, if it were a piece of information, how could you bank on the doctor's understanding what has been said? Indeed, if it is open to doubt "whether that is a hand," why isn't it also open to doubt whether the speaker is a human being who is informing the doctor of this? But this is not the only possible interpretation of what might be going on. One can imagine other possibilities where the remark is not superflous or even where it is superflous but not absurd and so forth. This gamut of possibilities is what Wittgenstein means by a range of cases. The point of the passage is to indicate that human activity is complex and cannot be understood according to one simple paradigm or model. In his new conception of philosophy, one of its tasks is to provide an accurate account of reality. Any such account must be sensitive to the range of differing cases that we find in "the language game," that is, in ordinary life. This lack of sensitivity is characteristic of traditional philosophy.

The third feature of the new method is its description and use of what Wittgenstein calls "language games." This concept first surfaced in the *Brown Book* of 1934. This is a work that Wittgenstein did not write but dictated to two of his students, Francis Skinner and Alice Ambrose. People who borrowed these notes made their own copies, and, as Rush Rhees states, "There was a trade in them." The *Blue Book* was based on lectures he had given a year earlier. The *Brown Book* contains seventy-three "language games." Each is said to be fully complete in itself, and each describes a possible situation, for example, in which a builder is speaking to an assistant. This concept became a key device of the later philosophy and is found extensively in such works as *Philosophical Investigations* and *On Certainty*. Curiously enough, a "language game" is neither *simply* a game nor *simply* a use of certain linguistic expressions, though both features are frequently present in language games. Rather, a language game is a description (depending on the context) of a slice of human everyday activity, including such practices as affirming, doubting, believing, following rules, and interacting with others in multifarious ways. Language games refer not only to individual human activities but to those that are common to the whole community. Their scope thus also comprises such institutions as governments, universities, banks, the military, and so forth.

With respect to such practices, Wittgenstein is urging the traditional philosopher not to think but to look and see what people actually do in the course of their daily lives. The *description* of such activities rather than a synoptic philosophical theory about them will give us an accurate picture of reality. Both the *Brown Book* and *Philosophical Investigations* open with a quotation from Augustine's *Confessions*. Augustine is describing how children learn to use language. He says in Book I, chapter 8, for example, "When they (my elders) named some object and accordingly moved towards something, I saw this and I grasped that the thing was called by the sound they uttered when they meant to point it out" (St. Augustine 1960:51). Wittgenstein says that Augustine is trying to give us "a particular picture of the essence of human language. It is this: the individual words in language name objects—sentences are combinations of such names. . . . In this picture of language we find the roots of the following idea: Every word has a meaning. This meaning is correlated with the word. It is the object for which the word stands" (1958:1). Augustine's picture of language is also Russell's in "Logical Atomism" and Wittgenstein's in the *Tractatus*. Recall *Tractatus* 3.203: "The name means the object. The object is its meaning."[7]

Wittgenstein's point here is not that this picture is absolutely wrong but rather that it is a restricted picture of how language functions in real life. As the collection of language games builds up in the *Investigations*, one can see that language has many other uses. This is what Wittgenstein means when he says that a picture held us captive and when he advises philosophers, "Don't think. Look!" To urge philosophers to look is to ask them to expand their conceptual categories, to see how words function in the stream of life. As Wittgenstein puts it in a brilliant metaphor: "Think of the tools in a tool-box; there is a hammer, pliers, a saw, a screw-driver, a rule, a glue-pot, glue, nails and screws. The functions of words are as diverse as the functions of these objects" (1958:11).

By providing a vast array of differing language games, Wittgenstein is reminding the philosopher of something he is well aware of as an ordinary human being—before becoming a deeply reflective philosopher like Augustine. The parade of language games will allow one to understand what such concepts as believing, doubting, proving, and justifying are. Consider knowing, for example. Wittgenstein produces dozens of examples in which "I know" is actually used in ordinary discourse. These can be contrasted with the philosopher's use. Moore, for instance, claims to know with certainty such propositions as "the earth is very old," or "other persons have existed and many now exist." He also claims that virtually every adult also knows these propositions to be true. According to Wittgenstein, Moore assumes his use of "I know" is standard. Yet in normal conversation one says "I know" in order to communicate information not known to others.

Suppose you are asked, "Are you sure that Smith was really there for the opening?" and you respond by saying, "I know he was." In that case, your intention is to give the interrogator information he did not previously possess. Had he possessed that information, he would not have asked the question. Generally speaking, the use of "I know" is pointless when you produce as things you know things that you know that everyone knows. Moore's use of it is thus a special kind of nonsense. This is the point

Wittgenstein is making when he writes, "But Moore chooses precisely a case in which we all seem to know the same as he" (1969:84). Or again, "The truths which Moore says he knows are such as, roughly speaking, all of us know, if he knows them" (p. 100). "Why doesn't he mention a fact that is known to him and not to *every one* of us?" (p. 462). "Thus, it seems to me that I have known something the whole time and yet there is no meaning in saying so, in uttering this truth" (p. 466). Moore has imposed a conceptual model upon the language game, a model that distorts actual human practice and behavior and results in a kind of nonsense. Such impositions of models are characteristic of traditional philosophizing. They should thus be replaced by the new method of looking carefully at, and describing accurately, everyday human behavior.

In the published materials we now have, Wittgenstein's writings range over a vast assortment of subjects, from the foundations of mathematics to discussions of Sigmund Freud, Sir James George Frazer, Gustav Mahler, Felix Mendelssohn, the human mind, psychology, ethics, aesthetics, and the nature of color. Many of his comments are narrowly directed, to misuses and proper uses of the concept of justification, for example. It is thus impossible to describe in a limited space all the topics he examined and his various approaches to them. But in his two most important later works, *Philosophical Investigations* and *On Certainty*, he has two targets in mind: Platonism and Cartesianism. It is clear that he regards these as central themes in the history of Western philosophy. From his perspective they provide virtually irresistible conceptual models and indeed in certain ways overlap and intertwine. Nearly all the major problems of traditional philosophy—the problems of change, universals, abstract ideas, skepticism, meaning and reference, the nature of the mind—derive from the thought of Plato and Descartes. We shall conclude this discussion of Wittgenstein with the brief accounts of his approach to Platonism and Cartesianism that we find in *Philosophical Investigations* and *On Certainty*. In both cases we shall find that misconceptions of how language functions play essential roles in these conceptual schemes. We shall begin with his treatment of Platonism.

The theory of forms is central to the Platonic model of the nature of reality. It includes as part of its vision of things views about the nature of meaning, knowledge, and change. According to Plato, reality is immutable, and since anything that exists in space and time changes, what is real does not exist in space or time. Because whatever information we have about spatiotemporal objects is derived from sense experience, such information, which is about the changing, can never be identified with knowledge. In order to acquire knowledge we must transcend sense experience and discover a world of unchanging objects. These are what Plato calls "forms," or "ideas." In a sense difficult to specify, the objects of sense experience (those existing in the world of appearance) participate in or somehow copy or exemplify the forms. Thus a blue sweater exemplifies the nonvisible form of blueness; a particular good action exemplifies goodness, and so forth. The forms are entities that particulars share; they are the common features or essences of those particular objects. They are "essences" in the sense that they define the nature of the particulars that participate in them. They are thus the entities that constitute reality. They are discoverable only by reason. This theory is Plato's rationalism; it holds that only reason and never the senses can discover reality.

Wittgenstein begins his analysis of this model via its conception of meaning as the essence lying behind each word or sentence. The *Blue Book*, for instance, begins with the question "What is the meaning of a word?" The *Brown Book* and the *Investigations*, as I previously mentioned, begin with a discussion of a view about meaning that Augustine holds. What Wittgenstein shows in a brilliant extended analysis is that the Platonic conception breaks down in a variety of ways. It fails to comprehend that one who understands a word or a sentence is not necessarily grasping some abstract entity but is able to *use* the word or sentence in various contexts for particular purposes. Instead of the Platonic model, with its emphasis upon the common features that words possess, Wittgenstein points out that linguistic expressions—for example, the word "game"—have a wide variety of different uses. Games take many forms; some have explicit rules, such as chess; some involve winning, some do not; some may be played by oneself, such as throwing a ball against a wall. There is no common feature they possess. Here in a famous passage is what he writes about the many uses to which language is put:

> But how many kinds of sentence are there? Say assertion, question, and command?—There are *countless* kinds: countless different kinds of use of what we call "symbols," "words," "sentences." And this multiplicity is not something fixed, given once for all; but new types of language, new language-games, as we may say, come into existence, and others become obsolete and get forgotten. (We can get a *rough picture* of this from the changes in mathematics.)

> Here the term "language-*game*" is meant to bring into prominence the fact that the *speaking* of language is part of an activity, or a form of life.
>
> Review the multiplicity of language-games in the following examples, and in others:
>
> Giving orders, and obeying them—
>
> Describing the appearance of an object, or giving its measurements—
>
> Constructing an object from a description (a drawing)—
>
> Reporting an event—
>
> Speculating about an event—
>
> Forming and testing a hypothesis—
>
> Presenting the result of an experiment in tables and diagrams—
>
> Making up a story; and reading it—
>
> Play-acting—
>
> Singing catches—
>
> Guessing riddles—
>
> Making a joke; telling it—
>
> Solving a problem in practical arithmetic—
>
> Translating from one language into another—
>
> Asking, thanking, cursing, greeting, praying—
>
> It is interesting to compare the multiplicity of the tools in language and of the ways they are used, the multiplicity of the kinds of words and sentence, with what logicians have said about the structure of language. (Including the author of the *Tractatus Logico-Philosophicus*) (1958:23)

In place of the Platonic view about essences, Wittgenstein says that we should think of most concepts as being related in the way that members of a family are related. There is no essence they all share, but there are heaps of overlapping features. Think of the hair color of members of a family. A and B may be blond, and blondness may take many forms. C and D, other members of the family, may not be blond, yet the texture and thickness of their hair may resemble those of A and B, and so forth. The notion of "family resemblance" is a descriptive term. It describes how words, such as "game," "tool," "rule," and "know," are actually used in daily life. As such it is an antidote to the Platonic view. In this conception we see the method of cases at work. Wittgenstein is urging that one compare and contrast cases in order to see how words like "game" and "tool" are used in ordinary life. The method is applicable to all the concepts that traditional philosophers have explored. It replaces the search for the essence of things and the need to "penetrate phenomena" by an example-oriented case-by-case description. This is how one arrives at an accurate understanding of reality.

The other target of Wittgenstein's new method is the Cartesian model, which turns critically on an inner-outer distinction, involving a two-substance theory of reality. Mind and matter are two substances. Everything is either one or the other and nothing is both. The distinction is thus both exhaustive and exclusive. As with all two-substance models, it generates a problem about how, if at all, the two substances can interact. In the Cartesian model the problem of interaction concerns how the mental world can somehow impinge upon (or know) the material world. How can something immaterial (mind) affect or cause something material (like an arm) to move when you decide to pick up a book, say? The problem about knowledge can be stated as follows. The model identifies the mental with what is inner, the inner with what is private (with what is directly accessible to one only, i.e., to the proprietor of a particular mind), and the private with that which is hidden from others. The model thus suggests that each human being is encapsulated within the circle of his or her own ideas. The problem is then how to emerge from this "egocentric predicament." According to the model, one has direct access to one's own ideas but no direct access to anything external, that is, to the material world, or even to the minds of others. Such access, if possible at all, is at best inferential and at most probable. In one's own case certainty about one's ideas and feelings is possible because no inference is required. But this is a very restricted kind of certainty. It is limited to one's own sensations. Compare such a model with Augustine's limited conception of the essence of language. So two "big" questions follow from the Cartesian picture. What reason does anyone have to suppose that there is a reality external to one's ideas? And even if there is such a reality, what reason does one have for supposing that one has accurate information (knowledge) about it? The threats of solipsism and skepticism are immediately entailed by this conception.

Wittgenstein was obsessed with these threats, and much of his later philosophy is devoted to analyzing their sources in the Cartesian model and then showing how they can be neutralized. In *Philosophical Investigations* and in *On Certainty* (written about fifteen years apart) he offers different ways of resolving the problem of the external world. Both solutions are ingenious and original. In the *Investigations* he argues that the Cartesian model can be reinterpreted in a linguistic form. As such it gives rise to the notion of a wholly private language. This is a language that presumably only one person could understand. That person would use words in a singular way. Each word would stand for a particular object, and only the user of the language would understand which object a particular word meant. He would thus be using a system of private rules for designating the references of his words.

Nearly half of part 1 of the *Investigations* (especially the segment from 143 to 250) is dedicated to showing that no such conception of language is possible. For something to be a language it must be rule governed. A linguistic rule is a piece of instruction about how various elements of the language are to be used. In their commentary on the *Investigations*, G. P. Baker and P. M. S. Hacker point out that rules must satisfy certain criteria: any rule can be expressed; it must be possible to follow or violate a rule; rules are creatures of the will; rules are standards of correctness or guides to action; and, finally, rules must be more or less transparent to participants in a rule-governed practice such as a language. Norman Malcolm adds to this that the existence of rules presupposes their use in a human community and that the meaning of the words in a rule-governed language are therefore independent of any particular person:

> To speak a language is to participate in a way of living in which many people are engaged. The language I speak gets its meaning from the common ways of acting and responding to many people. I *take part* in a language in the sense in which I *take part* in a game—which is surely one reason why Wittgenstein compares languages to games. Another reason for this comparison is that in both languages and games there are *rules*. To follow the rules for the use of an expression is nothing other than to use the expression as it is ordinarily used—which is to say, as it is used by those many people who take part in the activities in which the expression is embedded. Thus the meaning of the expression is *independent* of me, or of any particular person; and this is why I can use the expression correctly or incorrectly. It has a meaning independent of my use of it. And this is why there is no sense in the supposition

> that a forever-solitary person could know a language any more than he could buy and sell. (1989:22)

Malcolm's point is that any rule can be understood by anyone and therefore is public. So no linguistic system can be private in the Cartesian sense. Moreover, because every language is rule governed, mistakes in the application of its rules are always possible. If there were a "private language," the distinction between correctly and incorrectly following a rule would make no sense. There would be no objective way of determining, for example, when a mistake in reference had been made. Hence the Cartesian conception is not a language at all. It follows, more generally from this linguistic analogy, that the Cartesian model does not generate a sensible picture of the relationship of the human mind to the external world. One lives in a public world where one learns to use language in accordance with the prevailing social uses of words. These practices instruct us in how to use terms that apply not only to our own pains, feelings, and thoughts but also to the pains and feelings of others. So even if one's pain is not accessible to others in the way it is to the person who has it, it does not follow that a public language cannot be used sensibly to refer to such pains or that another's comprehension of what is being said about pains differs from one's own. As Wittgenstein says, "Inward phenomena stand in need of outward criteria."

## *On Certainty*

Wittgenstein develops a different approach to the Cartesian model in *On Certainty*. This notebook, which was only published in 1969, is now considered to be one of Wittgenstein's most profound creations. It was Wittgenstein's last work; he wrote the final seven entries only two days before his death on April 29, 1951. Though clearly unfinished, it represents a new stage in his thinking. In opposition to the Cartesian form of foundationalism, Wittgenstein develops a unique alternative, different from anything explicitly argued for in the *Investigations*. For Descartes, the cogito is foundational for the entire system of human knowledge. But it is a psychological principle. One reflecting on the cogito can *see* clearly and distinctly that it is true. In contrast Wittgenstein describes a form of foundationalism that is nonpsychological. It is also nonpropositional. As he says: "Giving grounds, however, justifying the evidence, comes to an end;—but the end is not certain propositions striking us immediately as true, i.e., it is not a kind of *seeing* on our part; it is our *acting*, which lies at the bottom of the language game" (1969:204).

In speaking of acting as lying at the bottom of the language game, Wittgenstein is asserting that an objective, nonpsychological foundation exists for ordinary life and its various practices. He refers to this as that which "stands fast for all of us" (116). The foundation is neither true nor false but the *ground* of truth or falsity. As he says, "If the true is what is grounded, then the ground is not *true*, nor yet false" (205). The foundation is neither justifiable nor unjustifiable, neither known nor not known, neither doubtable nor not doubtable. It is just there like "one's life." What is this "foundation"? It is partly composed of the inorganic features of the world: mountains, rocks, dirt, and mud. But it also consists of the community. Thus the mate-rial world and its human communities are the twin foundations for all human behavior. Unless they exist, none of our ordinary practices could exist. Thus one who does history is presupposing the existence and antiquity of the earth. One who does medicine presupposes that human beings die. Why they die is a question open to experimental inquiry but that they die is not. As a presupposition it makes any inquiry into the cause of death sensible. But it requires no experimental investigation itself. Moore would have said that we know such a proposition as "all humans die" to be true with certainty. Wittgenstein instead calls it a "hinge proposition." There is a vast range of such propositions. They are like hinges that stand fast and are the immovable mounts on which the doors of everyday human intercourse turn.

Hinge propositions, as presuppositions, are not susceptible to such ascriptions as being known, being true or false, being justified or not, or being doubted. Because ordinary propositions are the paradigms of things that can be true or false, it is doubtful that "hinge propositions" are really propositions. When Wittgenstein states that it is acting that lies at the bottom of the language game, he is moving away from the notion that any kind of proposition can be foundational. To speak of propositions is to over-intellectualize the depth of communal involvement. Our training in communal practices is nonintellectual. It is like the training we give animals. That which "stands fast" is thus not a kind of "seeing" on our part but a way of acting in accord with everyday practices.

This analysis leads to one of Wittgenstein's deepest criticisms of Cartesianism and the radical forms of skepticism to which it gives rise. All of us are reared in a community in which we learn to recognize certain persons, our parents and others, learn to speak a language, and eventually come to participate unself-consciously in a wide range of human interactions, practices, and institutions. Even as early as *The Brown Book*, Wittgenstein stressed the effect of rote training in language learning and the absorption of communal life: "The child learns this language from the grown-ups by being trained to its use. I am using the word 'trained' in a way strictly analogous to that in which we talk of an animal being trained to do certain things. It is done by means of example, reward, punishment, and suchlike" (1960:77).

Thus the community provides a background whose existence one cannot reject, revise, or sensibly doubt. Yet this is just what the skeptic is trying to do. But even the form of the skeptic's challenge—the linguistic format to which it must conform so that another can understand it—presupposes the existence of the community and its linguistic practices. The skeptic's doubts are thus self-defeating. They presuppose the existence of the very thing whose existence the skeptic wishes to question. Skepticism is thus a special form of self-annulling nonsense, and its challenge to the acquisition of knowledge and certainty by humans can be dismissed as such. Scholars agree that in *On Certainty* Wittgenstein has developed a highly original solution to the external world problem.

## Criticisms of Wittgenstein

As much as Wittgenstein has been extolled, he has also been criticized. Some of these criticisms are highly technical and we shall not discuss them here. Some are less so and vary in importance. I will consider three of these.

First, there were criticisms of Wittgenstein's influence on young philosophers. Von Wright mentions this problem in his "Biographical Sketch":

> To learn from Wittgenstein without coming to adopt his forms of expression and catchwords and even to imitate his tone of voice, his mien and gestures was almost impossible. The danger was that the thoughts should deteriorate into a jargon. The teaching of great men often has a simplicity and naturalness which makes the difficult appear easy to grasp. Their disciples usually become, therefore, insignificant epigones. The historical influence of such men does not manifest itself

> in their disciples but through influences of a more indirect, subtle, and often unexpected kind. (1984:17)

Gilbert Ryle mentions that veneration for Wittgenstein was so incontinent that Ryle's references to any other philosopher were greeted with jeers. As he says: "This contempt for thoughts other than Wittgenstein's seemed to me pedagogically disastrous for the students and unhealthy for Wittgenstein himself. It made me resolve, not indeed to be a philosophical polyglot, but to avoid being a monoglot; and most of all to avoid being one's monoglot's echo, even though he was a genius and a friend" (1970:11).

C. D. Broad was even more vitriolic. In his intellectual autobiography in *The Philosophy of C. D. Broad*, he writes: "The one duty which I willingly neglected was to attend the weekly meetings of the Moral Sciences Club. . . . I was not prepared to spend hours every week in a thick atmosphere of cigarette-smoke, while Wittgenstein punctually went through his hoops, and the faithful as punctually 'wondered with a foolish face of praise'" (1959:61). Even though Broad did not like Wittgenstein personally, when the issue of whether Wittgenstein should be appointed to replace Moore arose, he said, "To refuse the chair to Wittgenstein would be like refusing Einstein a chair of physics."

A second criticism was more substantial. Russell, in fact, set the tone for a raft of similar objections. Russell contrasted the "earlier Wittgenstein" with the "later Wittgenstein." The former, he stated, was profoundly aware of difficult problems and committed to intense thinking. The latter "seems to have grown tired of serious thinking and to have invented a doctrine which would make such an activity unnecessary." Russell said that for the kinds of issues Wittgenstein was now raising, one would do better to consult one's bed maker. Though the objection takes a sarcastic form, it can be posed in a less adversarial way. The author of the *Tractatus*, in this view, conceived of philosophy as having the rigor of logic and physical science. It is an endeavor in which the highest standards of professional tough-mindedness are brought to bear on conceptual problems. As such it is the kind of intellectual activity to which the "ordinary person" would have nothing to contribute. But the new Wittgenstein has relaxed those standards. Instead, it is almost as if anything the ordinary person would have said is all right. But if so, intellectual rigor has been compromised. Russell could not countenance this, and many philosophers whose standards of conceptual acuity are of a high order agreed. Of course, as we have seen,

Wittgenstein was doing something quite different in his new philosophy. From an older perspective it seemed lax and lacking rigor. In the United States, especially, and nowadays increasingly so in Western philosophy, this kind of criticism has become more vocal. But from a pro-Wittgensteinian perspective it amounts to bringing an older conception of philosophy to bear on a new and original approach. The important issue is whether Wittgenstein's later philosophy provides a new and deeper comprehension of philosophical practice and offers new solutions to traditional problems.

A variant of this criticism is often raised by those who are not unsympathetic to new approaches and even to what Wittgenstein is trying to do in his later philosophy. Their problem is that they cannot get a firm grip on exactly what is being argued, if anything is, and what the upshot of Wittgenstein's inquiries amount to. For these persons, Wittgenstein is maddening. Unlike some philosophers who write in a forbidding technical jargon, full of neologisms and other infelicities, Wittgenstein's language is elegant and clear. One can understand nearly all the sentences in the later philosophy. Wittgenstein's prose is comparatively untechnical and simple. The problem is that one is overwhelmed by words and by detail. One cannot seem to get the point of what is going on or, even after pages and pages of words, what has been accomplished. There is thus a slippery quality to the writing. It makes one feel as if one *should* be able to grasp what is being accomplished and yet that such a grasp is always just out of reach. Every aficionado of the later Wittgenstein can sympathize with this point of view. He is difficult to synthesize and thus difficult to explain. The answer—at least for some of us—is that reading the texts again and again is essential. One can begin to perceive patterns in the welter of words. One can even begin to identify a kind of overall dynamic in such works as the *Investigations* and *On Certainty*. The notion that Wittgenstein does not have a clear view of where he wishes to go thus begins to attenuate. The directions are there if elusive. One is helped to understand him by reflecting on what he says in the preface to the *Investigations*. His method, he tells us,

> is connected with the very nature of the investigation. For this compels us to travel over a wide field of thought criss-cross in every direction. The philosophical remarks in this book are, as it were, a number of sketches of landscapes which were made in the course of these long and involved journeyings. The same or almost the same points were always being approached from different directions, and new sketches

> made. Very many of these were badly drawn or uncharacteristic, marked by all the defects of a weak draughtsman. And when they were rejected a number of tolerable ones were left, which now had to be arranged and sometimes cut down, so that if you looked at them you could get a picture of the landscape. Thus this book is really only an album.

But, as Wittgenstein would have reminded us, the concept of an album has many uses. There are albums and albums, and his album is indeed remarkable. There is nothing like it in the history of philosophy. On that ground alone it is well worth looking through and reflecting on the meaning of the sketches it contains.

A third objection is to the therapeutic thrust of much of Wittgenstein's later writings. In *Philosophical Investigations* this theme is overt: "Where does our investigation get its importance from, since it seems only to destroy everything interesting, that is, all that is great and important? (As it were all the buildings, leaving behind only bits of stone and rubble.) What we are destroying is nothing but houses of cards and we are clearing up the ground of language on which they stand" (1958: 118).

The question raised by critics is, whose houses of cards is Wittgenstein clearing up? The answer: Only those occupied by professional philosophers. Wittgenstein's therapy is thus being applied to a limited number of persons and is designed to alleviate certain hangups induced by their professional activities. But then what do intelligent laypersons, nonphilosophers, learn from Wittgenstein? According to him, what they know or believe is in perfect order just as it stands. Therefore they need no therapy. So Wittgenstein has nothing to say to them. His views are thus of relevance only to a tiny coterie of intellectuals. The "great philosophers" of the past in contrast spoke to the multitudes, often with the aim of making them better human beings. There thus is no reason ordinary folk should read him or expect to benefit from his thought.

One response to this line of reasoning is to call attention to the fact that Wittgenstein's influence has spread beyond the confines of philosophy. As I mentioned earlier, his views about the nature of conceptual problems have been accepted by practitioners in a wide range of different disciplines. It can also be argued that any thoughtful person can be gripped by the kind of conceptual model that Wittgenstein regards as harmful. Wittgenstein's way of neutralizing any such model can thus be generally beneficial. But a still better response is that there is in his philosophy a positive, nontherapeutic strand, one that is difficult to discern because it is embedded in an avalanche of deflationary remarks. This positive philosophy consists of novel and original ways of looking at the world and its various features. His account of *that which stands fast* is a good example of such constructive thinking. It is, curiously enough, both a reminder of the obvious and a description of a facet of reality that no other philosopher has ever depicted.

Chapter Six

# Ryle and Austin: The Golden Age of Oxford Philosophy

Although Russell, Moore, and Wittgenstein lived through the Second World War, their best days were behind them, and by 1960 the great days of Cambridge philosophy were essentially finished. Wittgenstein died in 1951, and Moore wrote only two new essays between 1942 and his death in 1958. Russell's last major book--*Human Knowledge: Its Scope and Limits*—was published in 1948. C. D. Broad, R. B. Braithwaite, and John T. Wisdom, who were born in 1887, 1900, and 1904, respectively, made their most important contributions before 1955. G. H. von Wright inherited Wittgenstein's chair in 1947 but decided to return to Finland in 1952. At Oxford in the first half of the century the picture was entirely different. In an autobiographical essay Gilbert Ryle (1900–1976) gives a devastating description of the situation:

> During my time as an undergraduate and during my first few years as a teacher, the philosophical kettle in Oxford was barely lukewarm. I think that it would have been stone cold but for [H. A.] Prichard, who did bring into his chosen and rather narrow arenas vehemence, tenacity, unceremoniousness, and a perverse consistency that made our hackles rise, as nothing else at that time did. The Bradleians were not yet extinct, but they did not come out into the open. I cannot recollect hearing one referring mention of the Absolute. The Cook Wilsonians were hankering to gainsay the Bradleians and the Croceans, but were given few openings. Pragmatism was still represented by F. C. S. Schiller, but as his tasteless jocosities beat vainly against the snubbing primnesses of his colleagues, even this puny spark was effectually quenched.
>
> Logic, save for Aristotelian scholarship, was in the doldrums. Little was heard now even of the semi-psychological topics discussed in Bradley's mis-titled *Principles of Logic*. Russell's *Principles of Mathe-*

> *matics* had been published when I was three; twenty-five years later it and *Principia Mathematica* were still only the objects of Oxonian pleasantries. The names of Boole, De Morgan, Venn, Jevons, McColl, Frege, Peano, Johnson, and J. M. Keynes did not yet crop up in lectures or discussions. In the bibliography of the Kneales' *The Development of Logic* no Oxford entries, save contributions to scholarship, belong to the half century from Lewis Carroll (1896).
>
> The two branches of philosophy in which there was some life were ethics and the theory of sense-perception. It was from a consuming interest in sense-perception that Henry Price, with heroic sangfroid, migrated for a post-graduate spell to the university of Moore, Russell, and Broad. He thus made himself our first personal and doctrinal link with "the other place," and launched the idea that young Oxford could and should learn from Cambridge. Soon Oxford's hermetically conserved atmosphere began to smell stuffy even to ourselves. (1970:4–5)

Two things happened to arouse Oxford from its dogmatic slumbers. Ryle and a number of the other junior tutors began to attend meetings of the Mind Association and the Aristotelian Society at which they met colleagues from Cambridge, London, Scotland, Ireland, Wales, and the United States. On these occasions the winds of new doctrines began to cleanse Oxford's "hermetically conserved atmosphere." Moore was nearly always present at these sessions, and as Ryle humorously says, "his to us surprising readiness to explode at our sillinesses and to explode at his own, would have made the week-end, even by itself, a heart-warming and hair-raising experience." In 1929 Ryle met Wittgenstein and struck up a friendship that profoundly altered the direction of Ryle's philosophical thinking.

The second significant event was that Ryle organized an informal dining club, the "Wee Teas," whose other members were, "not all synchronously," H. M. Cox, Oliver Franks, W. F. R. Hardie, W. C. Kneale, C. S. Lewis, J. D. Mabbott, W. G. Maclagan, and H. H. Price. They were much influenced by the activities in Cambridge, and, as Ryle states, "Our tongues wagged more freely and our wits moved less deferentially in these evening sessions." The Wee Teas turned out to be a wonderful example of the mathematical theory of small groups. According to the theory, small groups exercise a disproportionate influence on larger units of which they are a part. In this case the activities of the members of the Wee Teas helped pave the way for the revivification of Oxford philosophy. Much is owed to

Ryle in particular for this historical change, both through the power and originality of his thought, and through his exquisite judgment as recruiter of talent. He was probably the single individual most responsible for making Oxford the center of world philosophy after the decline of Cambridge.

The postwar contingent at Oxford may have been the largest collection of first-rate philosophers ever to teach in one place: P. F. Strawson, James Urmson, Stuart Hampshire, Paul Grice, Herbert Hart, A. M. Quenton, David Pears, Michael Dummett, R. M. Hare, G. E. M. Anscombe, Isaiah Berlin, Brian McGuinness, and G. J. Warnock, among them. The two most creative and influential figures in this glittering assemblage were Ryle and his younger colleague, John Langshaw Austin. Each developed a style of philosophizing that attracted international attention. It should be remembered that though Wittgenstein's reputation as a "genius" was widespread in England, nothing except the *Tractatus* and his short paper on logic had been published before his death in 1951. Ryle was already a notable figure when Britain entered the war, but his reputation was to soar with the appearance of *The Concept of Mind* in 1949. Austin's career was meteoric and lamentably short. With the publication of his dazzling essay "Other Minds" in 1946 he joined Ryle as a superstar of British philosophy. In certain ways they were remarkably similar: both were "linguistic philosophers" of "the ordinary language" persuasion, and both wrote extensively about the other minds problem. But there were also differences in their methods and in their conceptions of what was important in the study of language.

## Ryle

### *Biography*

Much has been written about Ryle as a philosopher, but almost everything we know about him personally comes from his autobiography. It is an absorbing document: concise (fewer than fifteen pages), packed with information, and stylistically elegant. On the matter of brevity it is interesting to compare it with similar self-histories. Hume's death-bed statement, telling us "I now reckon upon a speedy dissolution," is only nine pages and is very moving. Moore, never long winded, tells us about himself in thirty-six pages, Carnap requires eighty, Quine more than five hundred, and Russell manages to fill three volumes. Ryle's account of his adolescence and family background is limited to three paragraphs and ends when he enrolls in Oxford at nineteen. His description of his life as an undergraduate is a masterpiece of wit and ruthless self-assessment: "For the first five terms I was working rather half-heartedly for Classical Honour Moderations. I lacked the ear, the nostrils, the palate, and the toes that are needed for excellence in linguistic and literary studies."

Ryle informs us that in his midtwenties he decided that philosophizing essentially incorporates argumentation and that any would-be philosopher would therefore need to study "the theory and technology of reasoning." Accordingly, he decided to peruse some of the books of England's most eminent logician, Russell:

> It was from this interest, and not from Price's interest in sense-perception that I 'went all Cambridge.' It was Russell and not Moore whom I studied, and it was Russell the logician and not Russell the epistemologist. Having no mathematical ability, equipment or interest, I did not make myself even competent in the algebra of logic; nor did the problem of the foundations of mathematics become a question that burned in my belly. My interest was in the theory of Meanings—horrid substantive!—and quite soon, I am glad to say in the theory of its senior partner, Nonsense. I laboured upon the doublets—Sense and Reference, Intension and Extension, Concept and Object, Propositions and Constituents, Objectives and Objects, Facts and Things, Formal Concepts and Real Concepts, Proper Names and Descriptions, and Subjects and Predicates. It was in Russell's *Principles of Mathematics* and not in his *Principia Mathematica*, in his Meinong articles and his "On Denoting," that I found the pack-ice of logical theory cracking. It was up these cracks that Wittgenstein steered his *Tractatus*. (1970:7)

The Russellian and Tractarian influences led him to do philosophy in a modified logical atomistic way. His most famous essay in that genre, "Systematically Misleading Expressions," first published in 1933, argues that ordinary locutions, such as "punctuality is a virtue," tend to mislead philosophers into thinking there exist abstract entities, such as punctuality and virtue. When these idioms are rewritten in a more perspicuous notation, for example, "for all x, if x is punctual, x is virtuous," the impulse to posit the existence of such abstractions is attenuated. The perspicuous notation in question came from Russell's theory of descriptions. Like Russell, Ryle presupposed that logic was an ideal language that could reveal the forms of facts in a way that ordinary English could not. After the war he would expressly disavow this approach. Yet, as many commentators have pointed out, one finds resonances of it even in the *Concept of Mind*.

Ryle's discussion of logical positivism explains why it first captivated the philosophers of his generation and then why they rejected it.

> Most of us took fairly untragically its demolition of Metaphysics. After all we never met anyone engaged in committing any metaphysics: our copies of *Appearance and Reality* were dusty; and most of us had never seen a copy of *Sein und Zeit*. On the other hand there was obviously something very important, though still disordered, in the Principle of Verifiability (and Falsifiability), quite apart from its Augean applications. We were not yet talking in the obsessive lingo of "criteria." But its cash-equivalents were already entering into our purchases and sales.
>
> There was a second quite unintended result of Logical Positivism. For by jointly equating Metaphysics with Nonsense and Sense with Science, it raised the awkward question "Where do we anti-nonsense philosophers belong? Are the sentences of which *Erkenntnis* itself is composed Metaphysics? Then are they Physics or Astronomy or Zoology? What of the sentences and formulae of which *Principia Mathematica* consists." We were facing what was in effect the double central challenge of Wittgenstein's *Tractatus Logico-Philosophicus* and the single central challenge of his future *Philosophical Investigations*. Neurath, Schlick, Carnap, Waismann, and for us, above all others, Ayer, had undeliberately raised a problem the solution to which was neither in the *Logical Syntax of Language* nor yet in the *Tractatus*. We philosophers were in for a near-lifetime of enquiry into our own title to be enquirers. Had we any answerable questions, including this one? The conviction that "the Viennese dichotomy, 'Either Science or Nonsense' had too few 'ors' in it" led some of us, including myself, to harbour and to work on a derivative suspicion. (1970:10)

That "derivative suspicion" was that, since philosophers of the past had said significant things, there was no reason why those of the present could not also do so. Though he conceded there was something important about the principle of verifiability, Ryle refused to accept the implication that science was the only key to reality. This suspicion hardened into certainty with his later work, which in effect affirmed the autonomy of philosophy as a discipline capable of making significant affirmations about the world. *The Concept of Mind* was a detailed illustration of this point of view.

Ryle alludes to his war service in nine words—"quite soon after I doffed my khaki in 1945"—and for the rest of the autobiography(another three pages) concerns himself with his subsequent activities as a philosopher, including the motivation that impelled him to write *The Concept of Mind.* The essay ends with portraits of two Oxford dons, R. G. Collingwood and Austin. The depiction of Austin is particularly interesting because it is here that Ryle draws a contrast between his conception of philosophy and Austin's. He points out that Austin's main interests were in the dictions, such as the particular utterances, that constitute promises, warnings, recommendations, and proposals and that differ from the statements and propositions that logicians focus on. Ryle's concerns, in contrast, were questions about what sorts of locutions make sense, or do not make sense, and why. He describes the difference between their approaches in the following (and last paragraph) of his autobiography:

> An examiner might pose two questions:—
>
> 1) Why cannot a traveller reach London gradually?
>
> 2) Why is "I warn you . . ." the beginning of a warning, but "I insult you . . ." not the beginning of an insult?
>
> On six days out of seven Question 1 would be Ryle's favorite; Question 2, Austin's. Each of us would think—wrongly—that there is not much real meat in the unfavoured question. But their meats are of such entirely disparate kinds that the epithet "linguistic" would apply in totally different ways 1) to the answer-sketch, "Adverbs like 'gradually' won't go with verbs like 'reach' for the following reason . . ."; 2) to the answer-sketch "To insult is to say to someone else pejorative things with such and such an intention, while to warn is to say. . . ." Anti-nonsense rules govern impartially sayings of all types. "Reach gradually" will not do in questions, commands, counsels, requests, warnings, complaints, promises, insults, or apologies, any more than it will do in statements. Epimenides can tease us in any grammatical mood. To an enquiry into categorical requirements references to differences of saying-type are irrelevant; to an enquiry into differences between saying-types, refer-

ences to category-requirements are irrelevant. Infelicities and absurdities are not even congeners. (1970:15)

Ryle is somewhat unfair here to Austin, who was not only interested in infelicities but also in absurdities, as we shall see. Diagnosticians of nonsense have been common in this century. Ryle had his "congeners" in Wittgenstein, Moore, J. T. Wisdom, Bouwsma, and Malcolm. But Austin invented the theory of infelicities in connection with his account of speech acts. It influenced such later writers as Paul Grice, Zeno Vendler, John Searle, and A. P. Martinich. In both Ryle and Austin these differing emphases were not in competition with one another but represented parallel, often overlapping, strands that "informal philosophy" could legitimately take in dealing with philosophical issues.

### *Philosophy*

In the twenty years between 1927 and 1947, Ryle published more than thirty articles, reviews, and critical notices but no books. His first venture into this larger format was *The Concept of Mind*. Apart from collections of his essays, he was to publish only two other books in his lifetime, *Dilemmas* in 1954, and *Plato's Progress* in 1966. Though these last two works are interesting pieces, they do not match the power and depth of *The Concept of Mind*. In an early review Stuart Hampshire declared that "this is probably one of the two or three most important and original works of general philosophy which have been published in English in the last twenty years. Both its main thesis and the mass of its detailed observations will certainly be a focus of discussion among philosophers for many years to come; and it has the distinction of style and the large simplicity of purpose which have always made the best philosophical writing a part of general literature" (1970:17).

In 1945 H. J. Paton invited Ryle to contribute a volume on any topic of his choice to the new series, Hutchinson's *Philosophical Library*, that he was editing. Ryle agreed to do so. His aim was to apply to some large-scale "philosophical crux" the answer to a question that had bothered him and his colleagues in the 1920s and '30s, namely, "What constitutes a philosophical problem; and what is the way to solve it?" As we have seen, this sort of meta-issue surfaced in the conceptions of philosophy advanced by the positivists and Wittgenstein. After mulling over various possibilities, one of which was the free will problem, Ryle finally settled on the relationship between the mental and the nonmental as his topic. The result was *The Concept of Mind.*

This book has two aspects: a negative deflationary one and a positive constructive one. The two approaches are tied together by an attack on a certain picture of the human mind and its relationship to the human body. Ryle gives different names to this picture: the Official Doctrine, the Cartesian Model, Descartes' Myth, the Ghost in the Machine, and The Para-Mechanical Hypothesis. The negative attack is to show that this picture is incoherent; the positive contribution is to give an accurate account (not a picture) of the relationship between mind and body. The positive account is detailed. It deals with the entire range of the mental: the will, knowing, emotions, dispositions and occurrences, self-knowledge, sensation, observation, imagination, and the intellect. The reader can obtain some sense of its high specificity by glancing at the index of topics covered in any of its ten chapters. In chapter 4 ("Emotion"), for example, Ryle explores such themes as feelings versus inclinations; inclinations versus agitations; moods; agitations and feelings; enjoying and wanting; the criteria of motives; and the reasons and the causes of actions. The book is thus a treasure house of detailed descriptions of all the major features of mentation.

Two further general comments. Ryle is one of the great stylists in the English language. In his writing he avoids jargon and is even more reluctant to use technical philosophical language in making a point. He is a master of metaphor and the striking phrase. Some passages I have quoted make it obvious that he is a writer of rare elegance. Second, note that there is not a single footnote in this long book. He once told me that if anything was worth saying, it was worth saying in the text. Ryle was a great admirer of Jane Austen. Just as one will find an absence of footnotes in her six novels, so one will find no footnotes in *The Concept of Mind.* The book is thus a felicitous mix of literary brilliance and substantive philosophical content.

What, then, is the official doctrine he is out to destroy? This doctrine, he contends, is given explicit expression by Descartes, but it is widely accepted by philosophers, psychologists, religious teachers, and many ordinary folk. It holds that every human being is both a mind and a body, which are ordinarily harnessed together but that after the body dies, the mind may continue to exist and function. Human bodies are in space and are subject to the mechanical laws of physics, chemistry, and biology. The body is a public object and can be inspected by external observers. But minds are immaterial and are not in space, nor are their operations subject to mechanical laws. The mind is an entity, to be sure, but an immaterial and invisible one that inhabits a mechanical body. This is why Ryle calls it the "ghost in the machine." It is *res cogitans* in Descartes' parlance. It is the thing that thinks, deliberates, decides, wills, and opines. Each mind is private—for example, only each person can take direct cognizance of the states and processes of his or her own mind. A person thus lives through two collateral histories, one consisting of what happens to his body, the other to what happens within his mind. The first is public, the second private. The Cartesian picture thus depends on the internal-external distinction. This leads to the problem of how the mind influences bodily action. Since the mind is construed as nonphysical and nonspatial, how does one's act of will, say, lead to a movement of one's legs—to the sort of thing called walking, for instance? Moreover, how are we to account for the knowledge we presume we have of the minds of others? If the Cartesian model is correct, observers cannot know with certainty what is taking place in the mind of another, because they are in principle cut off from any sort of direct cognitive awareness of the other's mental states or processes. The only direct knowledge any human has is of his or her own mental functions.

As plausible as this view may seem, it is absurd according to Ryle. As he states: "It is not merely an assemblage of particular mistakes. It is one big mistake and a mistake of a special kind. It is, namely, a category-mistake. It represents the facts of mental life as if they belonged to one logical type or category (or range of types or categories) when they actually belong to another. The dogma is therefore a philosopher's myth" (1949:16).

To illustrate what he means by a "category mistake," Ryle offers a number of examples. Here is one:

> A foreigner visiting Oxford or Cambridge for the first time is shown a number of colleges, libraries, playing fields, museums, scientific departments and administrative offices. He then asks 'But where is the University? I have seen where the members of the Colleges live, where the Registrar works, where the scientists experiment and the rest. But I have not yet seen the University in which reside and work the members of your University.' It has then to be explained to him that the University is not another collateral institution, some ulterior counterpart to the colleges, laboratories and offices which he has seen. The University is just the way in which all that he has already seen is organized. . . . His mistake lay in his innocent assumption that it was correct to speak of

> Christ Church, the Bodleian Library, the Ashmolean Museum *and* the University, to speak, that is, as if 'the University' stood for an extra member of the class of which these other units are members. He was mistakenly allocating the University to the same category as that to which the other institutions belong. (1949:16)

Ryle's point is that this sort of mistake is made by people who do not know how to employ the concept of a university. That is, their puzzle arises from an inability to use correctly certain items in the English vocabulary. According to Ryle, the Official Doctrine arises from a category mistake analogous to the preceding. It assumes that minds belong to the same category as bodies in the sense that both are rigidly governed by deterministic laws. The human body works according to mechanical principles: the heart is a pump, the veins are pipes, and the flow of blood is determined by the pressures that are described in fluid mechanics. The system is thus an assemblage of interacting parts that consist of fluids, solids, and electrical forces, all of which operate according to the laws of mechanics. All these forces usually work to some desired end, such as moving blood from one part of the body to another.

Minds also work in analogous ways. When I am hungry, a mental state, a desire, acts on my body and initiates those movements of hands and fingers that allow me to pick up and transfer food to my mouth. Accordingly, minds must be governed by deterministic laws. But minds are nonmaterial. They are not composed of solids, fluids, and electrical forces. So their laws, though deterministic, are nonmechanical. These Ryle calls "para-mechanical." The Official Doctrine invokes them as the analogues of the mechanical laws that govern the behavior of physical entities. But the concept of a paramechanical law is absurd. There are no such things as immaterial levers, valves, and pumps. Valves, levers, and pumps are solid entities that operate to effect bodily movements. To invoke the immaterial analogues of such entities to explain mental activity is thus to make a category mistake—to apply the concepts of mechanical forces and laws to a domain where they have no grip. Philosophers are thus like the person who does not know how to employ the concept of a university. It is this paramechanical model that Ryle attacks in the remainder of his book. Its existence indicates that these theorists do not know how to wield the set of concepts that characterize our mental functions.

The alternative he offers to the Official Doctrine is a detailed description of how mental concepts are used in everyday life. As he says: "The philosophical arguments which constitute this book are intended not to increase what we know about minds but to rectify the logical geography of the knowledge which we already possess." Ryle's purpose here is similar to Wittgenstein's in the *Philosophical Investigations.* In entry 127 Wittgenstein says, "The work of the philosopher consists in assembling reminders for a particular purpose." Ryle is also reminding us of what we have always known and also reminding us how philosophical conceits can blind us to the familiar. His description of the "logical geography" of mental concepts is thus a reminder of how we employ these concepts when we are not doing philosophy. Since any such employment is enormously complex, its "logical geography" will be detailed and specific. Given the vast number of such descriptions in *The Concept of Mind*, it is obviously impossible to run through the entire gamut he gives in that work. I will therefore pick one to illustrate his method.

In chapter 7 ("Sensation and Observation") Ryle says:

> However, these considerations will not satisfy the theorists who want to make the stream of a person's sensations, feelings and images the stuff of his mind, and thus to back up the dogma that minds are special-status things composed of a special stuff. They will urge, quite correctly, that though the oculist and the dentist can modify the patient's sensations by applying chemical or mechanical treatments to his bodily organs, yet they are debarred from observing the sensations themselves. . . . Only the wearer knows where the shoe pinches. From this is it argued, plausibly but fallaciously, that there does indeed exist the hallowed antithesis between the public, physical world and the private, mental world, between the things and events which anyone may witness and the things or events which only their possessor may witness. Planets, microbes, nerves and eardrums are publicly observable things in the outside world; sensations, feelings and images are privately observable constituents of our several mental worlds.
>
> I want to show that this antithesis is spurious. It is true that the cobbler cannot witness the tweaks that I feel when the shoe pinches. But it is false that I witness them. The reason why my tweaks cannot be witnessed by him is not that some Iron Curtain prevents them from being witnessed by anyone save myself, but that they are not the sorts of things of which it makes sense to say that they are witnessed or unwitnessed at all, even by me. I feel or have the tweaks, but I do not discover or peer

at them; they are not things that I find out about by watching them, listening to them, or savouring them. In the sense in which a person may be said to have had a robin under observation, it would be nonsense to say that he has had a twinge under observation. There may be one or several witnesses of a road-accident; there cannot be several witnesses, or even one witness, of a qualm. . . .

In saying that sensations are not the sorts of things that can be observed, I do not mean that they are unobservable in the way in which infra-microscopic bacteria, flying bullets, or the mountains on the other side of the moon, are unobservable, or that they are unobservable in the way in which the planets are unobservable to the blind. I mean something like this. Every word that can be written down, except words of one letter, has a spelling; some words are more difficult to spell than others and some words have several different spellings. Yet if we are asked how the letters of the alphabet are spelled, we have to answer that they cannot be spelled at all. But this 'cannot' does not mean that the task is one of insuperable difficulty, but only that the question, 'Of what letters arranged in what order does a given letter consist?' is an improper question. As letters are neither easy to spell, nor insuperably hard to spell, so, I argue, sensations are neither observable nor unobservable. Correspondingly, however, just as the fact that we may not even ask how a letter is spelled by no means precludes us from knowing perfectly well how letters are written, so the fact that we may not talk of the observation of sensations by no means precludes us from talking of the notice or heed that people can pay to their sensations, or of the avowals and reports that they can make of the sensations of which they have taken notice. Headaches cannot be witnessed but they can be noticed, and while it is improper to advise a person not to peep at his tickle, it is quite proper to advise him not to pay any heed to it. (1949:205–206).

In these passages, typical of a vast range of similar remarks, one finds a good example of Ryle's way of exorcising the ghost in the machine. The Official Doctrine presupposes that one has privileged access to a private realm consisting of one's own sensations, thoughts, and mental states and that such an access consists in the observation of one's sensations and states. Ryle shows that a distinction is properly drawn between one's tickles, tweaks, and qualms on the one hand and the cuts, bruises, and abrasions that a physician can observe on the other hand. What the physician sees can correctly be described as "observing." But the patient who feels a twinge or a tweak is *having* a certain sensation, and it would be nonsense to say that he or she is observing it. To say that one is observing something implies that one is using one's eyes, or certain kinds of observational aids such telescopes, stethoscopes, and torches. These instruments can be used for the observation of planets, heart beats, and moths. But we do not know what it would be like to apply them to felt sensations or to assert seriously that one can "observe one's headache." Since the Official Doctrine presupposes there is such a paramechanical analogue as observing, it can be shown to be a species of nonsense by comparing its requirements with our actual use of such mental concepts as tickles, qualms, and and headaches. What the comparison reveals is a category mistake. The concept of observation applies to the physical domain in a way it *cannot* apply to the mental. Note that the "cannot" here is the logical and not the empirical "cannot." Just as one logically cannot reach London gradually, so one cannot "observe" one's tickles and tweaks. In arriving at this result, Ryle is careful to distinguish heeding and noticing one's tickles and tingles from observing them. To heed or notice a sensation does not require the use of one's eyes or instruments, whereas observing does. Ryle's line of reasoning in these particular passages is a specimen of the kind of linguistic arguments we find in abundance in this book and whose thrust is to show that theorists have failed to deploy or have incorrectly deployed the ordinary concepts that describe human mental life.

### *Criticisms of Ryle*

*The Concept of Mind* created a sensation when it appeared in 1949. For at least a decade after its publication it was the single most discussed book in Anglo-American philosophy. Nearly every periodical carried long articles about it. It was translated into a host of foreign languages, was taught in virtually every major Western university, and within a short time seemingly had achieved the status of a philosophical classic. Yet a decade later it had fallen into obscurity, and for the past forty years it has hardly been referred to at all. What happened to occasion such a collapse? It is especially puzzling, given that the book was of superb philosophical quality, brilliantly written, and introduced such original and powerful distinctions as between knowing-that and knowing-how, and between a task word like running and an achievement word like winning; even more important, it was the first study to show in detail how the philosophy of language and the philosophy of mind are tied together. In this last respect it was a bellwether for work that was to be developed thirty years later.

There are several possibilities to explain what happened. One factor is that four years later Wittgenstein's *Philosophical Investigations* appeared. It covered much the same territory as Ryle's study and in greater depth. As brilliant as Ryle's book was, it paled in comparison to the power and insight of Wittgenstein's. So philosophers turned from Ryle to Wittgenstein. It was the latter and not the former who was now read: Ryle had simply gone out of fashion.

There is a second factor. Ryle claimed that in this work he was "charting the logical geography" of the many concepts used in speaking about the human mind. And though this was clearly an apt description, it was also patent that his work had a strong verificationist thrust. Ryle frequently and in crucial passages speaks about the testability of propositions about mental concepts. For example, he states: "For, roughly, the mind is not the topic of sets of untestable categorical propositions, but the topic of sets of testable hypothetical and semi-hypothetical propositions" (1949:46). Some critics have thus emphasized that Ryle's aim is to correct what other philosophers have said about the methods of *verifying* statements involving mental concepts, rather than trying to explicate these concepts themselves. The positivists, of course, identified the meaning of a statement with the method of its verification, and in many places in *The Concept of Mind* Ryle seems to presuppose that, in describing how certain propositions involving mental concepts are to be tested, he is explicating the meaning of those concepts. The book was thus eventually assessed as a sophisticated form of logical positivism, a view that, as we have seen, had lost its influence by the 1950s. Ryle's work was swept away with the rest of this movement.

Its behaviorism was a third factor. Ryle states that to give reasons for accepting or rejecting statements containing mental concepts will always involve hypothetical statements about overt behavior. In responding to the question "what knowledge can one person get of the workings of another mind?" Ryle answers that such knowledge is "how we establish, and how we apply, certain sorts of law-like propositions about the overt and the silent behavior of persons. I come to appreciate the skill and tactics of a chess player by watching him and others playing chess" (p. 169). Although Ryle always denied that he was reducing mind to behavior, and asserted instead that charting the "logical geography" of mental concepts was a philosophically neutral endeavor, his detailed analyses seemed to many philosophers to leave out the inward, felt quality of mental experience. For these philosophers such mental activities as deliberating or conjecturing, or such states as being in pain, were distinct from behavior. One could, for example, be in pain without evincing it in any mode of behavior. And even if one were to evince it, the pain itself was not to be identified with the behavior in question. A pain is not a grimace. So even if Ryle were correct in arguing that mental activity was exercised in various intersubjective situations, it did not follow that the behavior so exhibited was identical with the mental events in question. Unlike Ryle, who minimized internal experience, Wittgenstein emphasized and acknowledged the existence of such phenomena. His point was that one should not identify them with such features as meaning, expecting, thinking, and so forth. And this position was seen to be more compelling than Ryle's. In the end this may have been a decisive factor in the eclipse of Ryle's reputation.

## J. L. Austin (1911–1960)

### *Biography*

With the possible exception of Wittgenstein, Austin is unique among the philosophers we have discussed in not having left an autobiography or a diary. Wittgenstein's status is complicated. According to Ray Monk, toward the end of 1929 Wittgenstein thought of writing an autobiography, but nothing came of the plan. He did make notes for the next two or three years that attempted, as Monk quotes, "to expose the 'naked truth' about himself." Moreover, throughout his *Nachlass* there are scattered encoded secret remarks. These do not form a single document but when collected and deciphered provide snapshots of his private (often sexual) activities and of his psychological reactions to these episodes. It is difficult to know how to describe these secret writings. They cannot properly be called an "autobiography" or a "diary"—perhaps they are best characterized as one of those intermediate cases (*Zwischengliedern*) that he constantly urged philosophers to emphasize. He was also a voluminous writer of letters that range over a variety of topics, from his feelings of depression to scholarly worries about the English translation of the *Tractatus*. These missives have been published in *Letters from Ludwig Wittgenstein, with a Memoir by*

*Paul Engelmann* (1967a); *Letters to C. K. Ogden from Ludwig Wittgenstein* (1973); and *Letters to Russell, Keynes, and Moore by Ludwig Wittgenstein* (1974). On the basis of these various materials the philosophical historian can obtain a pretty good picture of Wittgenstein's thoughts and attitudes over much of his life.

But for Austin we have no written record of his own daily experiences and observations, no self-revelatory passages, and no autobiography. Practically everything we know about him is based on vignettes provided by acquaintances, such as his Oxford colleagues Urmson, Hampshire, Pears, Hart, and Ryle. Fortunately, we also have one excellent (if all too brief) biography. This was written by G. J. Warnock and is entitled "John Langshaw Austin: A Biographical Sketch." It originally appeared in *Proceedings of the British Academy* in 1963 and was reprinted in *Symposium on J. L. Austin* in 1969. Warnock's sketch provides a marvelous picture of Austin. It covers his early upbringing, his precollege and college student days, his career as an intelligence officer in World War II, and his later views about the nature of philosophical problems and how to deal with them.

Warnock tells us that even as a schoolboy Austin was recognized as an intellectual prodigy. Later at Oxford he won the Gaisford Prize for Greek Prose and other awards and came to philosophy via the study of Aristotle. Austin and Moore were both originally classicists, and this kind of training undoubtedly played an important role in the emphasis they put on ordinary language and in developing the keen sense that both displayed for subtle linguistic distinctions. It was Moore, rather than Russell or Wittgenstein, whom Austin most admired. Austin seems to have been less affected than Ryle by the dreariness of Oxford philosophy in the 1930s and, like Ryle, found Prichard the most stimulating thinker at that institution. Prichard had no general conception of the nature of philosophical problems and instead treated them in a piecemeal fashion. Whether this attitude rubbed off on Austin is not clear, but this was Austin's outlook as well throughout his career.

Austin reacted to the powerful invasive thrust of logical positivism in much the same way that Ryle did. He was generally sympathetic to its attack on the rhetoric, pretension, and obscurity that are often associated with metaphysical conceits and thus approved of the tough-minded outlook of *Der Wiener Kreis*. But he also distrusted the positivist commitment to a quasi-scientific technical vocabulary and, moreover, viewed positivism as just another general philosophical theory not so different from those whose pretensions it wished to demolish. Austin consistently held that if any generalization could be applied to philosophy, it was that both the formulations of and purported solutions to philosophical problems were vague, because philosophers were disposed to try to settle these matters too quickly. As Warnock says:

> He believed (like Moore) that, if progress was to be made, *many* questions would have to be raised, *many* facts surveyed, *many* arguments deployed step by step and narrowly criticized; questions ought to be distinguished and considered strictly one at a time, and no effort spared to make it *wholly* clear what question was being asked and *exactly* what answer was proposed to it. The effect, in discussion in the thirties, of this dogged resistance to haste has been described as 'powerfully negative', and so no doubt it was (if one remembers how philosophers are prone to go on); but conspicuously it was not dull, and above all, not negligible. (1969:7)

According to Warnock, no one outside Austin's family knew him well, and he attributes this to shyness. Shyness can often be confused with condescension and indifference, and that may well have been a factor in the way that some individuals perceived Austin. There is no doubt that his sharp intelligence and penetrating wit proved daunting to many of his acquaintances. Warnock broaches the issue and and agrees that Austin was "formidable" but denies that he was cold or remote:

> That he was, and could not help being, a formidable person is true; but that he was cold is not. It is because his kindness, his affections, and for that matter his aversions, were so real they could not, without falsity, have been indiscriminately displayed; and he was not capable of falsity.
>
> Above all it should be remembered that, formidable though he often was, there was in him no stiffness or stuffiness, no pedantic rigour. In conversation he was capable of, one might almost say, addicted to, the rashest flights of speculation and fantastic extravagance; he was always utterly without pomposity; his lectures and discussions, even when he was philosophically in dead earnest, were continuously entertaining, and sometimes wildly funny. His way of speaking—rather dry and slow, very clear and with all edges, as it were, very sharply defined—was splendidly expressive of both the characteristic merits of his matter, and the characteristic wit of his style. It was also, on occasion, an effective polemical instrument; for he could, and sometimes

> did, reduce philosophical propositions to helpless absurdity by simply reading them aloud. He was very far from thinking that philosophy was a form of entertainment; but he believed that its practice was all the better for being agreeable, and he accepted with relish the ample targets it offered him for ridicule. It seemed to him a short step from solemnity to pretentiousness and fraud, and he used his natural wit deliberately as a weapon against bogus profundities. In his hands philosophy seemed at once more serious, and more fun. (1969:20–21)

I find it difficult to believe that anyone who knew Austin personally could imagine him to be cold. I got to know him when he visited Berkeley in 1958. I had earlier received a nice note from him about a paper I had written shortly after receiving my doctoral degree. I was then teaching at the University of British Columbia, and I invited Austin to give a talk there while he was in California. We spent several days together, at the end of which time he invited me to join his seminar at Berkeley for its remaining two months. Before he arrived I had written a paper on rule following—a common topic among those who had recently read Wittgenstein's *Philosophical Investigations*—which for various reasons I wisely never published. Austin politely listened to my views about the matter and then made a perceptive comment. He said that issues about following rules were less important than the kinds of moral implications that the existence of rules entailed. As a fellow golfer, he reminded me that one who violated a rule was cheating, and it was this dimension that ought to be studied intensively. As far as I know he never published anything on this topic himself.

I was the only "professional philosopher," except Isabel C. Hungerland, whom he allowed to attend the class. At that time he was talking about the differences between effects, causes, and consequences (notions that obviously directly bear on utilitarianism, though he never mentioned the word at all). His teaching technique was unusual. Instead of lecturing, he involved the ten or so graduate students in a joint collegial inquiry into the subject. This consisted of a student's writing on the blackboard a sentence, such as "The effects of the explosion could be felt for miles," and then substituting for "effects" the words "results" and "consequences" to see if they fit. With respect to these replacements the whole class would be consulted and suggested options explored. Sometimes (depending on the sentence) such substitutions fit and sometimes they did not. When they did not, it led to a discussion of why this might be so. In each case further linguistic moves, often involving new sentences, were tried. Adjectives and adverbs were inserted into each sentence to see if there was any change of meaning and whether they did or did not make sense in that particular context. One might have tried "unfortunate" or "voluntary" before "effects," for example.

After weeks of such linguistic manipulations a penumbra of words was discovered to "hang together" with a particular term but not with the others. Gradually, as a cluster of such words was built up, the *sense* of each term was revealed. Austin's teaching technique was nondirective. Instead of issuing authoritative decisions, he would say, "Suppose we try this word here," or "What do you think if we insert this locution there?" and so forth. It was a fascinating and original form of teaching in my experience. Austin had also given this seminar when he visited Harvard in 1955. He urged Zeno Vendler, who participated in it, to write a paper on the topic. The result (not an effect or consequence) was a splendid essay, "Effects, Results, and Consequences," published in Vendler's *Linguistics in Philosophy* in 1967. Readers who wish to get a feeling for the powerful insights such an inquiry can produce should read Vendler's essay. Nothing in the previous history of Western philosophy will prepare them for the originality of his account of the complex relationships holding between causes and effects.

In the seminar and outside it Austin was gracious and hospitable and extremely witty in conversation. To give you some idea of his sense of humor, let me quote three brief passages from his writings. At the end of "The Meaning of a Word," he says: "On these matters, dogmatists require prodding: although history indeed suggests that it may sometimes be better to let sleeping dogmatists lie" (1970b:75).

The opening paragraph of "Truth" runs as follows:

> 1. 'What is truth?' said jesting Pilate, and would not stay for an answer. Pilate was in advance of his time. For 'truth' itself is an abstract noun, a camel, that is, of a logical construction, which cannot get past the eye even of a grammarian. We approach it cap and categories in hand: we ask ourselves whether Truth is a substance (the Truth, the Body of Knowledge), or a quality (something like the colour red, inhering in truths), or a relation ('correspondence'). But philosophers should take something more nearly their own size to strain at. What needs discussing rather is the use, or certain uses, of the word 'true.' In *vino*, possibly, '*veritas*', but in a sober symposium '*verum*'. (1970b:117)

In *Sense and Sensibilia* wit and philosophical insight are inextricably mixed.

> Then there are differences of another kind in the ways in which 'looks like' may be meant and may be taken. We are about to watch, from seats high up at the back of the stadium, a football match in which one of the teams is Japanese. I might say,
>
> (1) 'They look like ants'; or
>
> (2) 'They look like Europeans'
>
> Now it is plain enough that, in saying (1) I do *not* mean either that I am inclined to think that some ants have come on to the field or that the players, on inspection, would be found to look exactly, or even rather like ants. (I may know quite well, and even be able to see, that for instance they haven't got that very striking sort of nipped-in waist). (1962b:40)

Despite a vast number of passages like these, the impression existed during his lifetime that Austin was aloof and cold. Mistaken though it is, there may be reasons that explain this reputation. Compare Austin with Moore, for example. Austin was like Moore in being very much a family man. But unlike Moore, who effusively enjoyed eating and drinking, walking, gardening, talking with his friends, and playing the piano for them, Austin treated his home as a kind of shelter. He could entertain delightfully if the occasion required it, but in general he did not need or want the distraction of many acquaintances. He married in 1941 and had four children, two daughters and two sons. The marriage and his family were sources of satisfaction and happiness that, as Warnock relates, "he found nowhere else, and I have no doubt that this devotion explains in a large measure the impression of detachment, of remoteness even, which he sometimes made in other settings."

Austin's death in February 1960, at the age of forty-nine, was unforeseen and left a terrible gap at Oxford. Warnock's description is very moving: "His fine-drawn features—his face, as Shaw said of Voltaire's, was 'all intelligence'—had for some months looked rather worn and tired; but in the end he was scarcely known to be ill before it was clear that he was dying."

The cause of death was cancer. Austin was at the height of his philosophical powers when he died. It is interesting to speculate on how his thinking would have developed and what effect it would have had on analytic philosophy in the last half of the twentieth century. My own guess is that its consequences would have been momentous and that the course of mainstream philosophy would have been radically different had he lived for another two or three decades.

### *Philosophy*

Austin's publications were few in number, yet their impact on the profession was tremendous. What we have are the following: about fourteen or fifteen essays, a dozen of which have been collected and published under the title *Philosophical Papers*. Two books, *Sense and Sensibilia* and *How to Do Things with Words*, were posthumously reconstructed by Warnock and Urmson, respectively, from Austin's extensive lecture notes. To these we can add three or four minor pieces and a critical review, "Intelligent Behavior," of *The Concept of Mind* in the *Times Literary Supplement* in 1950. This brief review is Austin at his best—witty, trenchant, and profound. With respect to Ryle's claim to have expunged the ghost from the machine, Austin writes:

> Those who, like Professor Ryle, revolt against a dichotomy to which they have been once addicted, commonly go over to maintain that only one of the alleged pair of opposites really exists at all. And so he, though he does not believe the body is a machine, does believe that it alone, and not the "ghost," exists: he preaches with the fervour of a proselyte a doctrine of "one world." Yet what has ever been gained by this favourite philosophical pastime of counting worlds? And why does the answer always turn out to be one or two, or some similar small, well-rounded philosophically acceptable number? Why, if there are nineteen of anything, is it not philosophy? (1970a:47–48)

One of Austin's characteristic themes is contained in this paragraph. Why are philosophers addicted to a simple dichotomy or, even worse, to just one aspect of it? As he says: "Why, if there are nineteen of anything, is it not philosophy?" Is there a resonance here of Aristotle's comment in Book XII, chapter 8, of the *Metaphysics* that there are either forty-seven or fifty-five unmoved movers, not just one?

The bulk of Austin's writings falls into two groups. The first consists of a meticulous examination of four profound problems: other minds, freedom of the will, our knowledge of the external world, and the nature of truth. The second group is directed toward something new in the history of philosophy: an attempt to provide a theory or a general account of what he calls "speech acts"—what they are and how they function in human communication. Some of the writings deal with topics in both groups (e.g., "Other Minds"), but most do not. Austin's approach to the issues in the two groups is both deflationary and constructive. These are consequences that flow from his careful description of the ordinary uses of various linguistic idioms. The constructive aspect provides an accurate account of the meanings and uses of these locutions, and the deflationary aspect demonstrates how misleading, misguided, or even unintelligible many traditional philosophical treatments of some of these matters are.

I will list the main writings that belong to each group:

**Group I**

1. Other Minds
    a. "Other Minds," 1946
    b. "Pretending," 1958
2. Freedom of the Will
    a. "If and Cans," 1956
    b. "A Plea for Excuses," 1956–1957
    c. "Three Ways of Spilling Ink," 1958
3. Truth
    a. "Truth," 1950
    b. "Unfair to Facts," 1954
4. The External World Problem
    a. "Are There A *Priori* Concepts?" 1939
    b. *Sense and Sensibilia*, 1962

**Group II (Speech Acts)**

a. "Other Minds," 1946
b. "How to Talk: Some Simple Ways," 1953–1954
c. "Performative Utterances," 1956
d. *How to Do Things with Words*, 1962
e. "Performative-Constative," 1963

It would obviously be infeasible to attempt to discuss each of these topics here. Instead, I will concentrate on his method, which he believed could be applied to any philosophical concern. Though other writers, such as Moore, Wittgenstein, and Ryle, had emphasized the importance of studying ordinary language and its relationship to philosophical perplexities, no other philosopher explored this topic in the depth and with the care that Austin did. In practice his approach is thus something absolutely new in the history of philosophy. I shall first explain what it is and then show how it casts new light on two of the issues mentioned earlier: freedom of the will and the nature of speech acts. Austin was always reluctant, of course, to generalize about philosophical matters, but he did so in two places, first and extensively at the beginning of "A Plea for Excuses" and again, to a lesser degree, at the beginning of *Sense and Sensibilia*.

### *Austin's Method*

Austin's method rests on two tenets. I shall call them the "first word principle" and the "ontological applicability principle," respectively. Both are clearly expressed in "A Plea for Excuses."

1. The first word principle states that everyday language has a long history. It has been used for eons by people for a variety of purposes, among which are the drawing of various distinctions. It is a tool used in the practical business of life and, accordingly, has survival value. We distinguish males from females, the inanimate from the animate, friends from enemies, and in more sophisticated ways, edges from surfaces, circles from squares, and so on. The list of such distinctions is endless. The making of such distinctions is not arbitrary, but each distinction has a purpose that is connected with the mundane, ongoing activities of ordinary human beings. The essential feature of the first word principle is that ordinary language contains many distinctions and that these have come down to us in more or less intact forms.

2. The ontological applicability principle is a corollary of the first word principle. It states that these distinctions are more than verbal—namely, that they pick out or discriminate actual features in the world. Thus the distinction between male and female is not simply a linguistic contrast but actually marks out divergent physical and social traits whose discrimination is important in everyday life. Of course, some distinctions embedded in ordinary language may arise from superstition or ignorance and fail in this

respect. But these are exceptions. We can thus assume, at least prima facie, that if a distinction exists—and has existed for a long time—in ordinary discourse we can expect to find its correlate in the real world.

### *Excuses and Free Will*

With these two principles in hand, we can follow Austin's resolution of the free will problem. As we shall see, it is intimately connected to the observation that ordinary language discriminates various types of excuses from other forms of human behavior. The argument is subtle and complex. In "A Plea for Excuses" Austin begins by asking: "When, then, do we 'excuse' conduct, our own or somebody else's? When are 'excuses' proffered?"

The answer is that the situation is one in which someone is said to have done something bad, wrong, inept, or unwelcome. Thereupon he, or someone on his behalf, will try to defend his conduct or to get him out of it. In such a case the defense can take two lines: one can admit that one did the thing in question and argue that it was a good thing to do. A person who tried to murder Hitler might state in court that he was proud of his attempt. To follow this track is to *justify* the action. A different way of going about things is to admit that one did something untoward but to deny that one intended to. I was cleaning the gun and it went off. It was an accident. I didn't mean to do it and so forth. This is to give an excuse. Austin's initial move is thus to draw a contrast between a justification and an excuse.

Now, why is it important to study excuses? In ethics we study the good and the bad, the right and the wrong, the obligatory and the forbidden, and this to a great extent is connected with conduct—with the doing of actions. But it is important to realize that the concept of "doing an action," as used in philosophy is a highly abstract notion. Yet Austin stresses, " 'in sober philosophy' we need to ask such questions as: Is to sneeze to do an action? Or is to breathe, or to see, or to checkmate, or each one of countless others? In short, for what range of verbs, as used on what occasions, is 'doing an action' a stand-in?" (1970b:179). The study of excuses can throw light on these matters. To examine excuses is to examine cases in which something has been done, but in which an aberrance or failure occurred. These are then special sorts of doings. But if they are special, why study them? Austin answers: "As so often, the abnormal will throw light on the normal, will help us to penetrate the blinding veil of ease and obviousness that hides the mechanisms of the natural successful act" (p. 180). By analyzing excuses, one can thus obtain a more perspicuous view of the complexities involved in doing *any* action. Furthermore, he avers: "In examining all the ways in which each action may not be 'free', i.e., the cases in which it will not do to say simply 'X did A', we may hope to dispose of the problem of Freedom" (p. 180).

The previous paragraph contains a sentence whose significance may have been overlooked in a quick reading. Austin says: "As so often, the abnormal will throw light on the normal." He does not expatiate on this remark in the essay or indeed anywhere else, but it is a notable feature of his method—and one that no other philosopher had previously thought of, including Wittgenstein. This is the idea that by studying the deviant we cast light on the standard case. Austin does this throughout his writings: instead of discussing statements he discusses performatives, which are linguistic expressions that look like statements but are neither true nor false and play different roles from statements. Or again, in its canonical formulations the free will problem asks whether a person's behavior is wholly determined by antecedent conditions, and if so, whether that person can be held *responsible* for what she or he has done. Instead of investigating the notion of responsibility, in this essay Austin looks at its reverse side, those cases in which a person has done something but refuses to accept responsibility for it by pleading extenuating circumstances or proffering some other form of exculpation. The technique rests on the assumption that, by becoming clear about the reverse side of some concept or notions, we can become clear, or at least clearer, about its obverse side. He states that by means of this approach we can avoid a number of traditional blind alleys:

> First among these comes the problem of Freedom. While it has been the tradition to present this as the 'positive' term requiring elucidation, there is little doubt that to say we acted 'freely' (in the philosopher's use, which is only faintly related to the everyday use) is to say only that we acted *not* un-freely, in one or another of the many heterogeneous ways of so acting (under duress or what not). Like 'real', 'free' is only used to rule out the suggestion of some or all of its recognized antitheses. As 'truth' is not a name for a characteristic of assertions, so 'freedom' is not a name for a characteristic of actions, but the name of a dimension in which actions are assessed. In examining all the ways in which each action may not be 'free', i.e., the cases in which it will not do to say sim-

ply 'X did A', we may hope to dispose of the problem of Freedom. (1970b:128)

His solution to the problem of freedom is embedded in that paragraph. "Free," Austin says, is the name of a *dimension* in which actions are assessed. If it were the name of a property of actions, we could give a positive account of what makes an action free. But we cannot, because "free" is a word that acquires its meaning from the concepts it excludes. There are thus many ways in which an action can be free: "I shot the rat, he deserved it," or "I went there because I wanted to." Both exclude actions done under duress, but in the former case one explicitly accepts responsibility whereas in the latter the question of responsibility may not arise. There are also myriad ways in which actions may be unfree, and some of these involve excuses. "I have to wash my hands every ten minutes, I just can't help it," or "He held the gun to my head, so I had to open the safe," or "I stumbled and that's why I dropped the tray." All these are cases of being unfree, of one's being unable to control what one did, and in each case someone offers an excuse. But in each situation autonomy is absent in a different way. The former involves obsession, the second compulsion, and the third an accident. If we wish to explain to someone what it means to say "X is free," we will say such things as "X is not constrained," or "X is not compelled," and so forth. "Free" is thus used in ordinary speech as an excluder; it stands in contrast to such notions as "duress," "compulsion," or "constraint." In Austin's parlance it is a case where the negative use wears the trousers, where words like "duress" and "constraint" carry the meaning. We know what it is to tie somebody up—to constrain that person—and so forth. But we do not know, except by exclusion from such circumstances, what it is to be free. In cases where excuses are apposite, "free" is excluded though excluded in a gamut of different ways.

Given that "free" is a term of ordinary speech, and that it marks out a variety of contrasts, and given further that such distinctions capture features of human conduct, we can say that there are indeed cases of free action, just as there are cases of unfree action. According to the traditional puzzle about freedom, because every action has antecedent causes, no person could have chosen or behaved differently, and therefore no one is free. Though it may be true that every action is caused, it does not follow from that thesis that no actions are free. In fact, Austin draws the opposite conclusion from the conjunction of the first word principle and the ontological applicability principle. Together they entail that some actions are free and that some are unfree. The applicability of excuses in ordinary life reveals a gamut of differing kinds of unfree actions and, by contrast, a gamut of free actions. This result "disposes" of the problem of freedom.

Why do I call the first of these methodological maxims "the first word principle"? The answer is that Austin is very careful to emphasize that the appeal to ordinary language is not the *last* word. As he points out:

> Certainly ordinary language has no claim to be the last word, if there is such a thing. It embodies, indeed, something better than the metaphysics of the Stone Age, namely, as was said, the inherited experience and acumen of many generations of men. But then, that acumen has been concentrated primarily upon the practical business of life. If a distinction works well for practical purposes in ordinary life (no mean feat, for even ordinary life is full of hard cases), then there is sure to be something in it, it will not mark nothing: yet this is likely enough to be not the best way of arranging things if our interests are more extensive or intellectual than ordinary. And again, that experience has been derived only from the sources available to ordinary men throughout civilized history: it has not been fed from the resources of the microscope and error and fantasy of all kinds do become incorporated in ordinary language and even sometimes stand up to the survival test (only, when they do, why should we not detect it?) Certainly, then, ordinary language is *not* the last word: in principle it can everywhere be supplemented and improved upon and superseded. Only remember, it *is* the *first* word. (1970b:133)

One mistake some critics have made in discussing Austin's philosophy is to assume that ordinary language is the last word. Austin consistently denied that he ever held such a view, and indeed in his final work on speech acts he developed a taxonomy whose main terms—such as "locutionary," "illocutionary," and "perlocutionary"—do not belong to ordinary language at all. Thus he thought that there are circumstances in doing philosophy where ordinary language needs to be supplemented by a technical vocabulary. But he also never failed to stress that ordinary language is the first word. Any investigation should begin by considering its resources. In "A Plea for Excuses" Austin adds a dozen specific maxims to the principles I have mentioned. But these are too detailed to discuss here.

### *Speech Acts*

Austin's first discussion of this topic appeared in his 1946 paper "Other Minds." In this particular section he argues that although "I know" differs in various ways from "I promise," "I do," and "I warn," it resembles them in one respect. "I know" is one of those linguistic expressions that is typically used *not to describe or report* a state of mind but to perform a different function. For example, a person who says "I do" in certain circumstances is not describing his or her psychological attitudes or feelings but is using a traditional formula as part of the process of marrying someone. On such an occasion one's saying "I do" is a way of *doing* something, namely, of marrying. The term "speech act" appears for the first time in "How to Talk: Some Simple Ways," published in 1953.

In contrast to the six pages devoted to the topic in "Other Minds," the discussion in "How to Talk" is vastly expanded. Three years later Austin devoted a whole article, "Performative Utterances," to the topic. In 1962 Urmson edited a series of twelve lectures that Austin had given at Harvard University in 1955 and published them in book form under the title *How to Do Things with Words.* This work contains Austin's most extensive theory of speech acts; the entire doctrine is now reconstructed in a very sophisticated way. Austin distinguishes three different types of speech acts: the phonetic, the phatic, and the rhetic. The first of these is merely the act of uttering certain noises. The phatic act is the uttering of certain vocables or words, such as noises of certain types that belong to a certain vocabulary and conform to a certain grammar. The rhetic act is the performance of an act using those vocables with sense and reference. Thus "He said, 'The cat is on the mat'" reports a phatic act, whereas "He said that the cat was on the mat," reports a rhetic act.

These distinctions lead to another trio: that between locutionary, illocutionary, and perlocutionary acts. With respect to these the terminology of "acts" gives way to "forces." To speak of the "locutionary force" of an utterance is to speak about its meaning (sense). Austin describes this speech act by saying that in a sentence like "He said to me, 'Shoot her,'" he would *mean* by "shoot" shoot and by "her" her. An illocutionary act consists of words used in their standard senses to do what, in this particular case, one would say is *urging* or *advising* or *ordering* me to shoot her. Urging or advising is thus the force of the utterance. The perlocutionary act describes the result of such urging or advising, namely, that he *persuaded* or *induced* me to shoot her. Once again the persuading or inducing is called a "force" by Austin. By the twelfth lecture even these classifications are seen to be too simple. Austin now distinguishes (p. 150) five more general categories of utterance, classified according to their illocutionary force:

1. Verdictives
2. Exercitives
3. Commissives
4. Behabitives
5. Expositives

Austin explains each of these in detail—in the sort of detail we cannot pursue here. An example, however: verdictives, as the name suggests, are typified by the giving of a verdict—say, by a jury, judge, umpire, or arbiter. Such verdicts may take various forms, for example, they can be estimates, assessments, reckonings, or appraisals. Verdictives are thus special cases of what earlier philosophers called "uses" of language. The concept of "use" is thus deepened and greatly refined by Austin in this book.

As can be seen from this description, this mature account of speech acts had become enormously complex. Therefore, rather than trying to explain, via such a complicated system, what Austin is getting at by the notion of a speech act, I shall describe the theory in a somewhat simpler form, as expressed in the article "Performative Utterances" of 1956. It should be emphasized that some of the distinctions I will mention were eventually superseded in *How to Do Things with Words*.

### *Performatives*

Austin begins by describing what he calls "the traditional view" of language. In this conception the only interesting feature of any utterance is its capacity to be true or false. This view was doubtless influenced by thinking of ordinary language as if it were a logical calculus, consisting of declarative sentences. Philosophers thus concentrated on what they called "propositions," "statements," and "assertions" and more or less ignored other uses of language. A good example of this approach was to be found in the work of the logical positivists, who argued that every cognitively meaningful sentence is either true or false and, if so, is either logically determinate or empirically verifiable. Other sentential forms—imperatives, optatives—and their typical uses, to issue orders or express wishes and so forth, were paid lip service only; insofar as they were mentioned at all, they were regarded as literally nonsensical.

As we saw in chapter 3, the positivists, in responding to criticisms, eventually broadened their horizons and classified moral pronouncements, historical and literary remarks, and other nonpropositional forms as having emotive, hortatory, or poetic meaning. But none of these locutions was *cognitively* meaningful. That appellation was reserved for those sentences that are either true or false. Austin called this emphasis the "descriptive fallacy." The fallacy consists in relegating all sorts of utterances to the category of the nonsensical that do not belong there. His investigation in contradistinction was into a group of speech acts that look like statements and that grammatically might be classified as such, yet are neither true nor false while being perfectly meaningful. These he called "performatives." His identification of such a class was thus a major countercase to the positivist contention that only those locutions that are either true or false are cognitively meaningful.

Though performatives are neither true nor false, they sometimes imply things that are. For example, in saying "I do" under normal circumstances of marrying, one implies that one is not already married. To recognize that certain kinds of conditions must obtain or a speech act is null is an important insight into their logic. Austin labels such misfires "infelicities," and a substantial portion of "Performative Utterances" is concerned with identifying the rules whose violations lead to infelicitous speech acts. Austin lists at least seven such rules, while pointing out that the list may well not be complete. First, a procedure must actually exist if a performative is to be in order. Thus in England and the United States, unlike in Saudi Arabia, one cannot divorce one's wife merely by saying "I divorce you." That procedure is not extant in these countries. Second, certain circumstances must obtain or the act will misfire. "I appoint you consul," but you are already appointed or you are a horse. Or "I pick George," but George refuses to play. Third, one must carry the procedure through correctly. You say, "I nominate you the Queen Elizabeth," when you should have said "name." A fourth sort of flaw is insincerity: "I congratulate you," or "I promise to be there," when you do not mean it. A fifth kind of infelicity involves misunderstandings: you may not hear what I say or take me to be referring to something entirely different. Sixth are what Austin calls "unhappinesses," the doing of something under duress, and seventh are cases in which the act is not seriously performed (for example, in a play or as part of a joke—"Go catch a falling star").

How can one tell when x is a performative? Austin says we need a grammatical criterion. He notes that all these examples begin with a verb in the first-person singular, present active indicative (e.g., "I promise," "I order," "I warn you," etc.). This is often accompanied by the addition of the term "hereby" (e.g., "I hereby appoint you vice chancellor"). Here we seem to have a criterion. But not every performative has to take these two standard forms: "shut the door," and "there is a bull in the pasture" may be orders or warnings and so forth. To say "you are hereby warned there is a bull in the pasture" is simply more explicit than "there is a bull in the pasture." Another grammatical feature is the asymmetry between such first-person pronouncements and their third-person counterparts. "I promise" is performatory, but "he promised" is not; it is generally a report of what he did.

But even this list of rules and grammatical features is hardly sufficient to determine the character of a speech act. To these examples one must add such indexes as tone of voice, cadence, various gestures, and circumstances. Circumstances help one decide whether I am ordering, advising, warning, or cajoling. The upshot of his discussion is that even when all these different rules and other complexities are made explicit, the distinction between a statement and a performative is still not crystal clear. For example, is "hurrah" a performative? Is "I am sorry" a performative or a report of one's feelings? When the umpire says, "You are out," his remark is connected to the facts, and it is also a verdict. But most puzzling of all is: "I state that . . ." which seems to report an act of stating and therefore to be true or false and yet is also like "I order you . . ." and thus is neither true nor false. So it seems to be like both a statement and a performative. Moreover, statements are not just either true or false but are also subject to felicity and infelicity conditions. For example, "all John's children are asleep," but John doesn't have any children. In that case the locution seems very much like "I promise to go" when I have no intention to be there. In the case of John's children is the locution meaningless or nonsensical? It surely seems to be infelicitous, something like selling a property that does not exist.

Austin thus recognizes that statements have ills that parallel those of performatives. Therefore we can ask with respect to statements not only are they true or false but are they in order? The question also applies to performatives: are they in order? One can ask: was it a justified warning, a good estimate, a sound verdict? With statements: are they fair, adequate, not exaggerated, precise, and accurate? These reflections lead Austin reluctantly to conclude that "I state" is performing the act of stating, just as saying "I order you" is performing the act of ordering. Therefore in both cases, in saying something, one is doing something. But if so, is the original distinction between statements and performatives not viable? Austin ends the article without answering the question. But he does believe that we can still make a tenable distinction between the meaning and the force of an utterance and that this therefore is the direction that new research into speech acts should follow. This suggestion led to the elaborate theory in *How to Do Things with Words.* Part of that theory is that the distinction between statements (now called "constatives") and performatives is replaced by the distinction between the locutionary, illocutionary, and perlocutionary forces of utterances.

*Criticisms of Austin*

We have seen that Ryle differentiates between his work and Austin's by saying that six days out of seven he, Ryle, was concerned with questions of sense versus nonsense, whereas Austin was interested in such things as warnings, cajolings, and other types of speech acts. Ryle's remarks can be taken as a statement of fact, but they can also be read as a subtle criticism of Austin. As he says: "Each of us would think—wrongly—that there is not much real meat in the unfavoured question." But whatever his intentions, the facts do not bear him out. Austin's writings contain extensive discussions of questions of sense and nonsense, of the meaningful and the meaningless. It is true, of course, that he was also interested in speech acts. But the two interests are not incompatible, and both are well represented in his work. At the beginning of *How to Do Things with Words* Austin connects up his interest in speech acts with traditional concerns about nonsense. He writes:

> First, and most obviously, many 'statements' were shown to be, as KANT perhaps first argued systematically, strictly nonsense, despite an unexceptional grammatical form: and the continued discovery of fresh types of nonsense, unsystematic though their classification and mysterious though their explanation is too often allowed to remain, has done on the whole nothing but good. Yet we, that is, even philosophers, set some

> limits to the amount of nonsense that we are prepared to admit we talk: so that it was natural to go on to ask, as a second stage, whether many apparent pseudo-statements really set out to be 'statements' at all. It has come to be commonly held that many utterances which look like statements are either not intended at all, or only intended in part, to record or impart straightforward information about the facts. . . . Along these lines it has by now been shown piecemeal, or at least made to look likely, that many traditional philosophical perplexities have arisen through a mistake—the mistake of taking as straightforward statements of fact utterances which are *either* (in interesting non-grammatical ways) nonsensical *or else* intended as something quite different. (1962a:2)

Austin does not always use the term "nonsense" in making a particular point. He often says such things as "no modifying expression is permissible" or "in order" or that it does not make "good sense." But these idioms are equivalent to what Ryle means when he uses "nonsense." Consider the following example from "A Plea for Excuses":

> Expressions modifying verbs, typically adverbs, have limited ranges of application. That is, given any adverb of excuse, such as 'unwittingly' or 'spontaneously' or 'impulsively', it will not be found that it makes good sense to attach it to any and every verb of 'action' in any and every context: indeed, it will often apply only to a narrow range of such verbs. Something in the lad's upturned face appealed to him, he threw a brick at it—'spontaneously'? (1970b:190)

His writings are replete with such cases. Ryle's comments are thus not as telling as he thought.

A more serious criticism is the following. It has been suggested that Austin's approach is wholly introspective. This charge was made by W. V. O. Quine in the mid-1960s, and it has been echoed by many other commentators. The suggestion is that Austin asks himself, "What would I say when . . ." and provides an answer that may not represent what ordinary speakers would say at all. Austin, after all, was an Englishman, a trained classicist, a professor at Oxford, and a philosopher. He is not likely to have used the language in the way that "the man in the street" might. It is also true that in his classes Austin asked the other participants what they would also say, so that his approach was not purely subjective. But it is also a fact that these other individuals were looking inward to determine what each of them should say when. The complaint is that none of this is genuine research in the way that a field linguist might conduct it. Austin anticipated this objection and discussed it in "A Plea for Excuses." Here is how he responded to it:

> Well, people's usages do vary, and we do talk loosely, and we do say different things apparently indifferently. But first, not nearly as much as one would think. When we come down to cases, it transpires in the very great majority that what we had thought was our wanting to say different things of and in *the same* situation was really not so—we had simply imagined the situation slightly differently: which is all too easy to do, because of course no situation (and we are dealing with *imagined* situations) is ever 'completely' described. The more we imagine the situation in detail, with a background of story—and it is worth employing the most idiosyncratic, or sometimes, boring means to stimulate and to discipline our wretched imaginations—the less we find we disagree about what we should say. Nevertheless, *sometimes* we do ultimately disagree: sometimes we must allow a usage to be, though appalling, yet actual; sometimes we should genuinely use either or both of two different descriptions. But why should this daunt us? All that is happening is entirely explicable. If our usages disagree, then you use 'X' where I use 'Y', or more probably (and more intriguingly) your conceptual system is different from mine, though very likely it is at least equally consistent and servicable: in short, we can find why we disagree—you choose to classify in one way, I in another. If the usage is loose, we can understand the temptation that leads to it, and the distinctions that it blurs: if there are 'alternative' descriptions, then the situation can be described or can be 'structured' in two ways, or perhaps it is one where, for current purposes, the two alternatives come down to the same. A disagreement as to what we should say is not to be shied off, but to be pounced upon: for the explanation of it can hardly fail to be illuminating. If we light on an electron that rotates the wrong way, that is a discovery, a portent to be followed up, not a reason for chucking physics: and by the same token, a genuinely loose or eccentric talker is a rare specimen to be prized. (1970b:183–84)

For other criticisms I recommend the papers by Roderick Chisholm, C. G. New, John R. Searle, Jonathan Bennett, and A. J. Ayer that appear in *Symposium on J. L. Austin*, edited by K. T. Fann (1969). These cover most of the major objections to Austin's philosophy. It should be mentioned in concluding this chapter that though ordinary language philosophy at the end of the century has fewer practitioners than it did in the 1950s, 1960s, and 1970s, it still has some. But it is Austin's contributions to speech act theory that are still live topics in philosophy and linguistics today. The theory was extended and refined by Vendler in *Linguistics in Philosophy* (1967), by John Searle in *Speech Acts* (1969) and *The Construction of Social Reality* (1995); and by A. P. Martinich in *Communication and Reference* (1984). They independently showed that, via speech act theory, the philosophy of language can be construed as a branch of the philosophy of action. Speech acts are types of actions, involving intentional human behavior. Further advancing this line of thought, Grice later established that the philosophy of action can be construed as a subdomain of the philosophy of mind. Such a connection with the philosophy of language was already presupposed in Ryle's contributions, but it was greatly advanced by the work of Vendler, Searle, and Grice. As a result of these developments, the philosophy of language, which began with Frege and Russell has, via the doctrine of speech acts, virtually become absorbed into the philosophy of mind. This expansion of the philosophy of mind has been one of the most significant changes in analytic philosophy in the last half of the century. The seeds of these major developments are thus traceable to Austin's creation of speech act theory.

Like Wittgenstein, Moore, and Ryle, Austin's work was not overtly influenced by the developments in mathematical logic. The later Wittgenstein was antithetical to the use of formal logic in dealing with philosophical questions. Austin's attitude was that of tolerant neglect. He simply did not find it relevant to his particular concerns. With W. V. O. Quine, whom we shall discuss in the next chapter, the situation is entirely different. He stands firmly rooted in the traditions of Frege, Russell, and Carnap.

CHAPTER SEVEN

# W. V. O. Quine

With Quine the philosopher and with Quine the man we encounter paradox. Quine the philosopher has stated that science is self-conscious common sense and that his doctrines are an extension of science; yet he has also asserted that there are no meanings, no propositions, no attributes, no relations, no numbers, and no analytic truths. What could be more paradoxical than the claim that there are no numbers? How could anyone count unless there were numbers? And now the second paradox. This concerns Quine the man and the disparity between his professional and autobiographical writings. The former are invariably elegant and clever. He once said: "There is many a slip betwixt subjective cup and objective lip." In responding to Jaakko Hintikka's "Quine on Who's Who," he wrote: "Let me stress all flat-footedly, and not for the first time, that familiarity carries no presumption of clarity. It merely breeds contentment." Or consider this passage from "On What There Is": "This is the old Platonic riddle of non-being. Non-being must in some sense be, otherwise what is it that there is not? This tangled doctrine might be nicknamed *Plato's beard*; historically it has proved tough, frequently dulling the edge of Occam's razor" (1953:1–2).

Quine (1908–) has written two autobiographies, and one would expect them to reflect the engaging and facetious personality we find in his philosophical works. Surprisingly, they do not. The larger of the two, *The Time of My Life* (1985), is a carefully itemized, 499-page travelogue. Large stretches of it have much of the charm of a railroad timetable. The smaller, forty-six-page "Autobiography of W. V. Quine" is the opening segment of the *Philosophy of W. V. Quine* in the Library of Living Philosophers Series (1986). It is more personal and more interesting, especially when Quine describes his adolescence and then later his modus operandi as a philosopher. I shall therefore use it as a basis in what follows. It begins with his boyhood in Akron, Ohio, carries the reader from his undergraduate days at Oberlin College through his subsequent career at Harvard to his postretirement life. Like the bigger work, it contains an extensive itinerary of places he has visited. In neither is there the kind of wit one expects from Quine and very little substantive discussion of either people or places. It is surely paradoxical that his autobiographies should be less sparkling than his technical studies, and I shall try to explain why this is so. Here is a typical passage from the "Autobiography of W. V. Quine" by way of illustration:

> The spring and summer of 1970 were extraordinary, I said, but I have only begun to say why. In June I went to three commencements: to Columbia for a gold medal and to Temple and Oxford for my seventh and eighth honorary doctorates. (The earlier ones were from Oberlin, Ohio State, Akron, Washington, Lille, and Chicago.) Oxford meant going to Europe, so [Dagfinn] Follesdal suggested adding an Arctic jaunt and [Donald] Davidson a safari. Follesdal met me at Helsinki and we drove to the Arctic Ocean. Marge, Douglas, and Margaret joined us in the Arctic and we zigzagged through scenic Norway to a logic meeting at Oslo, where I spoke on predicate-functor logic. After Oxford we made rendezvous with the three Davidsons in Ethiopia and prowled East Africa seven strong, mostly in rented microbusses. The Davidsons had done complex and masterly prearranging. (1986:39)

During his forty-two-year career numerous famous personages visited Harvard. Whitehead was a faculty member when Quine became a graduate student in 1930. Russell, Carnap, and Tarski were there together in the 1940s, and Austin spent a year in Cambridge in 1955. Many of Quine's students became notable philosophers in their own right, among them Burton Dreben, John Myhill, Henry Hiz, Hao Wang, William Craig, Davidson, and Follesdal. In the 1960s Harvard went through the turmoil of the student protests against the Vietnam War. In his "Autobiography" Quine briefly comments on Alfred North Whitehead and H. M. Sheffer but otherwise proffers no evaluation of his instructors, colleagues, or students; of his teaching experiences; of what he thought of Russell, Tarski, or Austin; or of contemporary developments in epistemology or logic. Frege and Carnap, however, are exempted. I shall say more about Carnap shortly. With respect to Frege, Quine writes: "My celebration of Frege in *Mathematical*

*Logic* and in the classroom must have helped to bring people to see Frege as the father of modern logic. Russell had introduced him to us long ago, but we remained unaware of how many of the good things of logic had been done first by Frege" (1986:21).

His one reference to the student revolution is characteristically disengaged: "I got unpaid leave from Harvard for the spring of 1968 and spent a pleasant term as visiting professor at Rockefeller University. I wanted to see how I might like moving to Rockefeller if the Harvard administration failed to contain the mounting disorders" (p. 37).

In 1953 he was a visitor at Oxford, occupying the prestigious George Eastman Chair. He frequented seminars given by Strawson and Grice and attended Austin's Saturday meetings of dons. From his review of Strawson's *Introduction to Logical Theory* and his contribution to a symposium on Austin, we know that Quine disagreed with their approaches. Yet in the two autobiographies he says nothing personal about them and makes no assessment of their views. The account of his reaction to Oxford is limited to two sentences: "Marge and I dined happily in many homes and I in thirteen colleges. Marge bore a daughter, Margaret" (1986:31).

Next to Wittgenstein, Quine is the most influential and important analytic philosopher of the second half of the century. To explain why is to confront both paradoxes. Perhaps they are more apparent than real. Let us start with some things that Quine says about himself.

## Biography

As we have seen, Quine's focus in the "Autobiography" is not on those things that most diarists or autobiographers assume to be of central importance: their personal feelings about and interactions with others, including lovers; the political and social events of the time; and the main issues and players in their professional fields. He writes succinctly about his two marriages: "My first marriage had subsided *pari passu,* roughly, with the war. Late in 1948 I married Marjorie Boynton, formerly a lieutenant in my command. A sabbatical semester opportunely began, and we drove through Mexico, and flew around Central America. At Oaxaca we settled down for weeks of intensive work, and at Tuxtla and Taxco. I was writing *Methods of Logic,* the outgrowth of my mimeograms, and Marge was typing it." Instead, as this passage suggests, his concentration is upon his philosophy, mainly how it developed, what he was thinking about at a given moment, and what publications such reflections led to. Quine's work is thus the central theme of the "Autobiography." Obviously, this was of consuming importance to him. Everything else is subordinated to it. But its various descriptions are not designed for the general reader. They tend to be highly technical and directed to exegetes. Here is a passage illustrative of a larger set. It describes what he was working on in 1944:

> The core of "On the Logic of Quantification" was a monadic decision procedure, less transparent but more efficient than the [Jacques] Herbrand method in O *Sentido*; more like [Heinrich] Behmann's. Then I systematized polyadic schemata as follows. Those obtainable by substitution in valid monadic schemata I called *monadically valid*, noting that the decision procedure for validity of monadic schemata afforded a decision procedure for monadic validity generally. I showed that the rest of the valid schemata could be inferred from the monadically valid ones by universal generalization and *modus ponens*. I recount this because I can now prove more. Let us now count as monadically valid rather the universal closures of the schemata obtainable by substitution in valid monadic schemata. Monadic validity in this sense is still decidable; and from these closed schemata we can derive all valid closed schemata by *modus ponens* alone. This follows from *Mathematical Logic* as improved by [George] Berry, since the axioms of quantification there are all monadically valid and *modus ponens* is the only rule. (1986:25)

In its last four pages the "Autobiography" comes alive. Quine now describes *how* he works. It is obvious that Quine himself has a special interest in communicating his modus operandi to the general reader. That he works obsessively is perhaps his main message. As he says, "I do not work on schedule. Mostly I have simply worked, unless some social engagement intervened, or an attractive opportunity for travel. In my seven-by-ten-foot retreat at our summer place, intent on some absorbing project such as *Set Theory and Its Logic*, I sometimes worked nearly a hundred hours a week" (1986:44).

We are also given a sense of why the autobiographies do not expatiate on places and persons. Clearly, Quine is a loner, absorbed by his own thoughts. Depending on what they are, the intrusions of the outside world are tolerated and sometimes even enjoyed. But to try to understand them is not of pressing concern. They are less important than his own conceptual ambience. One can paint no better picture of the man than he does himself:

> Mostly I have worked alone. For years my work in logic was almost necessarily a lone venture, there being little appropriate company in easy reach. But I think the causes run deeper. This is suggested by my reactions to lectures, to reading, and to discussion.
>
> Generally I have found it hard to sit through lectures; hard to keep my mind on them. As a boy I would sit long hours bored in school, dreaming of slipping down through a trap door into the cool basement and running to freedom. This impatience has persisted.
>
> Books serve me better, but still imperfectly. I can escape contentedly into books of linguistics or popular science or into the encyclopedia, but I study writings in my professional sphere with less patience, preferring evidently to get on with it on my own. Thus it was that my early work with *Principia Mathematica* suited me so well. I was using the book as a tool rather than passively reading it. Often in my later logic efforts I have tried to prove something anew rather than search and study a book that I knew must contain a proof of it. Both in logic and in philosophy I have tended to write first and search the literature only afterward for anticipations to acknowledge. Sometimes I have stopped searching too soon. This indocile habit of mind has obvious drawbacks. Surely it has led to inefficiency and duplication of effort.
>
> What then of oral discussion? Take first the mathematico-logical side. If someone makes or challenges a technical point, the matter can usually be settled in short order and I am always then gratified, except perhaps for chagrin at having erred indelibly in print. If on the other hand someone raises a technical problem that takes long pondering, I do better to go away and think alone.
>
> With philosophy proper, I find private discussion wasteful and frustrating except with persons of kindred outlook and purpose. Worse still is private argument with one who is motivated by vanity or *parti pris*; I withdraw when I sense motives other than desire for truth. But not so in public discussion, oral or written. Public discussion even with someone with unworthy motives or a very alien outlook can be of value in clarifying matters for receptive third parties. If the defining feature of debate is the desire to win, then private debate is folly but public debate can still have its purpose. (1986:43)

But nobody can work all the time, and Quine is no exception. He says:

> Research and writing and reviewing can have boring phases, too, and at times I have indeed taken refuge in leisure reading on irrelevant subjects for a time. Sometimes also I have escaped from some boring task into logic, thinking up a logical idea for no other purpose, deep down, than the escape itself. This is a sly escape, for it deceives the conscience. I think a couple of my little logic papers probably began thus. (p. 45)

This passage occurs on the penultimate page of the "Autobiography." It and the previous quotation are worth reading carefully. In the former Quine speaks about "escaping" from his work into linguistics, or popular science, or the encyclopedia, and in the latter he talks about taking "refuge" in "irrelevant" subjects. Irrelevant to what? To his real mission in life: his work. He also mentions escaping into logic and describes it as a "sly escape, for it deceives the conscience." I think he means that he is doing something easy in entertaining logical ideas, that is, doing something more facile than serious work in philosophy demands. That demand is obviously all encompassing for him. The language of isolation, refuge, and escape is revelatory. It tells us something profound about Quine the man and thus about the myopic character of the two autobiographies. Because his inward life is everything, his outward life is as solitary as a monk's. Many analytic philosophers deny that solipsism is a view that makes sense and, accordingly, that nobody could be one, even in principle. Yet in a way Quine is a solipsist—not a theoretical solipsist who denies there is an external world but a practicing solipsist who isolates himself from it. We have a description of solipsism in Wittgenstein's *Tractatus* that in a startling way fits Quine. Wittgenstein writes: "Logic fills the world: the limits of the world are also its limits." . . . "In fact what solipsism *means*, is quite correct, only it cannot be *said*, but it shows itself. That the world is *my* world, shows itself in the fact that the limits of the language (*the* language which I understand) mean the limits of *my* world." . . . "The world and life are one." . . . "I am my world (The microcosm)" (5.61; 5.62; 5.621; 5.63).

Clearly, logic fills Quine's world. The limits of its language are the limits of his world. "I am my world," Wittgenstein says. Quine the worker is his world. *Der Mann ist seiner Arbeit.* The autobiographies do not *state* that he is his world, but they *show* it. That is why he only alludes to external things—other human beings, political events, places, the philosophies of Austin, Grice, and Strawson—but never explores them. In a significant sense they are not part of *the* world. The unusual nature of the autobiographies—our first paradox about Quine the man—can thus be explained as the confessions of a solipsist. But such an explanation only engenders a greater mystery. Why would a solipsist write not one but two autobiographies?

## Philosophy

Quine's philosophical career can be divided into three successive phases. We shall call the first the logic stage. It begins in 1934 with his *A System of Logistic* and continues without other distractions roughly up to 1950 with the promulgation of *Methods of Logic*. In the intervening sixteen years three other books on logic appear: *Mathematical Logic* (1940), *Elementary Logic* (1941), and *O Sentido da Nova Lógica*, first published in 1944. He also published about forty papers in this period, almost all of them dealing with similar matters. Some titles: "Set-Theoretical Foundations for Logic," 1936; "On the Logic of Quantification," 1945; and "On Natural Deduction," 1950. Even after 1950 Quine's interest in logical theory continues; among his later publications are *Set Theory and Its Logic* and *Selected Logic Papers*, first published in 1963 and 1968, respectively, and *Philosophy of Logic* (1970).

A second, concurrent phase starts in 1939 with "Designation and Existence" and reaches its high point in 1948 with "On What There Is." Let us call this the semantic stage. In this period his concern is with the ontological implications of logic—for example, with the relationship between quantification theory and what exists. The two most important books in this period are *From a Logical Point of View* (1953), which is a collection of essays, and *The Roots of Reference* (1974). As one can see from the dates of his writings, the first and second phases overlap, and that is also true of the third, which begins later but incorporates the earlier segments. Let us call this the epistemological stage. It commences in 1951 with the appearance of "Two Dogmas of Empiricism." This is certainly Quine's most famous essay. It has been reprinted in at least twenty textbooks and has been translated into nearly every Western language, as well as into a host of exotic languages. His major book, *Word and Object*, followed in 1960 and was succeeded by such notable works as *Ontological Relativity and Other*

*Essays* (1969); *The Roots of Reference* (1974); *The Pursuit of Truth*, published in 1990; and *From Stimulus to Science*, which appeared in 1995. Besides "Two Dogmas," this period includes a number of other consequential essays, such as "Epistemology Naturalized," 1969; "On Empirically Equivalent Systems of the World," 1975; and "Two Dogmas in Retrospect" (1991).

Philosophically, this last is the most interesting stage; it pulls together into a comprehensive system the main and sometimes modified contributions of all three increments, including his earliest work in logic. The system at its apex is *scientistic*, *empiricist*, and *behaviorist*. Together these three main categories cover a wide gamut of theses and theories, each of which has generated a rich literature. This gamut can further be divided into two contrasting categories: those in which Quine rejects a number of traditional or concurrent views, and those in which he is affirming his own position. Among the items rejected are traditional metaphysics, the analytic-synthetic distinction, reductionism, modal logic, essentialism, and skepticism. Because each of these doctrines in diverse ways requires the existence of meanings, propositions, attributes, relations, or numbers, these are discarded as well. The views affirmed include an enhanced common sense, naturalism (in contrast to mentalism), physicalism (in opposition to phenomenalism), holism (in opposition to reductionism and atomism), pragmatism, undetermination of theory, indeterminacy of translation, radical translation, inscrutability of reference, and ontological relativity.

This complex web of doctrines leads to what I earlier called a paradox. Quine asserts that science is a continuation of common sense and that his philosophy is an extension of science. He also asserts, as just mentioned, that there are no meanings, propositions, relations, or numbers, a proposition that seems inconsistent with what either common sense or science would say. Still, what at first glance strikes the reader as paradoxical and counterintuitive may come to seem less so as one explores the supporting grounds for this intertwined network of conceits. That we are dealing here with a *system* should also be emphasized. In this respect Quine is unusual in the analytic tradition, whose practitioners are prone to piecemeal inquiry. System building is normally the metaphysician's modus operandi. It is surprising to find a Weltanschaaung in such a hard-nosed antimetaphysician. Like all systems his has its advantages and disadvantages: on the positive side it offers a synoptic explanatory theory that encompasses a wide range of phenomena; on the negative side, if any of its essential features—

such as its behaviorism—is found to be untenable, the whole system is vulnerable to collapse.

The best way to grasp the development of this comprehensive assemblage of facts, principles, and theses is to discover its stimulus in Carnap's work. As I mentioned earlier, Quine's autobiographies do not expatiate much on personalities, with the exceptions of Frege and Carnap. That he esteemed Frege is clear, but it is nothing compared to his admiration for Carnap. In August 1932, having received a Sheldon Travelling Fellowship, Quine went to Europe and spent five months in Vienna where he attended meetings of the Vienna Circle. Carnap had just moved to Prague and Quine followed him there. He regularly attended Carnap's lectures and "read his *Logische Syntax der Sprache* as it issued from Ina Carnap's typewriter." This interaction was to have a decisive influence on his subsequent career. Here is how a young man of twenty-four describes his initial contact with a famous professor: "It was my first experience of sustained intellectual engagement with anyone of an older generation, let alone a great man. It was my first really considerable experience of being intellectually fired by a living teacher rather than by a dead book."

Shortly after Carnap's death in 1970, Quine wrote to his daughter, Hanna Thost-Carnap, saying: "I deeply sympathize with you over the death of your father. Carnap was my old and valued friend, besides being the greatest of my teachers. So I very much share your personal sense of loss, as well as the sense of an overwhelming loss to philosophy." And in that same year, in a memorial statement read to the Philosophy of Science Association, he declared: "Carnap is a towering figure. I see him as the dominant figure in philosophy from the 1930's onward, as Russell had been in the decades before. Russell's well-earned glory went on mounting afterward, as the evidence of his historical importance continued to pile up; but the leader of the continuing developments was Carnap. Some philosophers would assign this role rather to Wittgenstein; but many see the scene as I do."

Carnap and Quine's interaction in 1932 was to begin a lifelong friendship, marked by mutual admiration and affection. Yet within a generally shared outlook that was antimetaphysical, that vigorously exploited the resources of modern logic and science for philosophical ends, and that could be broadly characterized as "empiricist," they had profound conceptual differences. The epistemological stage of Quine's thought exhibits both the attractions of Carnap's methodology and a powerful negative reaction to some of its fundamental tenets. Quine's ambivalence is clearly expressed in such essays as "Two Dogmas of Empiricism," first published in 1951; "On Carnap's Views on Ontology," 1951; and "Carnap and Logical Truth," 1954. The 1951 paper on Carnap, for example, begins with this statement: "Though no one has influenced my thought more than Carnap, an issue has persisted between us for years over questions of ontology and analyticity."

At the end of "Carnap and Logical Truth" Quine expatiates on their disagreement:

> Now I urge that scientists, proceeding thus, are not thereby slurring over any meaningful distinction. Legislative acts occur again and again; on the other hand a dichotomy of the resulting truths themselves into analytic and synthetic, truths by meaning postulate and truths by force of nature, has been given no tolerably clear meaning even as a methodological ideal.
>
> One conspicuous consequence of Carnap's belief in this dichotomy may be seen in his attitude toward philosophical issues as to what there is. It is only by assuming the cleavage between analytic and synthetic truths that he is able to declare the problem of universals to be a matter not of theory but of linguistic decision. . . . What impresses me more than it does Carnap is . . . how little basis there is for a distinction.

As these quotations illustrate, the issue that has "persisted between us for years" concerns ontic commitment and the analytic-synthetic distinction. Quine thinks that their divergencies about ontology ultimately stem from their differences about the analytic-synthetic "cleavage." Now, even if this is so, why should the latter disagreement be so important? The answer, as Roger Gibson has pointed out in his excellent *The Philosophy of W. V. Quine*, is that it is absolutely central to their conceptions of empiricism. They are in agreement that empiricism is *the* philosophy that best explicates the nature of science, and they concur that science provides the best theory of the world. What divides them is whether empiricism requires the analytic-synthetic distinction. Accordingly, their quarrel is about the character of the philosophy that best explains the nature of reality ("as to what there is," in Quine's parlance). But this is a deep dispute. It goes to the heart of what they think philosophy is all about. Despite a voluminous correspondence that lasted until Carnap's death in 1970, neither ever abandoned his fundamental conviction. For a detailed account of the debate, see their letters in *Dear Carnap, Dear Van* (Creath 1990). Richard Creath's introduction to this correspondence brings out the nature of the controversy in a pellucid way.

Let us look at the argument from Quine's perspective. Quine and Carnap both believe all knowledge derives from sense experience. This is the classical statement of empiricism that can be traced to Locke and Hume. But to this provision Carnap adds another, which Quine does not accept, namely, that sense experience requires a philosophical "reconstruction" to explain the organized and coherent theories one finds in science. Such a reconstruction is also a justification. A justification is needed because science cannot be derived merely from observation. Even a simple generalization, such as the law of falling bodies, speaks about all bodies and thus about more bodies than anyone has observed or ever will observe. Science thus has a nonobservational component that gives it much of its scope and conceptual force.

The philosophical task, as Carnap sees it, is to reconstruct the steps that justify the derivation of science from its experiential basis. This, for him, is the prime function of an empirical philosophy. Such a reconstruction may work in either of two ways: it may begin from theory and trace its origins to sense-data. Quine calls this procedure "the reductive thesis." As we shall see, he will reject this claim in the form advanced by Carnap. The second way is to start from sense experience and to show by logical steps how theory is constructed from an evidential base. But these steps are not observations; they are deductive and hence logical in character. In effect, they are analytic statements (often taking the form of definitions). Thus to develop a reconstruction of the coherent body of theory called "science," the philosopher must presuppose the distinction between the analytic and the synthetic. According to Carnap, the framework (*Der Rahmen*) of a scientific theory derives from analyticity; it is not a function of sense experience but of a priori decision. Thus there can be alternative frameworks, such as the adoption of a physicalistic language or a phenomenalistic language, that apply to the same set of observational data. Synthetic statements depend on sense experience and occur within the framework. Hence for Carnap the analytic-synthetic contrast is essential to empiricism, conceived as *the* philosophy of science.

But it was also important for another reason. The analytic-synthetic contrast was regarded by Carnap—and indeed by all the members of the

Vienna Circle—as indispensable in their assault upon metaphysics, including any form of rationalism, that is, the doctrine that pure reason can issue in substantive truths about reality. According to Carnap and his positivist colleagues, all the truths of reason, in particular those of mathematics, are analytic and as such are tautologous. Hence unlike synthetic truths, none of them carries existential import. The analytic-synthetic distinction was thus essential to their defense of empiricism, in explaining how all nontautologous knowledge derives from sense experience.

Quine rejects the Carnapian/positivist construal of empiricism on the ground that it presupposes there are analytic truths. He also rejects Carnap's interpretation of the task of empiricism. He contends that no reconstruction or justification of science by philosophy is either needed or possible. To assume that such an *Aufbau* is required is to assume that philosophy has a privileged position from which it can infallibly judge science. This is to think of empiricism as a *normative* philosophy, as laying down the rules that science must follow. And this is to assume the existence of a first philosophy that is self-validating. Quine believes that this is a kind of fantasy, entertained seriously only by philosophers. His alternative, which he labels "epistemology naturalized," denies that empiricism is normative. Instead, it recognizes that science goes its own way in developing theory and pays no attention to any such Carnapian reconstruction. The task of an empirical philosophy is simply to describe what scientists do. As Quine writes in "Epistemology Naturalized": "But why all this creative reconstruction, all this make-believe? The stimulation of his sensory receptors is all the evidence anybody has had to go on, ultimately, in arriving at his picture of the world. Why not just see how this construction really proceeds? Why not settle for psychology?" (1969:75).

In asking "Why not just see how this construction really proceeds?" Quine reminds one of Wittgenstein. Wittgenstein tells us: "Don't think, look!" Quine agrees. Both are saying, "Don't theorize, just look at human practice." Quine's "naturalized epistemology" is the doctrine that no justification beyond scientific practice itself is possible. His advocacy of psychology—by which he means behaviorism—is an alternative formulation of the same point. It entails the disavowal of philosophical reconstructionism. He "settles" for behaviorist psychology on the ground that the only evidence one has for what a scientist does in "arriving at his picture of the world" is the scientist's actual practice. And if we look without preconceptions or preconditions at the behavior of scientists, we find that they do not engage in "all this make-believe." They rely only on "the stimulation of their sensory receptors." His naturalized epistemology thus amounts to a new conception of empiricism—one, he insists, that more accurately captures the nature of scientific activity. It is a philosophy purified of the dogmas of the analytic-synthetic cleavage and reductionism. The opening sentences of his celebrated "Two Dogmas of Empiricism" boldly declare his opposition to the Carnapian program:

> Modern empiricism has been conditioned in large part by two dogmas. One is a belief in some fundamental cleavage between truths which are *analytic*, or grounded in meanings independently of matters of fact, and truths which are *synthetic*, or grounded in fact. The other dogma is *reductionism*: the belief that each meaningful statement is equivalent to some logical construct upon terms which refer to immediate experience. Both dogmas, I shall argue, are ill-founded. (1953:20)

Interestingly enough, though Quine treats the two dogmas separately throughout most of his paper, he eventually arrives at the position that they "are, indeed, at root identical." In order to see how he arrives at this conclusion, let us follow the structure of his essay, which begins with an attack on the analytic-synthetic distinction and then turns to the reductive thesis.

## The Analytic-Synthetic "Dogma"

Quine wishes to show that the supposed distinction cannot sensibly be drawn and develops a panoply of arguments to this effect. Accordingly, when he himself speaks of "analytic statements," he should be understood as implicitly adding "putative" or "so-called" to each occurrence of this epithet. He begins with the traditional view, which discriminates between logical truths and analytic statements. By "general philosophical acclaim" this first statement is said to be a logical truth, and the second statement is said to be an analytic statement:

1. No unmarried man is married.
2. No bachelor is married.

Quine has no objection to the concept of logical truth. A logical truth is a sentence that remains true under all reinterpretations of its components other than the logical particles. If we replace "man" in the first statement by "woman," for example, the resulting statement, "No unmarried woman is married," is logically true. But the situation is different with the second statement. It does not have the same logical form as the first. Quine states that philosophers have assumed that every analytic statement can be transformed into a logical truth by substituting synonyms for synonyms, for example, in this case by replacing "unmarried man" by "bachelor." This move, however, rests on an unanalyzed notion of "synonymy." But this, he will show, is as much in need of clarification as "analyticity" itself. Accordingly, his next step is to ask if we can make sense of "synonymy."

Those who contend that we can "find it soothing to say" that analytic statements reduce to logical truths by *definition*; "bachelor," for example, is *defined* as synonymous with "unmarried man." "Who," Quine queries, "defined it thus and when? If we appeal to the dictionary we are putting the cart before the horse." As he explains:

> The lexicographer is an empirical scientist, whose business is the recording of antecedent facts; and if he glosses 'bachelor' as 'unmarried man' it is because of his belief that there is a relation of synonymy between those forms, implicit in general or preferred usage prior to his own work. The notion of synonymy presupposed here has still to be clarified, presumably in terms relating to linguistic behavior. Certainly the "definition" which is the lexicographer's report of an observed synonymy cannot be taken as the ground of the synonymy. (1953:24)

Because reports of usage presuppose the concept of synonymy, Quine asks whether other kinds of definitions might capture this notion. Such other types of definitions include what Carnap calls "explications" and what logicians call "abbreviations." Explication is a definitional process that attempts to improve on the commonly accepted but vague meaning of a term; hence there may be many explications of the same explicandum. As enhancements, none of these can be regarded as strictly synonymous with the original locution. Abbreviations occur in regimented languages, such as *Principia Mathematica*, where $(p \supset q)$ is defined as $(\sim p \vee q)$. Such stipulations will not do because they assume the concept of synonymy rather than explain it. So recognizing that the notion of definition does not hold the key to synonymy and analyticity, Quine proposes that we concentrate on synonymy itself and "say no more" of definition.

This leads him to consider the suggestion that the synonymy of two linguistic forms consists simply in their interchangeability in all contexts without a change of truth value—interchangeability *salva veritate* in Leibniz's phrase. Quine produces a host of counterexamples to this idea. I will mention two. First, consider the sentence:

"Bachelor" has less than ten letters.

To replace "bachelor" by "unmarried male" would turn a truth into a falsehood. Similar remarks apply to sentences containing such phrases as "bachelor of arts" or "bachelor's buttons."

Second, interchangeability *salva veritate* is not a condition that is strong enough to assure synonymity. "Creature with a heart" and "creature with kidneys" may be interchanged *salva veritate* in extensional contexts, but clearly these concepts differ in cognitive significance. Interchangeability will not in general preserve truth in nonextensional contexts.

Therefore, abandoning this approach, Quine considers another, again because of Carnap. Carnap argues in *Meaning and Necessity* (1947) and elsewhere that one can use the semantic rules of a regimented language to define "analytic." But Quine objects to this on the ground that the resulting definition is not for "analytic" per se but only for "analytic-in-L," where L is the regimented language in question. So Carnap's solution is rejected as insufficiently general.

Finally, one might argue that "analyticity" might be explained in terms of the modal notion of "necessity." This move would produce the following sentence:

Necessarily all and only bachelors are unmarried men.

But the addition of "necessarily" does not really help, because the traditional interpretation of such a sentence is that it holds in "all state descriptions" because it is analytic. But then we are back where we started, that is, left with the problem of trying to make sense of "analytic." The use of "necessarily" in this line of reasoning produces, as Quine puts it, "an argument that is not flatly circular, but something like it. It has the form, figuratively speaking, of a closed curve in space" (1953:30).

Quine concludes this first part of his paper as follows:

> It is obvious that truth in general depends on both language and extralinguistic fact. The statement 'Brutus killed Caesar' would be false if the world had been different in certain ways, but it would also be false if the word 'killed' happened rather to have the sense of 'begat.' Thus one is tempted to suppose in general that the truth of a statement is somehow analyzable into a linguistic component and a factual component. Given this supposition, it next seems reasonable that in some statements the factual component should be null; and these are the analytic statements. But, for all its a priori reasonableness, a boundary between analytic and synthetic statements simply has not been drawn. That there is such a distinction to be drawn at all is an unempirical dogma of empiricists, a metaphysical article of faith. (p. 36)

After surveying this list of attempts to explain the concept of analyticity, Quine concludes that "a boundary between analytic and synthetic statements simply has not been drawn." Note his final remark. He accuses those who are committed to the analytic-synthetic distinction of being "unempirical empiricists" and, even worse, of being metaphysicians. These pejorative epithets bring out his deep and irresolvable differences with Carnap and the other positivists.

## The Dogma of Reductionism

After stating that in the course of the previous "somber reflections, we have taken a dim view first of the notion of meaning, then of the notion of cognitive synonymy, and finally of the notion of analyticity" (1953:37), Quine asks whether a key to these problems might not lie in the verification theory of meaning. He thinks this might be so on the ground that the verification theory holds that the meaning of a statement is the method of empirically confirming or infirming it. An analytic statement is the limiting case that is confirmed no matter what. But then one can ask: what is the relationship between a synthetic statement and the experiences that contribute to or detract from its confirmation? The most naive view of this relationship is what he calls the dogma of "radical reductionism." This is the thesis that each meaningful statement is translatable into a statement (true or false) about immediate experience. It is the view held by Locke and Hume. They argued that every idea must either originate directly in sense experience or be compounded of ideas thus originating. Quine states that this view can be rephrased in semantic jargon as holding that a term, to be significant at all, must be either a name of a sense-datum or an abbreviation of such a compound. A more sophisticated, later version of this view maintained that our statements as wholes be translatable into sense-datum language but not that they be translatable term by term. According to this reorientation, the primary vehicle of meaning is the statement rather than the term. This position was explicitly held by Frege and also by Russell in his theory of descriptions.

Quine also mentions that Carnap espoused this point of view when he wrote the *Aufbau* but later abandoned it when he realized that statements about the physical world could not be fully translated into statements about immediate experience. Quine says this revised version of radical reductionism is genuinely holistic but is nevertheless insufficient. It still adheres to the idea that a unique range of possible sensory events is associated with each statement, such that the occurrence of any of them would add to or detract from the likelihood of its truth.

The dogma of reductionism in this modified form can thus be described as the doctrine that *each* synthetic statement, "taken in isolation from its fellows," admits of confirmation or disconfirmation. Though this is an improvement on the term-by-term empiricism of Locke and Hume, it does not account for the nature of theorizing in science. What one means by such terms as "mass," "electron," and "velocity" depends upon the synoptic theory in which they are embedded. Newton's understanding of "simultaneity" is thus different from Einstein's because this notion plays radically different roles in their respective theories. No account of science is acceptable that does not recognize theory construction as a fundamental aspect of science. Each such theory is holistic in character; its constituent sentences and their constituent words depend for their meaning on the character of the theory. We must thus give up the idea that it is the individual sentence that is the basic repository of significance. Rather it is whole theories that impinge "upon the fabric of experience." Or, as Quine now expresses the matter in "Two Dogmas of Empiricism": "Our statements about the external world face the tribunal of sense experience not individually but only as a corporate body." This corporate body, which Quine asserts is "the unit of empirical significance," is no less than the whole of science.

## Empiricism Without the Dogmas

Having reached this stage in his explication and rejection of the second dogma, Quine concludes his essay by describing his new version of empiricism—an empiricism without the dogmas. Although this final section of his paper is only four pages long, it is a literary and philosophical tour de force. Ideally, one should quote the whole of it, but space considerations preclude my doing so. Still, in order for the reader to get some feel for its literary and conceptual power, I will reproduce the section's first two paragraphs verbatim:

> The totality of our so-called knowledge or beliefs, from the most casual matters of geography and history to the profoundest laws of atomic physics or even of pure mathematics and logic, is a man-made fabric which impinges on experience only along the edges. Or, to change the figure, total science is like a field of force whose boundary conditions are experience. A conflict with experience at the periphery occasions readjustments in the interior of the field. Truth values have to be redistributed over some of our statements. Reevaluation of some statements entails reevaluation of others, because of their logical interconnections—the logical laws being in turn simply certain further statements of the system, certain further elements of the field. Having reevaluated one statement we must reevaluate some others, which may be statements logically connected with the first or may be the statements of logical connections themselves. But the total field is so underdetermined by its boundary conditions, experience, that there is much latitude of choice as to what statements to reevaluate in the light of any single contrary experience. No particular experiences are linked with any particular statements in the interior of the field, except indirectly through considerations of equilibrium affecting the field as a whole.
>
> If this view is right, it is misleading to speak of the empirical content of an individual statement—especially if it is a statement at all remote from the experiential periphery of the field. Furthermore, it becomes

> folly to seek a boundary between synthetic statements, which hold contingently on experience, and analytic statements, which hold come what may. Any statement can be held true come what may, if we make drastic enough adjustments elsewhere in the system. Even a statement very close to the periphery can be held true in the face of recalcitrant experience by pleading hallucination or by amending certain statements of the kind called logical laws. Conversely, by the same token, no statement is immune to revision. Revision even of the logical law of the excluded middle has been proposed as a means of simplifying quantum mechanics; and what difference is there in principle between such a shift and the shift whereby Kepler superseded Ptolemy, or Einstein Newton, or Darwin Aristotle? (1953:42–43)

What Quine has just described is his alternative to the reductive dogma. That alternative is a radical form of holism. It is depicted in graphic metaphorical language in which the unit of empirical significance is now likened to a manmade fabric or, giving this image a scientific twist, to a field of force that covers sense experience. This field has a center occupied by the basic laws of physics and logic. These are the most certain pieces of knowledge humans possess. Fading off from them toward the periphery are the kinds of knowledge we possess in geography and history, and still closer to the edge of experience are particular mundane truths: that there are brick houses on Elm Street. It should be noted that this holistic view also encompasses the analytic-synthetic cleavage. The difference between so-called analytic and synthetic truths is simply a matter of degree. Any statement can be held true "come what may" and no statement is "immune to revision." How we treat such statements thus depends on the findings of future scientific inquiry. If the experimental data require it, even a logical truth, such as the law of excluded middle, may have to be abandoned to accommodate the discoveries of quantum mechanics. Quine's holism enables him to explain why the two dogmas are at root identical. If our statements about the external world face the tribunal of sense experience, not individually but only as a corporate body, and if this corporate body is such that no statement belonging to it is immune to revision, then no statement holds come what may. There are thus no analytic statements in the traditional sense. Statements differ only in the degree of tenacity with which they are held, and that degree of tenacity turns "upon our vaguely pragmatic inclination to adjust one strand of the fabric of science rather than another in accommodating some particular recalcitrant experience" (1953:46). This flexibility in revising the corporate body of theory is Quine's pragmatism. It is an integral part of his empiricism. As he says: "As an empiricist I continue to think of the conceptual scheme of science as a tool, ultimately, for predicting future experience in the light of past experience" (p. 44).

I should mention that Quine modified the radical holism of "Two Dogmas" in his treatise of 1960, *Word and Object.* Though he still continues to speak of "our statements" as forming a "corporate body," the earlier thesis that the corporate body is the whole of science has been replaced in *Word and Object* by "moderate holism." This is the doctrine that the corporate body of statements consists of individual segments of science rather than the whole of science. This modification is also accompanied by the admission that some observation sentences are individually confirmable or disconfirmable. This moderate form of holism has two consequences: it blurs the boundary between speculative metaphysics and science, thus giving a kind of credibility to metaphysics that Carnap would never have countenanced, and it emphasizes the importance of pragmatism as an essential ingredient of the scientific outlook. Still later his pragmatism was even further emphasized. In "Two Dogmas in Retrospect" (1991) Quine's analysis of how science should respond when a theory is refuted by a critical experiment was expressed as follows: "the crisis can be resolved by revoking one *or* another sentence of the cluster. We hope to choose in such a way as to optimize future progress. If one of the sentences is mathematical, we will not choose to revoke it; such a move would reverberate excessively through the rest of science. We are restrained by a maxim of minimum mutilation. It is simply in this, I hold, that the necessity of mathematics lies: our determination to make revisions elsewhere instead." The outcome of these revisions was to admit a kind of legitimacy to the analytic-synthetic contrast but on wholly pragmatic grounds. Analytic statements are those to which the maxim of minimal mutilation applies. When they appear in a system contradicted by recalcitrant experiment, other sentences in the system will always be revised first. This consequence still allows for Quine's refusal to grant that some propositions are analytic in the strong sense of the term espoused by the positivists.

Let us return to "Two Dogmas of Empiricism." At the end of this paper

Carnap reappears. Quine's pragmatism even in this early essay is much in play. He says:

> Carnap, Lewis, and others take a pragmatic stand on the question of choosing between language forms, scientific frameworks; but their pragmatism leaves off at the imagined boundary between the analytic and the synthetic. In repudiating such a boundary I espouse a more thorough pragmatism. Each man is given a scientific heritage plus a continuing barrage of sensory stimulation; and the considerations which guide him in warping his scientific heritage to fit his continuing sensory promptings are, where rational, pragmatic.

## Quine's Behaviorism

I mentioned that the three main and closely interconnected features of Quine's philosophy are its scientism, empiricism, and behaviorism. It remains to say a few words about the last of these. After the publication of "Two Dogmas" in 1951, Quine began to emphasize the behaviorist-cum-naturalist aspects of his philosophy. The major document with this thrust is *Word and Object*. Why this stress in his approach to such topics as meaning, synonymy, properties, attributes, and relations—to the whole world of abstractions? The answer derives from his scientism, the doctrine that science alone is the key to reality. And by "science" Quine means "scientific theory." So the question for him is whether scientific theory requires the existence of various kinds of abstract *entities*. His descriptive naturalism tells him that it does not. In particular, it is the word "entity" that he bridles at. He has no objection to glossing such notions as meaning and synonymy in wholly scientific terms, because he believes that theory can accommodate these concepts without assuming that they stand for abstract entities. It can do so by translating the terminology of abstractions into the language of behaviorist psychology.

This view, in its most radical forms, denies that meanings are internal psychological states or Platonic entities that exist outside the space-time order. Hence to speak about the synonymy of two linguistic expressions, for example, is to describe the behavioral responses of human beings to various sensory promptings, such as verbal noises and perceived marks on paper. One does not need to probe into the internal world of the mind to discover the answer; one simply notes the reactions of those persons. All the evidence human beings have for attributing significance to various utterances is based entirely on observational data. A strictly empiricist philosophy can allow only these stimuli and the responses to them. Because science relies upon observational and experimental data, its approach to any problem is from a third-person orientation. This third-person outlook gives science its objectivity.

Therefore, according to Quine, if scientists wish to understand whether significance can be ascribed to verbal noises, they must look at language from an auditor's perspective. Viewed from this standpoint, the issue for a scientific philosophy is how an observer can come to understand what (if anything) a speaker means by the sounds he utters. But to obtain the proper grip on this problem, one should develop a thought experiment in which the auditor (now a field scientist) confronts a foreigner making verbal sounds. The extreme case would be that of a Martian who has arrived on Earth. Deciphering foreign Earth languages is simply a more familiar version of the problem. The question for the field linguist is how to correlate expressions in his or her language with noises that the Martian makes. Suppose the Martian utters the sound "gavagai" as a rabbit runs by. What does the Martian mean?

To answer the question the scientist must figure out how to ask the Martian appropriate questions, and this presupposes that some sort of Martian behavior must be correlated at least with yes and no in the field linguist's parlance. The auditor must thus formulate a set of conjectures directed toward this result. This is a complicated process. It must take into account not only what group of sounds correlates with those in his home language but under what conditions they were uttered and what beliefs and intentions the speaker may have had at the time. The linguist cannot assume, for example, that a nod of the Martian's head means yes, while shaking it means no. But let us suppose that eventually some Martian behavior can be interpreted as yes and other behavior as no.

Still, other difficulties remain. It is generally assumed that the primary expressions of a language are those that are tied to observable things. One utters "papa" in the presence of a father, "white" in the presence of white, and "rabbit" in the presence of a rabbit. Now a rabbit appears, and the alien utters the noise "gavagai." The linguist may infer that the proper translation of this noise is "rabbit." But this hypothesis is consistent with other translations: It could mean "there is a rabbit," or "more rabbit," or "there's an undetached rabbit part." One way of attempting to resolve the question of whether "gavagai" is not only meaningful but also refers to rabbits, or, alternatively, to undetached rabbit parts, would be to point successively to two parts of the rabbit and ask whether the one gavagai is the same as the other gavagai. But even to ask this question, the field scientist must have already learned a considerable portion of Martianese. In particular, he would have to know which Martian sounds correspond to "is the same as" in English. He has heard the alien say "gavagai momotaro gavagai" when a rabbit is present. But can he be *sure* that "momotaro" means "the same as" rather than "is an undetached part of the same rabbit"? Quine says no.

Quine claims that no matter how many variations the linguist may try in attempting to decipher what this noise signifies, other (perhaps even incompatible) construals are possible. His point is not to deny the impossibility of translation but its uniqueness—that is, that any particular translation is the only correct one. The problem is that "rabbit," "undetached rabbit part," "here is a rabbit," and so on may all be acceptable translations of "gavagai." This is what Quine means by the indeterminacy of translation. He argues that every translation procedure rests on a general theory or hypothesis that the linguist imports from his or her home language. But because there may be a multiplicity of such hypotheses, the imposed theory may fail to capture other translation possibilities. In such a case the linguist cannot decide between the competing construals.

The important conclusion Quine draws from this thought experiment is that linguistic meaning is a function of a particular system and not of its subunits. Term-by-term or even statement-by-statement translation is infeasible. But this is simply his holism in a different terminological guise. A particular segment of the corporate body of science is the unit of significance in this new holistic view. By looking at the problem of translation we can now see how Quine's chief doctrines come together into a cohesive project. Because his scientism leads to his new form of empiricism, and that to his holism, and that in turn to his behaviorism, the latter falls out as a special case of his scientism. His behaviorist orientation in turn accounts for his rejection of meanings, attributes, and relations. When the elements of this complex system are spelled out, his affirmation that his philosophy is simply an extension of science seems less paradoxical than it originally appeared. But whether that is true of common sense is more problematical.

## Criticisms of Quine

As one might expect, any philosophy having so many congruent and interdependent features will have its censurers. The range of criticisms is so broad that it cannot be dealt with here. Noam Chomsky, for example, has argued that no stimulus-response theory such as Quine proffers can explain what he calls the "projection phenomenon," namely, that children can construct perfectly grammatical sentences they have never heard before. Chomsky's alternative is to pose the existence in every human being of internal mental structures that do not derive from experience. He thus defends a view he calls "Cartesian Linguistics."

Other scholars have argued that Quine's description of how language is acquired—that it is analogous to figuring out what an alien means—is not at all like the situation in which children learn language. Their parents and congeners are not aliens in that sense. Children do not bring a theory of the world to this process and especially do not bring a scientific theory to it. As Wittgenstein points out, language learning is more complicated than Quine suggests and at least involves a kind of rote training comparable to the way that animals learn to obey commands. There is also a widespread objection to Quine's holism. To many it smacks of a kind of idealism in which the whole is not only prior to its parts but cannot be reduced to them. This is just the sort of view that Russell rejected in favor of logical atomism. Another criticism points out that Quine is an "armchair" philosopher in the classical metaphysical sense. He does no experiments but simply provides an imaginative account of how language learning must take place. According to this objection, Quine is doing something analogous to what Rousseau did in the *Second Discourse on Political Inequality*, which has a highly persuasive account of how human beings learn language that is based upon no facts whatsoever. A variant of this point is that Quine's scientism leaves no room for philosophy. Yet what he is doing is not experimental science and indeed is a case of doing philosophy in just the sense he rejects. As I have mentioned, it is impossible to explore any of these criticisms in detail here. And because they are readily available in the existing literature, I shall say no more about them.

In what follows, I will instead offer three criticisms, some of which differ, I believe, either in substance or at least in presentation, from those found in the literature.

I will begin with two objections to Quine's behaviorism. The first is familiar. Like Ryle's less radical form of this notion, Quine's cannot handle the internal world of introspectible phenomena: feelings, sensations, thoughts, intentions, and beliefs. These, to be sure, may be manifested in behavior, but they cannot be identified with it. A man who is irritated may not exhibit any manifestations that an observer can identify as irritation, yet he may well be irritated and be aware that he is. Second, Quine thinks that we can identify what an utterance means with an auditor's reaction to it. But this thesis is susceptible to a serious objection. For an auditor to respond to an utterance, he must already understand what it means. Thus the expression "there is a bull in the pasture" will only elicit a reaction if its auditor understands it—for example, takes it to be a warning or a statement and so on.

It follows that behavior cannot be identical with meaning or understanding but presupposes these notions. A variation of this point deals with Quine's claim that two utterances are synonymous if the behavioral responses to them are identical. But in order to know whether two behavioral reactions are identical, one must already know what "identical" means. Again, meaning is presupposed in such a case and cannot be elicited from the response per se. More generally, my objection is that semantic properties, such as meaning, truth, or reference, cannot be identified with behavior. If one flees on hearing someone say, "There is a bull in the pasture," the physical movement has nothing to do with the truth or falsity of the remark. The objection also applies to the central concepts of logic, such as those of logical truth and validity. It is difficult to see how the concept of logical truth can be unpacked in behavioral terms. A logical truth is one that cannot *possibly* be false, and possibility cannot be identical with any *actual* response. The same point can be made about the concept of validity. In standard logic an argument is valid if it is not possible for its premises to be true and its conclusion false. There is no behavioral analogue of validity. Indeed, the objection I am now voicing to behaviorism itself rests on the notion of possibility. I am contending, in opposition to Quine, that it is *impossible* to explicate semantic concepts in purely behavioral terms. But if I am right, then we can also defend the traditional account of the analytic-synthetic distinction. The difference can be defined as follows: It is impossible for analytic statements to be false and possible for synthetic statements to be false. The difference is thus one of kind, after all.

My second criticism concerns Quine's holism. As we have seen, he proffers it as an alternative to the two dogmas. In fairness I should reiterate that, as I said before, in his later writings Quine modified the radical doctrine we find in "Two Dogmas." However, my objection also applies to the mitigated form of his view. I believe a compelling case can be made that his treatment of the analytic-synthetic distinction is inconsistent.

It rests on strong textual evidence. The evidence is that in "Two Dogmas" he expresses his rejection of the analytic-synthetic distinction in two different ways. Sometimes Quine asserts that the distinction is one of degree rather than one of kind. In this connection he says: "But I have been urging that this difference is only one of degree, and that it turns upon our vaguely pragmatic inclination to adjust one strand of the fabric of science rather than another" (1953:46). At other times he asserts that there is no such distinction: "But, for all its a priori reasonableness, a boundary between analytic and synthetic statements simply has not been drawn" (p. 37). Read literally, the first formulation says there is a distinction, whereas the second denies there is. The question for the exegete is whether these statements amount to two different ways of saying the same thing or whether they represent inconsistent conceptions. The matter is delicate and difficult to decide. After considerable reflection I am inclined to opt for the second reading. Here is my reasoning.

Quine's initial description of "the fabric of science" and of the roles played by various statements within it does not entail there are no analytic sentences. According to this formulation, scientific theory is a complex fabric containing many kinds of propositions, including conjectures, statements of low or moderate probability, well-established physical laws, and the theorems of logic and mathematics. In this view what are traditionally called "analytic propositions" would, along with physical and logical laws, be the last to be abandoned in the face of recalcitrant experimental evidence. How different propositions are held in the light of obdurate experience is thus a matter of degree. One will attempt other modifications of the theory before rejecting well-established physical laws, analytic statements, or the laws of logic. But it should be noted that in this interpretation there *are* analytic statements. To be sure, they differ from synthetic statements. But because they do, we can distinguish between them. We can even identify examples of each. We are thus left with the analytic-synthetic distinction after all, though now construed as a distinction of degree. In this interpretation the thrust of Quine's position is to deny that there is a distinction of *kind* in the fabric of science rather than no distinction at all.

In the second formulation he is maintaining that no distinction can be drawn between these supposed categories of propositions. As he says, it "becomes folly to seek such a boundary." If he literally means this, then it follows that nothing is being picked out by the traditional contrast between the analytic and the synthetic. It is simply a spurious dichotomy. The case is very much like trying to distinguish between different medieval humors, or between caloric and phlogiston. One cannot make such supposititious discriminations because there are no such things. The reason Quine gives for saying there is no distinction is that any attempt to define "analyticity" is circular, involving such interdefinable terms as "synonymity," "interchangeability," and "necessity." The process has the same difficulties as one who attempts to define "war" as "not peace" and "peace" as "not war." No meaningful distinction is being drawn by the use of these interconnected locutions. One is here reminded of Austin's comments about "material object" and "sense-datum." As Austin says, "Each takes in each other's washing." And so it is with "analytic" and "synthetic." A consequence of this position is that there are no analytic statements. Accordingly, it differs from the previous formulation.

As I read "Two Dogmas," it thus contains two different holistic views. The first says there is a distinction between the analytic and the synthetic, but it is one of degree. The second denies there is any such distinction. The first entails the existence of analytic statements, and the second does not. I am dubious that the two positions can be reconciled.

Finally, I have severe reservations about Quine's scientism, and since everything he advocates turns on this doctrine, my objection goes to the heart of his philosophy. The matter is complex. Let us start from ground zero. From his earliest epistemological writings to his latest, Quine has been consistent in stating that he is an empiricist. As we have seen, his quarrel with Carnap is over what it is to be an empiricist. The central challenge for any proponent of that position is the external world problem. The difficulty is clearly posed by Benson Mates in *The Skeptic Way*: "Ultimately the only basis I can have for a claim to know that there exists something other than my own perceptions is the nature of those very perceptions. But they could be just as they are even if there did not exist anything else. Ergo, I have no basis for the knowledge-claim in question" (1996:99–100).

As this passage reveals, Mates wishes to defend skepticism. Note that Mates is explicitly speaking about the impossibility of obtaining *knowledge* from the available data. Quine does not agree with Mates's skepticism. Quine's point of view begins with the realistic assumption that we do have such knowledge. His problem is to show how this is possible—to trace the steps that lead from one's sensible promptings impinging on nerve endings to reliable information about objective reality. The following passage clearly reveals this point of view.

> Science itself teaches that there is no clairvoyance; that the only information that can reach our sensory surfaces from external objects must be limited to two-dimensional optical projections and various impacts of air waves on the eardrums and some gaseous reactions in the nasal passages and a few kindred odds and ends. How, the challenge proceeds, could one hope to find out about that external world from such meager traces? (Quine 1974:2)

All the major and subordinate theses of Quine's complex philosophy are directed toward meeting this challenge, that is, of giving an accurate account of the relationship "between the meager input and the torrential output," as he has so strikingly described it elsewhere. The passage just quoted says that this is his purpose. Yet, as we shall now see, he gives various formulations of the problem that subtly but substantially change its character. I will argue that as a result of these changes the problem he eventually tries to solve is less important than the classical conundrum and is not a solution to the greater one. I will also argue that these changes are driven by his scientism.

Let us begin by considering four formulations of the external world problem. The first of these is to be found in Locke and Hume, the second in the passage from Quine just quoted. The third and fourth are to be found elsewhere in Quine's writings. By comparing these we shall see a step-by-step distortion of the classical problem.

A. The standard formulation: *How do we acquire knowledge of external objects?*

B. Quine's first formulation: *How could one hope to find out about the external world from such meager traces?*

C. Quine's second formulation: *How do we acquire our theory of the world?*

D. Quine's third formulation: *How does science acquire its theory of the world?*

Quine's first formulation is close to what we find in Locke and Hume. However, instead of the word "knowledge," which occurs in the standard formulation, Quine uses the phrase "find out." Earlier in that passage Quine also speaks about obtaining "information." The concepts of finding out and information are not equivalent to that of knowledge, of course, since either or both might be equated with some degree of probability less than knowledge. But let us minimize these potential differences. What is important in Quine's first formulation is that he uses the term "one." He seems to be asking: How could *anyone* hope to find out about the external world from such meager traces? This brings his query very close to that of the standard formulation. In that formulation "we" is usually interpreted as referring to each human being and not just to scientists. Locke, Hume, and Mates take it as obvious that everyone has a certain dilemma. According to them, each person believes there are external objects, but since the supporting evidence consists only in the apprehension of one's own subjective sensations, how can each of us justify such a belief? As skeptics, Hume and Mates doubt that we can. Locke is not a skeptic, but his commitment to the "way of ideas" forces him to face the specter of skepticism. Locke, Hume, and Mates are not just speaking of philosophers, though it is philosophical reflection that raises the problem in an acute and explicit form. But the problem exists for everyone: it is a general dilemma.

Also note that for all these formulations, what is to be acquired is knowledge. Now consider Quine's second formulation. In it the word "theory" has been substituted for "knowledge" in the standard formulation. But "we" has been retained. This formulation implies *that everyone has a theory of the world.* This is a thesis that Wittgenstein (and I) would deny, but I will not contest it here. To do so would require another chapter. I have argued the matter in chapter 10 of my *Wittgenstein and Moore on Certainty,* and I refer the reader to that discussion. Quine's scientism is very much in evidence here. His view is that common sense is a kind of inchoate theory that science refines. The resulting scientific theory is a more profound account of the world than any "theory" that common sense can provide. Because he perceives only a difference of degree between common sense and science, it is easy for him to transmute questions about each and every person into questions about science. We see this transformation in his third formulation, where "we" is replaced by "science." This shift turns the implausible implication that everybody has a theory of the world into an implication that is more persuasive—that theory construction is a function of science. This is an assertion that is hardly contentious. Nevertheless, in terms of the standard formulation it has severe liabilities. The reference to knowledge in the standard formulation has now given way to the notion of a theory. Clearly, not all scientific theories are specimens of knowledge. Theories can be mistaken but knowledge cannot be. Thus a fundamental and profound question—whether *we* have ***knowledge*** of the external world—has been substantially altered. It has now become: how does science obtain its theory of the world? But nobody would deny that theory construction is a legitimate function of science. That is a platitude. What is not a platitude is the claim that *each of us has knowledge of the external world.* Accordingly, Quine has avoided the original problem. I submit therefore that Quine's scientistic philosophy does not confront, let alone meet, what many regard as the central challenge of epistemology.

## Chapter Eight

# Direct Reference Theories

In chapter 2, I briefly compared and contrasted the Fregean and Russellian views on meaning and reference with those of direct reference theorists. I said then that in this chapter I would examine direct reference theories in more detail, and I will now turn to that task. The direct reference approach has its roots both in modal and nonmodal logics. The nonmodal roots are essentially Russellian rather than Fregean. For those who wish to explore these connections, I recommend Ruth Barcan Marcus's superb book, *Modalities* (1993). It consists of a series of essays in which she discusses these relationships both historically and analytically. There is thus no need to repeat that material here. Instead, my focus will be on the theories of meaning and reference themselves, in particular those that deal with so-called proper names, ("Poland," "John," etc.) and those that deal with natural kind terms ("water," "aardvark," etc.). I should at the outset, however, inform the reader that my approach in this chapter will differ from that in previous sections of this book. Because the direct reference theory is in the forefront of controversy today, I am going to examine the theory critically and thus will, in effect, be participating in the ongoing debate.

In what follows I will separate the account of proper names from that of natural kind terms. I do so because most advocates of the theory hold that proper names are meaningless but accept, or at least imply, that natural kind terms are meaningful. The arguments in support of these differing positions thus require separate consideration. I should also like to remind the reader that the theories of meaning and reference developed in the twentieth century are designed to solve a series of traditional puzzles, some of which have their antecedents in ancient Greek philosophy. These theories are thus not merely of technical interest but go to the heart of a number of profound philosophical challenges: the status of the ontological argument, Plato's puzzle in the *Sophist* about how one can speak meaningfully or truly about nonbeing, the atheist's conundrum of how one can deny the existence of God without assuming his existence, and Frege and Russell's query about how it is possible for true identity sentences to differ in cognitive significance. One can immediately illustrate the connection between modal logic and the theory of reference in terms of the last of these. Consider the following principle:

> Given a true identity statement linking two terms, one term may be substituted for the other without altering the truth value of the statement.

Thus in the proposition 2 + 3 = 5 we can replace "2" with "1 + 1," and the resulting statement will remain true. Yet what seems like an obviously true principle is subject to counterexamples, such as the conclusion to the following argument:

1. Necessarily 9 = 9.
2. The number of planets = 9.
3. Therefore, necessarily, the number of planets = 9.

Although both premises are true, the conclusion is false. The number of planets happens to be nine, but this is a contingent, not a necessary, truth. One arrived at a false conclusion by following the substitutional principle. The modal logicians are able to solve this problem. In a purely extensional language, such as we find in the propositional calculus of *Principia Mathematica*, or in standard arithmetic, the substitutional principle holds. Terms that have the same extensions can be exchanged *salva veritate* (i.e., preserving truth value). But in certain modal contexts, involving such notions as necessity and possibility, extensional interchangeability *salva veritate* is not possible. The paradox arises from two sources. The first is the various modal notions such as necessity and possibility. The second source is the different roles played by proper names and definite descriptions. In the argument "9" is the name of a number, but "the number of planets" is not the name of 9. It is a description that happens to be true of the number of planets. So built into modal theories is the familiar Russellian distinction between proper names and descriptions. If we adhere to this distinction, we can modify the substitution principle as follows:

> If entities X and Y are identical, then the *names* of X and Y should be interchangeable insofar as they are being used as names.

As we saw in chapter 2 this is precisely what Russell says. He states that when "Sir Walter" and "Scott" are being *used as names*, the sentence "Scott is Sir Walter" is just as trivial as "Scott is Scott." This is because a proper name means its bearer. If "Scott" and "Sir Walter" are both proper names, they are the names of a single bearer; hence they mean the same thing. And for that reason "Scott is Sir Walter" is trivial. But Russell also stresses that the case is different where "Sir Walter" is being used as a descriptive phrase, that is, as an abbreviation for "the person called 'Sir Walter.'" In such a case the sentence "Scott is Sir Walter" is not trivial and indeed is not even an identity sentence. The cognitive difference between the two sentences is accounted for via his theory of descriptions. In his analysis "Scott is Sir Walter" (where "Sir Walter" is an abbreviated description) is to be analyzed into a set of general sentences containing at least one existential sentence. It is thus not an identity sentence at all but a sentence of a different logical form. All direct reference theorists who are concerned about the role of proper names in ordinary language begin as Russell does, by distinguishing proper names from descriptions. They do so because they have in mind the Frege-Russell problem of identity and the other problems I have mentioned. It is these difficulties that their theories are designed to solve. Similar remarks apply to their treatment of natural kind terms.

## Proper Names

Let us then begin our discussion with the direct reference treatment of proper names. We shall set the discussion against a background involving one of the problems already mentioned, namely, how it is possible to speak meaningfully and/or truly about the nonexistent. We shall even narrow the issue to the *fictive* nonexistent. Today, one who says, "The present king of France is wise," is speaking about something that does not exist, but the alleged referent is not a fictional entity. But one who says, "Odysseus was landed on Ithaca deeply asleep" is referring to a character in a work of fiction, the *Odyssey* of Homer. As we shall see, the analysis of fictive talk will prove an especially difficult hurdle for direct reference theorists.

Let us begin at the beginning. What does it mean to say that any linguistic expression is *directly* referential? The key word in the question is "directly." So how is it used by these theorists? The answer is that they are concerned with the relationship between language and what language is about, or, as some writers have stated the matter, their concern is with the relationship between language and the world. As the solera system model reminds us, this is also an ancient problem, discussed by Plato in the *Cratylus* and *Sophist*. The theorists want to know how it is possible to use bits of language to speak about, mention, pick out, or refer to various kinds of things, such as colors, liquids, particular places and persons, and so forth. The answer to their query seems to turn on what it is that such pieces of language mean or how what they mean is connected with what they are used to refer to or mention. Thus, to take a simple example, if I say to my wife, "The cat scratched the table again this morning," my words mean something. In meaning what they do, they enable me to refer to a cat, a table, and the scratching of a table. There is thus some sort of connection between them, as so used, and the objects and processes being talked about. But what sort of a connection is it?

This query is the starting point for the philosopher of language. An initial sophisticated move is to distinguish between ways of directly referring to features and processes in the world and ways of referring to them indirectly or in a roundabout way. If in 1999 I said of the incumbent American president, "The occupant of the Oval Office is from Arkansas," I would not be mentioning Bill Clinton directly but in an oblique way. I would be assuming, in using this locution, that the occupant of the Oval Office is the president and that the president is Bill Clinton. Such locutions as "the incumbent president" or "the occupant of the Oval Office" are intercessors between me and the person I wish to mention, identify, pick out, or refer to. I could have simplified what I said if I had remarked, "Bill Clinton is from Arkansas." The name "Bill Clinton" is not an intercessor in the way that the description "the occupant of the Oval Office" is. Intuitively, it thus seems that a proper name provides a more direct referential route to a person than a description does.

Theorists seize upon this intuition, and it is the basis of the direct reference view. It begins, that is, by distinguishing between proper names and definite descriptions. But an argument supports the intuition. The argument is that a name attaches to its bearer in a special way. It is like a decal or a label. Imagine some furniture in a storehouse. The proprietor places adhesive labels of different colors on chairs and tables. If he wishes to correlate sets of furniture for shipping purposes, he can simply arrange them according to the color of their labels. The labels have no special meaning. They are simply devices for picking out various pieces of furniture. Now, according to direct reference theorists, proper names function exactly in this way. They are like labels that, via an original naming ceremony, one sticks on a person or a place. In this respect they differ from definite descriptions. "The 1999 occupant of the Oval Office" refers to Bill Clinton; after the year 2000 it will refer to a different person. It is thus not like a label that is attached to, and picks out, exactly one individual. The argument concludes that the same description may have different referents or no referents at all. But each label or decal—each proper name—must have a bearer and exactly one.

Direct reference theorists also emphasize that, although descriptions are not names, their grammatical and linguistic roles are similar to those of names and that, because this is so, traditional philosophy has often confused them. One can speak of "the occupant of the Oval Office" or of "Bill Clinton" and be understood in both cases as referring to or mentioning the same person. So these different idioms play similar roles. Yet similarity is not identity, and nearly all philosophers of language emphasize the distinction. In chapter 2 we considered a number of arguments by Russell to show that one cannot in general substitute a description for a proper name while preserving truth value, and I will not repeat those arguments here. The contemporary discussions of such differences are even more subtle than the accounts we find in Frege and Russell.

There are two versions of the direct reference theory today. In somewhat different ways both treat proper names as decals or labels. The first was developed by Ruth Marcus, who calls proper names "tags," and the second by Saul Kripke, who calls proper names "rigid designators." The two versions are similar in six respects and differ in three. The similarities are as follows:

1. Both, as mentioned earlier, sharply distinguish between proper names and descriptions. They also agree that proper names and descriptions can be used for purposes of identification and reference but that in such cases their logical roles differ. In particular, in the case of names the route from name to bearer is direct, whereas with descriptions it is indirect (i.e., one identifies or picks out the object through the intermediation of the descriptive phrase).

2. Both hold that a proper name is what is ordinarily meant by "proper name." As Kripke says: "By a name here I will mean a proper name, i.e., the name of a person, a city, a country. . . . We will use the term 'name' so

that it does not include definite descriptions . . . but only those things which in ordinary language would be called 'proper names'" (1980:24). In holding to this second point, Marcus and Kripke are anti-Fregean. As the reader may recall from chapter 2, Frege uses "name" in a broad sense to include declarative sentences, definite descriptions, common nouns (including natural kind terms), and proper nouns. In opposition to Frege, Marcus and Kripke deny that descriptions and declarative sentences are names.

3. Both agree that a true identity sentence whose flanking expressions are proper names (tags) is necessary and not contingent. They thus reject Quine's idea that if one tags the same object twice, and by different names, say, the planet Venus by "Phosphorus" and "Hesperus," the identity sentence "Phosphorus is Hesperus" is contingent. According to Kripke, Quine was confusing the concept of contingency with that of a posteriority. It was an a posteriori discovery that one had tagged Venus twice, but because, necessarily, Venus is Venus, it follows that "Phosphorus is Hesperus" is necessary and not contingent.

4. Both agree that tagging and rigid designation require the existence of the object tagged or designated and that descriptions do not. It follows from their accounts that one cannot tag or rigidly designate a nonexistent entity, like the present king of France or Odysseus. You cannot put a label on a nonexistent chair.

5. Both agree that linguistic expressions that have the grammatical form of definite descriptions may sometimes function as proper names. Marcus explains this point as follows:

> In fact it often happens, in a growing, changing language, that a descriptive phrase comes to be used as a proper name—an identifying tag—and the descriptive meaning is lost or ignored. Sometimes we use certain devices, such as capitalization with or without dropping of the definite article, to indicate the change in use. 'The evening star' becomes 'Evening star', 'the morning star' becomes 'Morning Star', and they come to be used as names for the same thing. Singular descriptions such as 'the little corporal', 'the Prince of Denmark', 'the sage of Concord', or 'the great dissenter', are, as we know, often used as alternative proper names of Napoleon, Hamlet, Emerson, and Oliver Wendell Holmes. (1993:11)

Kripke agrees. He writes:

> It should not be thought that every phrase of the form 'the x such that Fx' is always used in English as a description rather than a name. I guess everyone has heard about The Holy Roman Empire, which was neither holy, Roman nor an empire. Today we have The United Nations. Here it would seem that since these things can be so-called, even though they are not Holy Roman United Nations, these phrases should be regarded not as definite descriptions, but as names. (1980:26)

6. Finally, both agree that proper names are strictly meaningless. In this respect they differ both from Russell and Frege. Frege held that proper names must have a *Sinn* and in natural language may or may not have a *Bedeutung*. In a regimented well-formed language they would have both. Russell denies that proper names have intensional meaning, or *Sinn*, but insists they mean their bearers, so they mean in an extensional sense. Marcus says in opposition: "A proper name (of a thing) has no meaning." And Kripke, with Marcus and Paul Ziff in mind, concurs: "There are writers, I think, who explicitly deny that names have meaning at all, even more strongly than I would" (1980:32).

Despite these overlaps, the two views differ in certain respects.

1. Marcus denies that tagging is to be identified with rigid designation. As she states, "Proper names are not assimilated to what later came to be called 'rigid designators' by Saul Kripke, although they share some features" (1993:xiii–xiv). She does not explicitly state why she distinguishes between tagging and rigid designation, but an easy explanation is at hand. Kripke gives the following definition of "rigid designator": "It is a term that in every possible world designates the same object" (1980:48). Since Marcus says that a proper name tags the same object in every possible world, it would seem that her conception and Kripke's do not differ that much. But they do. Kripke believes that certain definite descriptive phrases in arithmetic are rigid designators. Thus "the sum of 2 + 3" rigidly designates the number 5. Marcus explicitly denies that any descriptions are tags. Second, as we shall see later, Kripke also holds that certain natural kind terms, for example, "water," are rigid designators. Marcus withholds the concept of tagging from such common nouns; in effect, she restricts this notion to proper names. Tagging, for her, is thus a narrower concept than rigid designation.

2. Kripke holds that natural kind terms are meaningful but that they lack intensions in the Fregean sense of the term. Their meaning is thus wholly extensional. Marcus does not discuss the question directly in *Modalities*, though in one of its essays, "Nominalism and the Substitutional Quantifier," she has explored a modified nominalistic theory in which proper names are *not* eliminable, though common nouns (predicates) that express abstract concepts may be. But she emphasizes that this exploration is simply an exploration and is not necessarily her settled opinion. We can thus say that, with respect to the meaningfulness and referentiality of common nouns, her outiook remains open in a way that Kripke's is not.

3. Their views about how to deal with fictive names like "Hamlet" and "Odysseus" also differ. Both deny that fictive names are tags or rigid designators since fictive objects do not exist. But Kripke refuses to speculate on how such names are to be analyzed. He says: "Concerning rigidity: In many places, both in this preface and in the text of this monograph, I deliberately ignore delicate questions arising from the possible nonexistence of an object" (1980:21). Marcus is also reluctant to explore the issue in detail, but at the end of an essay, "Possibilia and Possible Worlds," she seems to opt for a variation of Russell's theory of descriptions, according to which fictive names are to be regarded as purely syntactical expressions and thus as having no existential implications. She says in this connection:

> One might assign true to the sentence 'Pegasus is a winged horse' in a given world, and the existential generalization to 'Something is a winged horse' will mean nothing more than that some substitution of a syntactical item, for example, the syntactical name 'Pegasus' for 'x' in 'x is a winged horse' generates a sentence that is assigned true. . . . Such a view has certain interesting uses in a semantics for fictional or mythological discourse and for discourse about putative possibilia freed of a "commitment" to mythical or possible objects. But it misses a metaphysical point. Identity, which is a feature of *objects*, cannot be defined in such a semantics. Intersubstitutivity of *syntactical* items *salve veritate* does not generate objects, which must be *given* if identity is to hold. The intersubstituting of 'Father Christmas' and 'Santa Claus' even if truth values are preserved no more generates identical objects than does the intersubstituting of 'not' and 'not not not,' which also holds *salve veritate*. (1993:213)

Looked at from an historical perspective, direct reference theories can be traced to an early version of Russellian semantics that he later abandoned. As I pointed out in chapter 2, Russell originally drew a distinction between proper names and descriptions, using examples like "Scott," and "the author of *Waverley*." In attempting to deal with the proper names of nonexistent objects, such as "Medusa" and "Odysseus," Russell argued that what ordinary persons regard as proper names are really abbreviations for descriptions. In his modified view logic still requires proper names in order to instantiate singular sentences, such as "Fa." His candidates for "a" were thus adverbs and demonstrative pronouns, words like "now," "here," "this," and "that." That such words can be regarded as proper names is clearly counterintuitive and simply represents a last-gasp attempt to apply logical formulae to ordinary language. The direct reference theorists are much more sensitive to the relationship between logic, including modal logic, and everyday speech. They take proper names to be what in ordinary discourse would be called proper names. Their modification of Russell's view is to return to his original distinction in which "Scott" is a proper name and "the author of *Waverley*" is not. This result has all sorts of advantages. It enables them to explain in a way that Russell could not how misidentification using descriptions can occur. In the case of proper names ostension is required, and this means, according to Marcus, that the "referent of a proper name remains fixed, even where attributions claimed by narrative are in error." As she writes:

> On this account, "proper name" is a semantical, not merely syntactical, notion. Reference is supposed. We may mistakenly believe of some syntactically proper name, say, 'Homer', that it has an actual singular referent and is a genuine proper name, but if its use does not finally link it to a singular object, it is not a genuine name at all. (1993:203)

Therefore, a designator cannot be a proper name unless there exists a particular individual that it tags. As we shall see in a moment, the idea that there is a direct link between a proper name and its referent creates a serious problem for the theory in speaking about fictive objects. As Marcus emphasizes: "It is not, I will propose, the general absence of 'identification *conditions*' that makes possibilia problematic. It is that possibilia cannot be objects of reference at all" (p. 204).

Fictive entities are possibilia in Marcus's sense, so they cannot be the objects of reference. Keith Donnellan, who espouses a variant of the direct reference theory that he calls "the historical explanation theory," is well aware of the problem. As he says in "Speaking of Nothing": "What is to be excluded from consideration here is an account of discourse about fiction. (This is not, of course, to say that such an account is not in the end needed)" (1977:218).

## The Problem

In evaluating the direct reference theory, one must assess its capacity to deal with the problem of fictive names. The problem is easy to explain. Fictive objects seem to have what are commonly recognized as proper names, (e.g., "Santa Claus," "Medusa," and "Odysseus"), and yet if such "objects" do not exist, they cannot be tagged or labeled. One cannot attach tags to mere possibilia, as Marcus emphasizes. Possibilia are not like tables or chairs. There is literally nothing to hang a tag on. It follows that fictive "names" cannot be rigid designators or tags. But if that is so, then direct reference theorists face a dilemma. Here are some options for them:

1. To accommodate ordinary discourse, they could abandon the thesis that all proper names are tags or rigid designators.

2. They could propose a variant of Russell's theory of descriptions. This theory would hold that in fiction so-called proper names are abbreviations for descriptions, whereas in standard discourse they are tags or rigid designators. Such a proposal would have two consequences. First, descriptions would not be abbreviations for the names of existing entities. Second, this proposal would result in a nonhomogeneous theory about the role or roles of names in ordinary speech. The first consequence would allow for ordinary names to be tags or rigid designators, which is a welcome suggestion. But the second would be undesirable, since it would run counter to the view that in everyday speech fictive names are indeed names.

3. They could argue that in fiction so-called proper names have a symbiotic, derivative, or secondary use. This option would differ from the second option as follows. To say that fictive names have a derivative use does not imply that they have to be analyzed as definite descriptions. A fictive proper name would thus be what ordinary speech regards as a proper name, only its referential function would not be direct—it would not be a

tag or rigid designator. The difficulty with this proposal consists in explaining the referential function of fictive names without treating them as abbreviated descriptions.

4. They could maintain that discourse about fictive objects presupposes a "fictive existence operator," so that fictive objects do exist in fiction and therefore can be tagged by fictive proper names. Similar remarks could be made about heraldry. Tagging would thus be relativized to a particular body of discourse. One could appeal to a theory of contextual implication, differing versions of which are found in the writings of Grice, Searle, and Martinich.

This set of options does not exhaust the possibilities, of course, but it does bring out the nature of the difficulty that the direct reference theorist faces. For none of these options is attractive. To abandon the notion that names are tags is, of course, simply to abandon the theory. To accept the Russellian account that fictive names are descriptions is to abandon the notion that proper names are what ordinary persons describe them as being. No ordinary speaker would accept that "the male protagonist in *The Magic Mountain*" is the name of Hans Castorp.

To adopt the notion that fictive names are derivative or symbiotic, and are about fictive objects in some secondary sense of "about," simply begs the question. Strawson advocates such a view in "On Referring." He says: "It would not in general be correct to say that a statement was about Mr. X or the so-and-so unless there were such a person or thing" (1960:35). Clearly, this option begs the question; it presupposes what is at issue, whether a fictive name is really a referring expression unless the "object" it purports to name exists.

To accept the fourth option, that one can tag fictive objects in fiction, obviously involves an extended or quixotic use of "tag." The proposal obviously runs counter to a principle that all direct reference theorists accept, namely, that one cannot tag the nonexistent.

Let us summarize the problem. It arises because the following theses, all of which are essential to the direct reference theory, seem to be in conflict.

1. Proper names are tags (or rigid designators).
2. Tags (or rigid designators) require the existence of something to be tagged.
3. Fictive objects do not exist and therefore cannot be tagged.

4. Fictive objects in ordinary discourse have proper names.
5. A proper name is what is ordinarily meant by a proper name.

## The Direct Reference Theory Assessed

In what follows, I will offer a series of criticisms of the direct reference theory and eventually a solution to the preceding dilemma. In setting the stage, I recommend that we alter our perspective about fictive names since it is conditioned by a long ontological tradition and its problems. Let us focus instead on how ordinary persons think and talk about names. Of course, one must concede at the outset that the famous "plain man" or his female counterpart does not think very deeply, if at all, about the problems that vex philosophers of language. It is also dubious that such folk, whether male or female, have anything that could be called a "theory" about proper names. Still, they do talk about, and on occasion reflect deeply, about the names they choose for all sorts of things: babies, streets, cities, and dogs (see T. S. Eliot's *The Naming of Cats*). Moreover, the ordinary use of names is much more complex and subtle than most theorists have acknowledged. Take, as an example, the claim made by Marcus that "linguists exclude proper names from the lexicon altogether." This is a contention with which many philosophers agree, among them Kripke and Paul Ziff. But are they right?

Just turning to the L's in my dictionary, I find entries for a large number of what philosophers call "proper names," including the names of fictive entities: Laban, La Belle Dame Sans Merci, La Bohème, Lachesis, La Coruna, La Crosse, Laertes (the father of Odysseus). Some philosophers, as we have seen, have held that proper names are meaningless. In support of this thesis they contend that dictionaries don't give the meaning but the origin of the name. Yet dictionaries tell us that "Sarah" in Hebrew means "princess," that "Svensen" in Norwegian means "the son of Sven," that "Momotaro" in Japanese means "the son of a peach," and that "Polaris" means (denotes) the polestar, or North Star. Some philosophers have even stated that proper names do not belong to any language. Yet, clearly, "Marco" is Italian, "Mark" is English, and, of course, the same name may belong to more than one language, for example, "Francis."

Indeed, ordinary speakers may well have important things to tell us about names that philosophers have overlooked or ignored. If one were to ask such a person what he or she thinks about the aforementioned five steps that seem to be in conflict, one would elicit some instructive answers.

First, a reflective, thoughtful person would certainly reject step 5. This states that a proper name is what is ordinarily meant by a proper name. That person would point out that in ordinary speech the term "proper name" is hardly ever used. Clearly, the ordinary person would be right. "Proper name" is a technical term invented by grammarians, linguists, and other specialists in language. In such disciplines it is used metalinguistically to speak about the grammar of particular object languages and in particular to distinguish nouns that apply to individual persons, places, and things from so-called common nouns, like "tiger" and "gold." Ordinary speakers are not in the grammar business and hence do not employ (or need) this metalinguistic terminology. Accordingly, they do not say of persons or places that they have proper names. Instead, they speak about the names *simpliciter* of such entities and objects. They will ask, "What is the name of the city you visited last year?" not "What is the proper name of the city you visited last year?"; or "What is his name?" and not "What is his proper name?" An ordinary person hearing the question "What is his proper name?" would be puzzled by it. Is the interrogator suggesting that the person is using a pseudonym or an alias or a nickname, for example? Apart from such special contexts, the question may not be understood at all.

Second, an ordinary person would accept premise 4, that fictive objects in ordinary discourse have proper names, but only if the premise were modified. The modification would consist of dropping the word "proper" and thus concurring that in ordinary discourse fictive objects have names. That is, they would say that words like "Sherlock Holmes" and "Odysseus" are just as much names as "Bill Clinton" or "Bertrand Russell." If asked by a philosopher what "Sherlock Holmes" and "Odysseus" supposedly are the names of (and assuming that the person knows the relevant literary references), the ordinary person might be puzzled by the question. It seems obvious that these are the names of Sherlock Holmes and Odysseus. Before considering the other three steps in the argument, one might also pursue the point further, in Meno-like fashion, seeing whether one could elicit an argument in support of step 4 as modified. Here are two that might emerge from the process.

Suppose a philosopher were to ask an ordinary individual to pick out the proper names in the following list:

Paula

the discoverer of America

a metal

Santa Claus

Columbus

Zeus

chief of staff

Assuming that he understood the question, because it uses the locution "proper name," the person would select "Paula," "Santa Claus," "Columbus," and "Zeus" and would reject "the discoverer of America," "a metal," and "chief of staff" as names. One cannot imagine naming a new born child "The Discoverer of America," for example. Because two selections on the list are the names of fictive entities, Santa Claus and Zeus, one can conclude that for ordinary speakers such entities have what philosophers would regard as proper names.

Now a second argument. Suppose a person were looking through a book of names in order to select one for a newborn male child. That list might include "Sherlock," "Lancelot," and "Hamlet." These are names made famous in Western fiction, yet they can be used as the names of existing persons. So why think they are not names when used in fiction? A name is a name is a name in any context, as Gertrude Stein might have said. An ordinary person would find no obstacle in identifying these words as names. Playing the philosophical game, we could even add that they are "proper names."

Direct reference theorists would probably not accept this argument. They might contend that it rests on a confusion, namely, that a list or a book of names does not contain proper names in a strict sense of the term, for proper names are the actual names of existing individuals, whereas what a book gives us are only potential names. Potential names become proper names only when they are applied to particular persons, and then they function as tags. It is therefore misleading to think of potential names as proper names per se. This response is interesting, but I believe it begs the question. It assumes that which is in dispute: that N is a proper name only if N is applied to an existing person, place, or thing. It is therefore not a compelling objection.

## The Axiom of Referring

We shall resume our inquiry by considering the remaining three premises of the argument from a philosophical perspective and thus leave the ordinary man to go about his daily activities. I accept premise 3, that fictive objects do not exist and therefore cannot be tagged. I also accept premise 2, that tags require the existence of something to be tagged. Marcus is clearly right in asserting both 2 and 3. Fictive objects are mere possibilia, and possibilia cannot be tagged. I also accept the ordinary person's modifications of premises 4 and 5. So in order to provide a solution to the direct reference's dilemma, which arises from accepting all five premises, I must reject premise 1, namely, that proper names are tags. In explaining why, I must begin by reiterating what it is that direct reference theorists mean in describing a proper name as a tag. A proper name is used—and here the terminology varies depending on the theory—for identifying, picking out, speaking about, mentioning, or referring to a particular person, place, city, object, and so forth. Let us speak for the moment only about referring. The theory thus rests on a principle that is assumed by all direct reference theorists and even by many nondirect reference theorists such as Strawson and Searle. I call this the "axiom of referring." It can be formulated as follows:

> One cannot refer to that which does not exist.

Though Searle is not a direct reference theorist, his version is almost identical with the preceding. He writes in *Speech Acts*:

> Whatever is referred to must exist. (1969:77)

This axiom has a number of variants. Strawson's version states:

> It would not *in general* be correct to say that a statement was about Mr. X, or the-so-and-so, unless there were such a person or thing. (1960:35)

We find a still different, more radical formulation in *Derrida and Wittgenstein* by Newton Garver and Seung-Chong Lee. They say:

> In philosophy, it is no good talking about something that is not there. (1994:115)

The principle can be traced to the pre-Socratics, but its locus classicus in philosophy of language can be found in Frege. In a famous passage he asserts:

> He who does not acknowledge the nominatum cannot ascribe or deny a predicate to it. (1949:90)

I call this principle, with its variations, an "axiom" because it is never in fact supported by arguments, reasons, or evidence. It is simply assumed to be true. It is then imported into theories of reference and plays a crucial role in them. Yet, although accepted as true by virtually all philosophers of language, it is patently false. The irony of the situation is not merely that it is false but that it is obviously so. For it is a plain fact that we do use language to refer to nonexistent (including fictive) objects by name and to make true (or sometimes false) statements about such objects. It is plainly true to say that Odysseus was married to Penelope and that Hamlet was not married to Ophelia and false to say otherwise. Literary critics, and indeed just ordinary readers, frequently discuss the characters of fictive personages, for example, Emma in the eponymous novel by Jane Austen. In doing so, they use all the resources of everyday speech that they would use in talking about real persons, alluding to places where such personages live, identifying those places by name, historical origin, and so forth. Those fictive names are transferred by a causal chain from generation to generation in just the way that the names of real historical persons are.

In such contexts one is speaking about fictive objects not in any secondary sense of "about," if there be such, but in the same sense of "about" in which I have been speaking about Saul Kripke and Ruth Marcus in this book. It is true, of course, as Marcus has pointed out to me in private correspondence, that there is a radical difference between fictive and real things with respect to the verification of statements. With the former the process of verification terminates in human (mostly literary) constructs, with the latter in facts. Holmes is what Conan Doyle says he is, but Doyle is what he is. But it is also true that counterfactuals about fictive characters are possible. It has been argued, for instance, that Dr. Watson was a woman, though no such identification appears in the Conan Doyle texts. More generally, what is true is that all the linguistic expressions that are used about real persons, things, and events can and indeed are used in fiction. Thus the language of meaning and reference is broader than its application to the existing world. In that sense whatever can be said about nonfictional objects can be said about fictional ones, and whatever can be said in our daily talk outside fiction can be said within or about fiction. Such talk includes every possible use of ordinary discourse: jokes, lies, true and false statements, direct and indirect references, asides, and the application of names to characters, places, and things.

## The Solution

What is the significance of these remarks for direct reference theories? I submit that we should abandon the axiom of referring in any of its forms because it is palpably false. This would clear the way for a better account of names, including what the tradition calls "proper names," and also of statement making. In its place I now propose an alternative account that has manifold advantages over direct reference theories and none of their liabilities. This will be my solution to the dilemma described earlier.

First, the account would specify that the names used to refer to fictive entities, such as Sherlock Holmes and Odysseus, really are names and are not to be distinguished from the names of nonfictive entities, such as Ruth Marcus and Saul Kripke. One would thus have a uniform, rather than a fractionated, account of names.

Second, it would entail that we abandon the notion that proper names are tags. I have agreed that if a tag is a label that one applies to an object, one cannot tag things that do not exist or that are mere possibilia, as Marcus correctly states. Thus by abandoning the notion that proper names are tags (premise 1 of the dilemma), we can then use such names to refer to fictive entities in just the way that ordinary speakers do. We would thus need no special theory about the use of so-called proper names in fiction.

Third, it would specify that we do not have to construe so-called proper names as abbreviated descriptions in fictive contexts. Even better, it would entail that such names are not abbreviations for descriptions, whether used in fictive or nonfictive contexts. Whatever the context, they would just be names in the ordinary sense of that term. The Russellian and direct reference options would thus both be rendered otiose.

Fourth, it would entail that there is no difference in referential power between names and descriptions. The idea that so-called proper names refer directly and that descriptions do not is a red herring. Misidentification can occur with the use of names and in other ways as well. I can refer with "equal directness" to a neighbor as "the young man next door," or as "Donald Wilson." Which I do will depend on various contextual factors, such as whether I know the name of the person next door. But naming has no special referential sanctity in such cases. Depending on circumstances, either can do the job equally well.

Fifth, it would entail a greater sensitivity to the nuances of everyday discourse. One serious liability of the direct reference doctrine is that it attempts to find one and only one relationship—tagging—to explain how names refer. My view says that reference via names is multifarious, having various forms. In particular, we should distinguish between such notions as mentioning X and referring to X, and between both of them and such notions as picking out X and identifying X, which should also be discriminated from one another. These are all different actions. I can pick out persons, say, males from females in a group, without being able to identify any particular individual, and each of these actions is different from mentioning or referring to someone or something. I can perform both of the latter without picking anything out or identifying anything or anyone. I can mention by name, say, that Jack the Ripper was the serial killer who murdered X, without being able to identify Jack the Ripper and certainly without being able to pick him out of a group of suspects in a police lineup. Picking out, mentioning, speaking about, referring to, identifying, and other modes of discriminating things from one another are all ways that names work in everyday speech. There is thus no single form of specification, such as tagging, that is the key to understanding how names are used in human communication.

Sixth, we can dismiss the Meinongian fantasy that fictive objects must exist in some sense or other or we could not name them, refer to them, or make true statements about them. My view has the advantage of acknowledging, without hedging, that fictive objects are nonexistent. Finally, we do not need any such artificial ways of categorizing language as to say that there are assumed "existence operators" for fiction, mythology, or heraldry. Supporters of such a program would ask us to say such things as " 'Odysseus' is a proper name in fiction" or "That Odysseus was married to Penelope is true" means that this statement is true in fiction. My account does not divide the language into such labyrinthian and artificial compartments. Ordinary language is one indivisible body of discourse that we use to speak about many different kinds of things, including mythological, heraldic, and fictive entities. In using it for such purposes we need no "existence operators" for marking off spurious boundaries.

I believe that the axiom of referring is the source of much philosophical pathology. It is interesting to speculate on why philosophers have almost universally and uncritically accepted it. No doubt, a full explanation would require another essay. But it is obvious that it is their ontological and metaphysical concerns that lead them to the mistaken ideas that proper names are tags and that only existent entities can have proper names. Their philosophy of language is thus driven by ontological considerations. If, instead, we begin from the perspective of language itself—asking what counts as a name in everyday speech and how such names are used—all sorts of philosophical misconceptions will vanish. Among these are the notions that proper names are tags and that one can only refer to the existent.

## Natural Kind Terms

I will now examine an extension of the direct reference theory to so-called natural kind terms,that is, to the common nouns that refer to species or substances found in nature, as opposed to artifacts such as tables and chairs. The two major proponents of this version of the theory are Hilary Putnam and Kripke. In a paper, "Identity and Necessity," first published in 1971, and in his influential book, *Naming and Necessity* (1980), Kripke developed a series of arguments to show that natural kind terms are rigid designators. About the same time, in "Is Semantics Possible?" and in "Meaning and Reference," first published in 1970 and 1973, respectively, Putnam was propounding the same thesis. Both theories are directed against the Fregean view that every common noun has a sense (*Sinn*) and also in most cases a referent (*Bedeutung*).

For Frege the *Sinn* that the noun expresses is a concept, and it is via that concept that one can identify or pick out the referent. Frege's way of describing the relationship between the meaning of a linguistic expression and its referent is to say that meaning determines reference. Both Kripke and Putnam reject this view. As Putnam wittily puts the matter, "Cut the pie any way you like, 'meanings' just ain't in the head" (1977:124). If one were to use Fregean parlance in describing their views, Putnam and Kripke would be insisting in opposition to Frege that the meaning of a natural kind term is its *Bedeutung*, rather than its *Sinn*. According to the Putnam-Kripke view, the relationship between language and the world is the same whether one is speaking about proper nouns or common nouns; in both cases those words pick out their referents directly. To be sure, we can draw a distinction between proper and common nouns: the former are labels and hence meaningless, whereas the latter do have meaning—they mean the substances or species to which they refer. Thus the meaning of "water" is the substance water.

## The Twin Earth Argument

In "Meaning and Reference" Putnam provides what has become the most famous argument—the so-called Twin Earth scenario—in support of the direct reference view of natural kind terms.

Putnam asks us to imagine a twin of Earth, a planet exactly like ours, except in one respect that I shall mention in a moment. It will be the same size, have the same appearance, have on it counterparts of each person who now exists on Earth. There will thus be a Twin Earth Hilary Putnam and a Twin Earth Avrum Stroll and so on. Indeed, an observer, even a god, looking at the two planets from an external standpoint would find them indistinguishable. So early in the history of Twin Earth there would have been a Twin Thales and a Twin Vergil, and one of them would have claimed that everything is water, and the other would have written a book identical in name and content with the *Aeneid*. On Twin Earth there will also be a substance that Twin Earthlings call "water." In terms of its observable properties and its uses it will be indistinguishable from water. It will be a transparent liquid that is highly viscous and fluid. But there will be one difference between these two worlds. When this substance on Twin Earth is subjected to chemical analysis, it will be found not to be composed of hydrogen and oxygen but of another combination of chemicals, which we shall call XYZ and that are not identical with $H_20$.

According to Putnam, this is a possible scenario; we can easily imagine such a twin world. But if it is a possible scenario, then certain inferences about the theory of reference follow from it: (1) that Earthling and Twin Earthling can have the same concept of water in mind, namely, that water is a substance having such observable properties as liquidity, transparency, fluidity, and viscosity; and (2) that the reference (extension) of that concept is a liquid that is $H_2O$ on Earth and XYZ on Twin Earth (where XYZ is different from $H_2O$); (3) that the liquids referred to by the same term, "water," are therefore different substances; (4), that the Fregean view is therefore mistaken; (5) that because Earthling and Twin Earthling were grasping the same concept (i.e., had the same meaning in mind), and because that concept picked out two different references, $H_2O$ and XYZ, it follows that meaning does not determine reference, as Frege had claimed.

Seventh, and even deeper, his view was wrong in holding that "water" *meant* "the liquid having certain observable properties." What "water" meant had nothing to do with any such Fregean sense or meaning but was wholly determined by what water is, and this in turn was determined by the chemical composition of water.

Eighth, the nineteenth-century scientific discovery that water is composed of $H_2O$ resolved the question of what water is. Finally, English speakers who lived before the nineteenth-century chemical discovery that water is $H_2O$ were mistaken in thinking that water was *the* liquid defined by certain overt properties, for the Twin Earth narrative indicates that two different liquid substances exhibited those very same properties.

Putnam concludes that the observable properties of any natural kind do not determine its real nature. By a "natural kind" he means something found in nature as distinct from something created by human beings. Chairs are not natural kinds, but gold, water, and tigers are. It is thus possible to imagine an albino tiger that is not striped and is not beige in color, yet its genetic makeup, not its observable features, determine it to be a tiger. Some substances, such as iron pyrite, look exactly like gold, yet they have a different chemical composition, so they are not gold. There are some minerals, such as chrysoprase, that with the naked eye cannot be distinguished from jade but are not jade. Once again the phenomenological characteristics of these natural kinds do not determine their true natures. This is true of every natural kind: of tigers, elms, gold, and so on. In the case of water its nature is determined by a chemical analysis, which found it to be composed of $H_2O$. Because that was not the composition of the liquid on Twin Earth, it follows that, despite its appearance, the latter is not water. It also follows that as used on Twin Earth, "water" does not mean what "water" as used on Earth means.

In effect, then, the scenario shows that "water" is a homonym—a word with the same sound but with different meanings. The word "bank" in English is a homonym; it can refer to the sharp slopes between which a river runs or to a commercial institution in which money is deposited.

That a word has the same sound does not entail that it has the same meaning. So "water" means XYZ on Twin Earth and $H_2O$ on Earth and is therefore a homonym. This is a compelling analysis, almost universally accepted by philosophers of language and philosophers of science. But in my judgment it is wrong, and I will now try to show why. Let us concentrate specifically on their analysis of the word "water."

## A First Criticism of the Direct Reference View

As the Twin Earth scenario shows, Putnam is dealing with two different questions: what the word "water" means and what water is. Both he and Kripke frequently tend to conflate these questions, because they presuppose that the debate about what the word "water" means will be settled once it is determined what water is.

So what do they take water to be? Kripke answers as follows:

> I want to go on to the more general case, which I mentioned in the last lecture, of some identities between terms for substances, and also the properties of substances and natural kinds. Philosophers have, as I've said, been very interested in statements expressing theoretical identifications; among them, that light is a stream of photons, that water is $H_20$, that lightning is an electrical discharge, that gold is the element with the atomic number 79. (1980:116)

Putnam's view is indistinguishable from Kripke's. As Putnam puts it: "Once we have discovered that water (in the actual world) is $H_20$, *nothing counts as a possible world in which water isn't H20.*" (1977:130).

I think both Kripke and Putnam would agree that the expression water is $H_20$ exactly captures what they intend. Moreover, both take this locution to be an identity sentence, so that the word "is" means "is identical with." Let us simplify what they intend by using the formula: "Water = $H_20$." I do not believe that anything substantive in the theory is affected by this notational simplification.

Kripke states he is speaking of "identities" between terms for substances and adds that "philosophers have been very interested in statements expressing theoretical identifications." Clearly, both writers mean that water is identical with $H_20$.

But if that is so, the theory is unacceptable, as the following counterexample shows:

1. Water = $H_20$
2. Ice = $H_20$
3. Therefore, Water = Ice

The conclusion follows as an instance of the valid formula that if A = B and B = C, A = C. But because the conclusion of the argument is false, at least one of its premises must be false (in fact both are). That the conclusion is false is obvious. Clearly, water is not identical with ice. If I ask you to put some ice in my glass, I am not asking you to put water in my glass. Water is a liquid and ice is not; water is transparent and ice is not. Indeed, water and ice stand in a virtually unique relationship to one another. Nearly all other liquid substances have solids that are more dense than they are. But water is more dense than ice and therefore ice will always float in water. Ice could not in truth, and perhaps not even meaningfully, be said to float in water if ice and water were identical. Neither can ice and steam be phases of water, that is to say, subsets of water, because something cannot be ice (a cold solid) and warm (a liquid) at the same time.

Note that the argument could be extended by adding the premise:

Steam = $H_20$

If we add this premise, and reason validly, we can infer that ice = steam, which is clearly false. It follows that it is false that steam is identical with water, even though the chemical composition of steam is $H_20$. If Putnam believes that water is identical with $H_20$ and steam is identical with $H_20$, he would have to subscribe to the belief that ice is identical with steam since both have the same chemical composition.

What is the import of such counterexamples for the Putnam-Kripke theory? Because water is patently not identical with ice, or ice with steam, and because both water and ice, and steam and ice, have the same chemical composition, it follows that the difference between them cannot be accounted for in terms of their chemical composition. The difference will have to be explained in terms other than those that refer to their common microcomposition—indeed, as I have shown, in terms of their observable physical differences. And in order to do that we shall have to employ the locutions that ordinary nonscientific humans have used for this purpose since time immemorial. The phenomenological properties denoted by those locutions are what allow us to make the distinction: these tell us that when water freezes, it becomes ice, that ice is invariably cold but that water is not, and that water is transparent whereas ice is not. None of these features is an underlying chemical component of water in the way that $H_20$ is. Yet they serve to allow us to distinguish water from ice and steam from ice. Any scientific analysis more finely grained in terms of crystallinity, say, will have to recognize and conform to these macroscopic features. It follows that water is not identical with $H_20$ and that water is not identical with ice or ice with steam. All this is consistent with maintaining what is true, namely, that the chemical composition of water is $H_20$, for that statement, which speaks about the composition of water, is not an identity sentence.

Putnam-Kripke's basic mistake is to think that it is: we can say that their error is to have inferred from the chemical composition of water—two parts of hydrogen and one of oxygen—that it is identical with the union of those components. But as my counterexample shows, this is a sheer mistake, having such paradoxical consequences as that steam and ice, and water and ice, are identical.

Their idea, that one can state what a natural kind is in terms of a simple identity sentence, is not an uncommon error; indeed, it permeates the literature on direct reference, and we can find it in other authors as well. Here, for instance, is what J. J. C. Smart says:

> Consider lightning. Modern physical science tells us that lightning is a certain kind of electrical discharge due to ionization of clouds of water vapor in the atmosphere. This, it is now believed, is what the true nature of lightning is. Note that there are not two things: a flash of lightning and an electrical discharge. There is one thing, a flash of lightning, which is described scientifically as an electrical discharge to the earth from a cloud of ionized water molecules. (1962:163–65)

This error arises, at least in part, from a failure to make certain distinctions that are crucial in understanding the science involved. Speaking from the point of view of a philosopher of science, Putnam says:

> Suppose, now, that I have not yet discovered what the important physical properties of water are (in the actual world)—i.e., I don't yet know that water is $H_20$. I may have ways of *recognizing* water that are successful (of course, I may make a small number of mistakes that I won't be able to detect until a later stage in our scientific development), but not know the microstructure of water. If I agree that a liquid with the superficial properties of "water" but a different microstructure *isn't really water*, then my ways of recognizing water cannot be regarded as an analytical specification of what *it is to be* water. (1977:129)

We can contrast what Putnam says with what chemists tell us about water. But first note that in the passage quoted Putnam asserts that water is $H_20$ and that it is to be identified with its "microstructure," implying with this last remark that $H_20$ is the microstructure of water. Further, what we have been calling the "phenomenological" or "observable" properties of water Putnam calls the "superficial properties" of water. But scientists would deny both that the microstructure of water is $H_20$ and that the observable properties, which they also call the "gross," or "physical," properties of water, are superficial. If they were superficial in Putnam's sense, any chemist would tell you that you could not distinguish steam from ice.

In contrast to Putnam scientists distinguish the gross or physical properties of a substance, such as the rigidity of iron, from its chemical properties, such as its disposition to rust when, in the presence of air, it comes in contact with water. Its properties, whether gross or chemical, are to be distinguished from its chemical structure. The term "structure" is used to speak both about the internal spatial arrangements of atoms within a molecule and about the internal spatial arrangements of the molecules within a substance. If one is speaking about a molecule of water, then the microstructure of that molecule would be the particular (and characteristic) arrangement of the hydrogen and oxygen atoms within it. If one is speaking about a natural kind such as pure water, the microstructure of the substance will be certain characteristic spatial relationships between its molecules. In the case of steam this is a virtually random set of relationships—the molecules are apart and move almost independently of one another. In the case of water the molecules are condensed into a disordered and complex system characterized by much molecular movement and tumbling; in the case of ice the molecular arrangement is regular and crystalline.

Putnam's term, "microstructure," blurs these distinctions and leads to serious confusions. The basic point is that there is not a one-to-one correspondence between the physical, chemical, or gross properties of water and its chemical components. Thus water, ice, and steam all have the same chemical components. Each is composed of molecules containing two atoms of hydrogen and one of oxygen. Yet their gross properties are different, ice being rigid and water not. The example is directly relevant to the point we have been stressing. Ice, water, and steam are all identical in chemical composition, but their physical properties are distinct. If each of them were identical with its chemical composition, each would be identical with the other, and then by Leibniz's Law each would have identical gross properties. Since they obviously do not, it follows that none of them is identical with its chemical components (or with its "microstructure," as Putnam uses that term). One cannot therefore distinguish between them in terms of their chemical composition. It follows that Putnam is wrong in holding that water is identical with $H_20$ and indeed that natural kinds in general are to be identified with their chemical composition. His mistake stems, as I have indicated, from not distinguishing the propositions—water is identical with $H_20$, and water is composed of $H_20$—from one another. The "is" in "water is $H_20$" is not the "is" of identity but the "is" of composition.

One can make the same point by adopting a technique made famous by Kripke. Kripke will ask: Can you imagine a situation in which a liquid can have all the properties usually associated with water, such as being transparent, non-viscous, and the like and yet not be composed of $H_20$? Because the Twin Earth narrative gives one good grounds for saying yes, both Putnam and Kripke would argue that water cannot be identified with the liquid that has those phenomenological properties. Both infer therefore that water must be the single liquid composed of $H_20$. But this is a non sequitur, as my counterexample shows. Can one, I now ask, imagine something composed of $H_20$ that is not water? Of course, I answer: ice and steam. That shows by an argument parallel to that of Kripke and Putnam that water cannot be identified with its compositional constituents.

## Rebuttal by Kripke and Putnam

How might Kripke and Putnam respond to these criticisms? I can think of two arguments they might offer. The first I will call "the meltdown argument." Take an ice cube, they might say, and just leave it on a counter. In a few minutes it will begin to melt and the result will be water. Nothing in the ice cube has changed. It was water to begin with and it is still water after melting. When they say that $H_2O$ is the "essence" of water, they are referring to something that all forms of water have in common. The conclusion to be reached is that all forms of water, such as ice and steam, are combinations of hydrogen and oxygen. That is the point of the identity thesis, and it is supported by what science has discovered about $H_2O$.

This argument has a strong initial plausibility, but it is unsound for several reasons. Most important, it contains a false premise—that nothing in the ice cube has changed. In fact, the contrary is true. Ice is rigid; therefore, the cube that began with a crystalline structure has altered its internal structure in becoming a liquid. In phenomenological terms an object that is inert, hard, opaque, and cold to the touch has changed into a fluid that is transparent, tepid, and flows. What is true, as I have stressed, is that ice and water are both composed of $H_2O$. But that truth does not entail that they are therefore internally (or, for that matter, externally) the same.

The second I will call "the linguistic argument." According to it, there are two uses of "water." In the first use it denotes a fluid that is transparent, tasteless, and odorless. But the second use is generic: one can speak of frozen water, water vapor, and liquid water. In that use, ice is frozen water, steam is water vapor, and the familiar fluid is liquid water. Each of these items is thus water but in different states. Astronomers might describe Mars, for example, as possessing frozen water at one of its poles. The argument concludes that the common element of a solid, a gas, and a fluid is water in this generic sense.

This argument has something to be said in its behalf. It is true that people sometimes do refer to ice as frozen water and to steam as water vapor. I have never heard the term "liquid water" used in ordinary speech, but perhaps in scientific contexts it is employed. I grant, then, that there are such uses as "frozen water" and "water vapor." The argument gets some of its authority by suggesting that a frozen Eskimo is an Eskimo and, pari passu, that frozen water is water. But can we say that a vaporized Eskimo is still an Eskimo? It is dubious. More generally, my objection is that from such usages it does not follow that ice is identical with water or that steam is identical with water. The reason for th s is the introduction of three new complex terms. Each contains "water" but also a phenomenological term, such as "frozen," as a second constituent. We thus do not have one term, such as "water," that is common to descriptions of ice and steam but three different terms that cannot in each case simply be reduced to "water." It is like the difference between olive oil and baby oil. The former is made from olives, but the latter is not made from babies. What has happened here, in effect, is that "water" has been substituted for "$H_2O$." What proponents of this position really mean is that ice is frozen $H_2O$, and with that I agree. As I have stressed throughout this chapter, the common constituent of ice, steam, and water is $H_2O$. But it is not water, *simpliciter*.

There is a second objection to the argument. In referring to ice as "frozen water" and to steam as "water vapor," one is mentioning the phenomenological features of these things. One is no longer characterizing ice and steam simply as $H_2O$ but as having such and such observable features. The existence of these features is determined by various states of the world, such as whether the temperature is below zero degrees Celsius and so forth. By introducing such terms as "frozen" and "liquid," the Putnam-Kripke approach gives the game away. They are now agreeing with me that to discriminate ice from water we must refer to their phenomenological properties. I conclude that this argument, like the first, carries no conviction.

## Three Additional Criticisms

The Twin Earth argument holds that water is necessarily $H_2O$, and accordingly, it is not possible for "water" in Earth English to mean something other than $H_20$. The argument is thus a modal argument, employing such terms as "necessary" and "possible." Thus direct reference theorists are using modal logic here for linguistic and ontological purposes, just as they did with respect to proper names. But the argument in this case is not valid. The premise that water is necessarily $H_2O$ is false, but even if it were true, the conclusion derived from it, that "water" *must* mean $H_2O$, is a non sequitur. I will now show why the premise is false and why even if it were true the conclusion would not follow from it. I do not believe the direct reference theory can deal with these objections. These will be new arguments. I call them the "isotope argument," "the functional argument," and the "argument from isomers," respectively. I will begin with the isotope argument. In considering it, one should keep in mind that when Kripke-Putnam claim that water is necessarily identical with $H_20$, they mean, as Putnam explicitly states, that each and every water molecule is $H_2O$. They take this thesis to be significant and not a mere tautology. It is nontautologous in the sense that, despite what ordinary persons mean by "water" (the liquid that falls from the sky as rain and collects in pools, etc.), chemical theory shows that water is (ignoring impurities) necessarily $H_2O$. The isotope argument that now follows will show this claim to be false.

In 1931 Harold Urey discovered that the liquid most people call "water" is not only composed of $H_2O$ molecules but of molecules composed of deuterium and oxygen. For this achievement Urey later received the Nobel Prize. Deuterium is an isotope of hydrogen that has an atomic weight double that of ordinary hydrogen. When it combines with oxygen, it forms deuterium oxide, or $D_2O$. The collection of $D_2O$ molecules is also called "heavy water," which is visually indistinguishable from normal water. Deuterium oxide has a molecular weight of about 20 (twice the atomic weight of ordinary hydrogen, which is 1, plus oxygen, which is 16), whereas $H_2O$ has a molecular weight of about 18. Heavy water is comparatively rare, because ordinary water contains only one atom of deuterium for every 6,760 atoms of hydrogen.

In 1934 Ernest Rutherford, M. L. Oliphant, and Paul Hartreck bombarded deuterium with high-energy deuterons (the nuclei of deuterium atoms) and discovered another isotope of hydrogen, which they called "tritium." This also bonds to oxygen, forming a molecule, $T_2O$, that is heavier than deuterium oxide and rare in nature. To complicate matters still further, there are molecules containing Oxygen 17 and Oxygen 18 that bond with various isotypes of hydrogen to form molecules that differ from any described here.

If one were to eliminate all sand, oils, salts, metals, and such from the liquids found in the Pacific and Atlantic Oceans, one would obtain what Kripke and Putnam call "pure water." This they define as $H_2O$. But pure water would not be composed solely of $H_2O$. As the aforementioned history of chemistry shows, it is a mixture of various kinds of molecules, such as $H_2O$, $D_2O$, and $T_2O$, all closely resembling one another but nonetheless different. These various molecules have different properties (e.g., boiling points, molecular masses, and so forth) and are therefore not identical. The statement that pure water is $H_2O$ is neither a necessary nor an empirical truth, since heavy water is not identical with $H_2O$. Pure water is thus like jade. What is commonly called "jade" is composed of two different sorts of micromaterials. Like jade, water also comes in various forms, not all of which are composed of $H_2O$ molecules. The Kripke-Putnam thesis that water = $H_2O$ can be rejected because, like many philosophical conceits, it is based on too limited a gamut of samples. Moreover, since pure water is not identical with the total collection of $H_2O$ molecules, it does not follow, even on their own semantic account, that "water" means $H_2O$. Their account, which I do not accept, would entail that "water" means the aggregate of $H_2O$, $D_2O$, and $T_2O$, through the whole range of molecular combinations of hydrogen and oxygen. But independently of the theory of direct reference we shall find other reasons why "water" does not mean $H_2O$.

The instance of jade is interesting for another reason. Along with the fact that what is called "jade" has two different compositional elements, it gives us good grounds for suggesting that, in general, overt considerations, including the functions that certain natural kinds serve, are decisive in overriding microfeatures in determining what a word means. As I said earlier, this example will provide good grounds for rejecting the claim that there is always—I stress "always"—a direct connection between what a word means and what the substance named by that word is composed of. In the argument that follows—my so-called functional argument—we shall show that the meaning of the word has little to do with the composition of the item but depends on the function it serves.

Let us take as our example the common noun "table." This is, of course, not a natural kind word, but the point is applicable to natural kind words such as "water" and "jade." The term "table" refers to objects composed of glass, steel, wood, plastic, and other materials. The microstructures of tables vary according to the material of which the table is made. Yet function determines whether we subsume objects with such diverse microstructures under the rubric "table." What counts as a table is the use to which the item is put, not the material of which it is made. The meaning of "table" is thus determined by function or use and not by material composition or microstructure. This is also true of "jade." What passes as jade has two different microcompositions. But because the appearance of these two compounds is indistinguishable, each is used equally for cosmetic purposes. It is thus their function and appearance and not their microstructures that determine whether they are called "jade." Now it is easy to extend he point to other natural kind terms, such as "water." Consider the following modification of the Twin Earth scenario by way of illustration.

Suppose that for centuries now there has been considerable interaction between Earth and its twin. People have been flying between these planets for eons, and for some time now planes leaving Earth have been stocking up on what Earthlings call "water" and which they use for drinking, washing, cooking, and other purposes. Planes returning from Twin Earth have been supplied with what Twin Earthlings call "water," and this liquid is used for the same set of purposes on the return trip. But let us suppose that before 1999 nobody had performed a chemical analysis of the fluids they respectively call "water" on the two planets, but in that year that was done. It was then determined that the liquid on Earth was composed of $H_20$ and that the liquid on Twin Earth was composed of XYZ. Would the persons moving between the planets stop calling one of the fluids "water"? I doubt it. I think they would say that water is composed of different ingredients, depending on where it is found, or perhaps they would say it comes in two different forms, like jade. They would thus treat the word "water" in the way we now treat the word "table." Function, plus appearance, would override microcomposition in such a case. The example shows that there are plausible alternatives to Kripke's contention that the microcomposition of a substance is always decisive with respect to what we call that substance. This counterexample thus indicates that it cannot be a necessary truth that water is identical with $H_20$.

We can now turn to the argument from isomers. As I have been asserting in this essay, and as their own remarks abundantly confirm, Putnam and Kripke aver that the microcomponents determine the nature of any natural kind, as well as the meaning of the term denoting that kind. Let us move away from the case of water because it raises special problems about the relationship between $H_2O$ and the various forms it assumes under different conditions of temperature and pressure. But isomers involve a different set of relationships. Isomers are not phases or states of substances but independent substances. As such they provide a decisive counterinstance to the thesis that we can identify a natural kind, or indeed any substance, with its microcomposition.

Isomerism was first discovered at the beginning of the nineteenth century. The dominating chemical theory of the time held that all differences in the qualities of substances were the direct result of differences in their chemical composition. But in 1824–1825 two chemists (Justus von Liebig and Friedrich Wöhler), analyzing two different substances (fulminic acid and cyanic acid, respectively), discovered that the composition of both compounds proved to be absolutely the same. Jöns Jacob Berzelius

(1779–1848) shortly afterward introduced the term "isomerism" (from the Greek, meaning composed of equal parts) to denote the existence of substances that have different qualities, both in chemical and physical behavior, yet are identical in chemical composition. These phenomena were consistent with the atomic theory of matter because a compound that contains the same number of atoms of carbon, nitrogen, oxygen, and hydrogen as another might differ in internal structure by the different binding arrangements of those atoms in the molecules they form.

Water, ice, and steam are, of course, not isomers, but the mistake of identifying them with $H_20$, and thus by the transitivity of identicals with one another, is analogous to the mistake one would make if one were to identify isomers with one another. Isomers are substances that have exactly the same chemical components but with radically different arrangements of those ingredients. Thus ethyl alcohol, whose chemical formula is $C_2H_5OH$, and methyl ether, whose chemical formula is $CH_3OCH_3$, are each composed of two carbon atoms, six hydrogen atoms, and one oxygen atom. But the atoms bind to each other in different ways.

The substances in question are pure substances, that is, they are not interconvertible and are wholly different from one another, having different physical properties, such as their melting and boiling points, potability for humans, and so forth. There is no way of predicting these differences merely from knowing their chemical composition. Because they are pure substances, we can use the Kripke-Putnam vocabulary and call them natural kinds. The example shows that Putnam and Kripke are wrong in holding that natural kinds are identical with their chemical components since these are the same in all cases of isomers. The error of making such an identification was exposed nearly two centuries ago by the scientists I have mentioned and by now, of course, is accepted scientific doctrine.

## An Alternative Account

We have seen in this chapter that there are serious difficulties with either form of the direct reference theory. Does this mean that we are forced to fall back on a Fregean, Russellian, or Quinean view about meaning and reference? As I have also shown, these have their own difficulties. In the first part of this chapter I proposed an alternative account to these views with respect to proper names. I will now suggest an account about natural kind terms that also differs from those. It has recognizable Wittgensteinian resonances. Coming as it does at the end of a long chapter, it must perforce be brief, a mere sketch of such an account.

Suppose we wish to explain to a child what the word "water" means. How do we in fact go about it? We can exclude the direct reference myths that we do this by showing a child a glass of water and saying, "This is water," or by telling a child that what we now call "water" in the twentieth century is $H_20$. The notions of explaining, understanding, and meaning are connected elements in an ongoing instructional process designed to promote communication between human beings. Meanings play a crucial role in this process. They are the links that tie the chain of communication together. But the process is complicated. In teaching a tyke its native language, including what words mean, we do not begin with definitions, ostensive or otherwise. We train children in the way we train animals—to obey and to follow orders. We do not begin the training of animals with definitions. Moreover, early training is less designed to explain what words mean than to explain what things are. In training children the emphasis is upon teaching them what water is, not what the word "water" means. We say, "Don't spill the water," "Bring me a glass of water," "There is too much water in the glass, pour some out," and so on.

As Wittgenstein writes, "Children do not learn that books exist, that armchairs exist, etc. etc.—they learn to fetch books, sit in armchairs, etc." (1969:62). These kinds of training procedures initiate a child into a community united by common linguistic practices. Their effect is to provide modes of explanation that are not totally explicit but that, through a cumulative developmental process, eventually endow a child with the understanding of what words mean and what persons mean by the words they use. This process can succeed only if the young can observe the things and their features that are being referred to. In the case of water that means observing its overt properties: its potability, fluidity, transparency in small amounts, and so forth.

The outcome of the process is that the child, in an effort to communicate his or her thoughts to others, and to understand theirs, learns to use the word "water" in a way that is consonant with community practice. Children learn, that is, to apply the word to a liquid having certain perceptible properties and, beyond that, to use the word in a variety of other ways, as an active verb, for instance.

This learning process extends through time. At first a child may only understand "water" to mean a fluid that is tasteless and colorless and that is given to him or her to allay thirst. Later he or she may learn that this fluid, which is colorless in a glass, takes on a bluish hue in thick layers, that muds and salts dissolve in it, and yet that the word "water" is still applied to it. The child may also discover that when sufficiently cold it is transformed into a different substance, which his elders call "ice." How should one describe these supplemental pieces of information? Are they additions to the meaning of "water"? Let us not try to decide the matter here. What is clear is that such additional pieces of information allow for fuller communication between the child and others. The important point is that at this level of education all the components of the meaning of a word like "water" that a child grasps are phenomenological—they consist of such concepts as being liquid, fluid, transparent, odorless, potable. Meaning thus arises as a function of what the child observes and experiences. And what the neophyte observes are the gross properties of water. As a child's education proceeds, the youngster may eventually come to learn (though not by seeing or experiencing) that water is composed of $H_20$. Shall we say, as Putnam and Kripke insist, that children only know what "water" means at the end of this process—that is, when they learn that water is composed of $H_20$? Why should we? We do not and we should not.

If Putnam and Kripke were right, no native speakers of English before 1800 could have known what "water" meant. This follows from their thesis that "water" means the same as "$H_20$" and that nobody knew that the composition of water was $H_20$ before 1800. But if so, they could not have communicated with one another; they could not have sensibly given or obeyed such commands as "Don't spill the water," and "Bring me a glass of water." But since they did communicate with one another in saying these things, and without knowing anything about the molecular structure of water, it follows that they did know what "water" meant. Accordingly, the theory advanced by Putnam and Kripke is mistaken.

Putnam and Kripke have reversed the order of nature. Instead of beginning with the fact that early speakers of English communicated with one another and asking how that is possible, they have developed an a priori theory that makes the fact of such communication inexplicable. Here we have philosophical paradox in its strongest form.

For contrary to what they say, these early training procedures do not make use of the techniques of direct reference. They do not rely upon ostensive definitions, and they do not initially teach a child that water is composed of $H_20$. Instead, they teach a child what "water" means by reference to what the child observes and manipulates.

The direct reference doctrine cannot account for the developmental process I have described, or for the role that the phenomenological features of water play in determining the meaning of "water," or for the historical fact that early speakers of English in using the word "water" obviously communicated with one another. These thus comprise decisive reasons for rejecting the direct reference doctrine.

# Chapter Nine

# Today and Tomorrow

At the beginning of this book I argued that analytic philosophy, despite frequent claims by some of its practitioners to be "scientific," is essentially a humanistic endeavor. As such it is intimately tied to its past in a way that science is not. As I have emphasized throughout this study, many issues analytic philosophers deal with now and have dealt with since the time of Frege have ancient antecedents: How is it possible to speak meaningfully or truly about the nonexistent? How with consistency can one deny that something exists? How is it possible for two true identity sentences to differ in meaning? And, is existence a property?

I suggested in chapter 1 that a metaphor for explicating the relation between present philosophical practice and its trailing past is the solera system for making sherry. Using that analogy, we can say that old philosophy has the power to educate and improve new philosophy. And new philosophy not only preserves the quality and character of old philosophy but has the capacity to refresh it. Intermingling, preservation, and refreshment are thus the characteristics that define the relationship between contemporary philosophy and its intruding history. I also asked in chapter 1 whether the solera metaphor fits the facts. Is twentieth-century analytic philosophy like new wine? Or is it like old wine that has lost its freshness? After a lengthy depiction of the main developments in the twentieth century, from the time of Frege to the present, we are in a better position to address these queries.

But let us make them more specific. I have divided this chapter into two parts. In the first I look retrospectively at the preceding period, asking two questions: have we learned anything important from a whole century of logical analysis, or has it been a period of scholastic quibbling over this or that myopic refinement? And are any of the figures discussed of first-rate importance—comparable to Descartes, Hume, or Kant, for example? In the second part of the chapter I discuss some recent trends in analytic philosophy. These concern two long-standing topics—materialism and perception—that have been given what seem to be new twists, and I will determine whether they represent real advances over traditional approaches. I then conclude the chapter with a look at the situation as we move into the twenty-first century. The questions here are whether there are any dominant movements or personalities in the way there were earlier in the century. Some critics have said no. I shall critically examine their reasons for this judgment.

## Part 1

With the solera metaphor in mind, then, I will turn to my first two questions. Has the past century been a period of substantive philosophical achievement? Have any of the persons discussed been of first-rate importance? A number of contemporary authors have answered each of these questions with a resounding no. Some, echoing Hegel's claim in *Glauben und Wissen* that "God is dead," lament that "philosophy is dead." Others assert that it is alive but flaccid, while others see vitality, and even ferment, but all of it confined to in-house discussion. From this last perspective twentieth-century analytic philosophy has been *Ein Glasperlenspiel*, a game without practical application or social utility, that is, just another version of art for art's sake.

The first question is the more complicated, having such subparts as what have we learned from a century of analytic philosophy, whether analytic philosophy is a self-centered activity, or, even if it is, whether substantial achievements have nonetheless been made within that circumscribed field, and to what degree the various practitioners have been original thinkers. I think the critics are right in saying that analytic philosophy is self-contained in the sense that it is almost wholly an academic activity. But even this point requires careful assessment. Russell, for example, is one of the philosophers of the century whose work has had an impact in general society. Such books as *Why I Am Not a Christian, The Conquest of Happiness, Marriage and Morals, Justice in Wartime, Roads to Freedom: Socialism, Anarchism, and Syndicalism*, and a host of essays, such as "Anti-Suffragist Anxieties," "The Place of Science in a Liberal Education," "When Should Marriage Be Dissolved," "Chinese Civilization and the

West," and "A Free Man's Worship," have spilled well beyond the confines of academia. It is also true that most of these pieces do not involve what he called "analysis" in the strict sense, that is, the sort of approach we find in "On Denoting," "The Nature of Truth," "The Relation of Sense-Data to Physics," *Introduction to Mathematical Philosophy*, and *The Analysis of Mind.* These last are essays and studies written for professionals and have little external influence. It is possible the critics are thinking of such authors as John Dewey and William James, whose work had important societal implications. But neither of these persons was an analytic philosopher in the usual sense of the term. As with so many fields, there is a division of labor in philosophy, and analytic philosophy is one of those divisions of the subject that does not carry with it much social or political import. Carnap is a good example of a philosopher who distinguished between his analytic activities and his political views. He thought the former had very little relevance for the latter.

The cases of Moore and Wittgenstein are further illustrations of how narrow the concerns of analytic philosophers typically are. To be sure, Moore influenced a literary circle, the Bloomsbury group, and Wittgenstein's ideas have been disseminated widely through all the corridors of the academy, as I mentioned at the beginning of chapter 5. But he is hardly known to most people. A famous story illustrates how isolated from public awareness the analysts tend to be. In 1951 Moore was awarded the Order of Merit, the highest honor that a man of letters can receive in the British Empire. The presentation was made by King George VI, who chatted with Moore for a while and then arose, indicating that the ceremony was at an end. Moore returned to the cab where his wife was waiting for him and, leaning over excitedly, said to her: "Do you know that the king had never heard of Wittgenstein!" As far as I know, the contributions of most of the philosophers we have discussed in this book—Frege, Ryle, Austin, Carnap, Quine, Marcus, Putnam, and Kripke—are wholly academic and would not have been known to George VI or any of his royal progeny.

But just as those pursuing art for art's sake have made important contributions to art, so many of those I have just mentioned have made genuine contributions to philosophy. Probably no century has seen such original ideas as the theory of descriptions, speech act theory, the concept of family resemblance, rigid designation, and, most important, the development of mathematical logic. That these have turned out to be of interest mostly to philosophers does not detract from their intellectual power and sophistication. There is thus some weight to the criticism that analytic philosophy is a circumscribed activity. But even granting the point, one should not infer that nothing of intellectual significance occurred in the period under consideration. If something is important only to philosophers, it may still be important.

Another thing may be said in the defense of analytic philosophy. It, more than many other branches of the subject, is a continuation of the deepest and most profound tradition in philosophy. From the time of the ancient Greeks, philosophers have been interested in intellectually challenging issues: how motion is possible if reality is static, whether there is a first cause to the universe, whether space has boundaries, whether time is real, how language hooks up to the world, and so forth. The philosophers discussed in this book have been interested in many of these same problems; they have inherited the tradition and kept it alive. That these issues can be viewed as narrow intellectual puzzles is not so much a criticism of twentieth-century philosophy as a complaint about mainstream philosophy itself. If one thinks that the tradition is important, then it is not justifiable to criticize those who have carried on that tradition. The solera metaphor allows us to depict accurately the relationship between the tradition and its modern exponents. The latter take old wine and refresh it with new wine. The two intermingle in inextricable ways, and if the former is a justifiable activity, so is the latter.

The second question—has the century produced any real heavyweights?—is less complex but more conjectural, because it involves predictions about how the figures we have spoken about will be regarded, if at all, in the centuries to come. In this connection history teaches us two things: that local reputations may be inflated in their own time and that because philosophical fashions tend to fade once a thinker has died, the chance that his or her reputation will persist is unlikely. We already have plenty of evidence that history is right on both points. In 1939 the Library of Living Philosophers initiated a series of books dedicated to the proposition that "if great philosophers could be confronted by their capable philosophical peers and asked to reply," it would help to "eliminate confusions and endless sterile disputes over interpretation." The series thus discriminated between "great" philosophers and their "capable" peers and of course presupposed that the books to appear in the series were about the work of great philosophers.

Since the promulgation of the first book, devoted to the philosophy of John Dewey, twenty-five volumes had appeared as of 1999. It has been announced that P. F. Strawson, Donald Davidson, Jürgen Habermas, and

Seyyed Hossein Nasr (whom I have never heard of) will be the subjects of new volumes. The twenty-five individuals in the existing series are John Dewey, George Santayana, Alfred North Whitehead, Ernst Cassirer, Sarvepalli Radhakrishnan, Karl Jaspers, C. D. Broad, Martin Buber, C. I. Lewis, Brand Blanshard, Jean Paul Sartre, Gabriel Marcel, Charles Hartshorne, A. J. Ayer, Paul Ricoeur, Paul Weiss, Albert Einstein (taken as a philosopher), Hans-Georg Gadamer, Karl Popper, Rudolf Carnap, G. E. Moore, Roderick Chisholm, G. H. von Wright, and W. V. O. Quine. Most of these "greats" (e.g., Broad, Whitehead, Radhakrishan, Jaspers, Lewis, Blanshard, Weiss) are rarely alluded to today. Those who are—Gadamer, Popper, Carnap, and von Wright, for example—are mentioned because of their work on special topics such as, in Russell's case, the theory of descriptions. The main exception to the ravages of time so far seems to be Quine, and I will say more about him later. Gilbert Ryle and J. L. Austin are not even in the series. More interesting is the fact that there is no volume on Wittgenstein. This omission may be because he published only the *Tractatus* and a short paper on logical form in his lifetime. The series is based on the idea that eminent philosophers will have an opportunity to respond to their critics. But because Wittgenstein's later, most important, writings were published only posthumously, he was not a candidate for such a volume.

Thus history deals harshly with the eminent. How shall we assess the chances of "immortality" for the analytic philosophers we have dealt with in this study—Frege, Russell, Moore, Carnap, Wittgenstein, Ryle, Austin, and Quine? Will any of them turn out to be the Descartes or the Kant of the twenty-first or the twenty-second century? My own guess is that only Wittgenstein is a plausible candidate for that status. Here is why I think so. I believe that there are four or five criteria for greatness: the philosopher must have contributed to all or nearly all the main fields of the discipline, be original, leave a legacy whose content and size engender a scholarly corpus of commentary, have an influence on related disciplines in the humanities, and is such that if she or he had not lived, the field would be wholly different. Clearly Plato, Aristotle, Hume, and Kant satisfy all these conditions. Descartes did not contribute to all fields and yet he satisfies the other criteria. How do our twentieth-century candidates fare in light of these requirements?

Let us begin with the reasons for excluding all except Wittgenstein. We have already seen the etiolation of the reputations of Russell, Moore, Carnap, and Ryle. We can therefore set them aside. Those remaining include Frege, Austin, Quine, and Wittgenstein. I think Frege and Austin will continue to be remembered in the future but mostly, again, for specific achievements—Austin for his emphasis on ordinary discourse and the invention of speech act theory, and Frege historically for the creation of mathematical logic and philosophically for his linguistic theories. Frege's work has produced scholarly commentaries and Austin's has not. Each is an original thinker, but each will fail the criterion of scope. Their focus has been too narrow for imperishability. Accordingly, I believe that neither will achieve the reputation of Hume or Kant. To be remembered for antiquarian reasons or for specific achievements is not likely to be sufficient for inclusion in the pantheon of the philosophical gods. We are thus left with Quine and Wittgenstein.

Quine's future is hard to assess because he is still alive (at this writing), still producing books and papers, and speaking at conferences. It is thus difficult to know whether his current high reputation will persist after his death. Nonetheless, there are good reasons for thinking it will not. Let us begin with the reasons why he might be considered a candidate for canonical status. As I mentioned in chapter 7, he is one of the rare analytic philosophers—perhaps the only major figure of the century—who has a complete integrated system of philosophy. Thus, unlike Frege, Austin, and even Russell, his work will probably be judged in synoptic, rather than in piecemeal, terms. If he is remembered, it will be for constructing such a complex system.

Furthermore, Quine is certainly the most influential living philosopher in the analytic tradition. Although he is less discussed now than before his retirement in 1978, his influence on the profession continues to be great. Another factor is that his many students and acolytes—Davidson and others—have themselves become notable and influential thinkers. Although they often disagree with Quine on this or that specific point, they continue in general to represent his scientistic point of view, and their students in turn represent both theirs and Quine's. So future generations of philosophers may well elevate Quine to the canonical status we have been describing here. Furthermore, like that of Hume, Kant, and Aristotle, Quine's work has produced scholarly explanatory treatises. Finally, one must stress that we live in a scientific age par excellence. The influence of science on contemporary philosophers has been and continues to be enormous. Quine is the most articulate spokesman for this point of view. In this respect he represents the temper of the times. There is every reason to believe that the impact of science on society will continue in the future. If so, it is a plausible conjecture that Quine will continue to be its spokesman. On that ground alone, he may become ensconced as a memorable figure.

But there are also countervailing considerations. The very generality of Quine's approach means that it is vulnerable to rapid dissolution if its main theses are found to be wanting. Even among those who generally support a scientistic outlook, and who regard Quine as a major figure, severe objections to his holism and behaviorism arise. I mentioned some of these criticisms in chapter 7 and will not repeat them here. If future generations find them compelling, Quine's reputation may well plummet. In addition, Quine fails the criterion of scope. His writings, extensive as they are, are essentially limited in focus to scientific and logical issues. When compared with Hume and Kant, for example, who explored the whole range of philosophical questions, Quine has been myopic. As a result he has had virtually no influence on the other humanistic disciplines. But the greatest obstacle to his future reputation is the criticism that his philosophy is not original. No doubt, all will agree, its blend of ingredients is impressive, and some of these are certainly new, but looked at under the aspect of eternity it is essentially a familiar mixture of empiricism and logical analysis. From this perspective it belongs to a long tradition, starting with Locke and Hume and continuing to the present. Frege, Russell, and Carnap are also representatives of that tradition, but each of them is more original than Quine. All of them see in the blend of logic and science a solution to most philosophical problems, but their diverse approaches are each inventive in ways in which Quine's philosophy is not. He is, instead, a kind of synthesizer of the differing ingredients we find in that tradition. Just as there is a magnum of Humean wine in Russell, and a double magnum of Humean-Russellian wine in Carnap, there are jeroboams of Humean-Russellian-Carnapian wine in Quine. Quine thus exemplifies the solera system perfectly. That there is plenty of that sort of wine on philosophical shelves may in the end militate against his membership on the list of deities. Indeed, that is my conclusion.

In my opinion Wittgenstein is the strongest of all the candidates. More than any other analytic philosopher, he has changed the thinking of a whole generation. Like Plato, Aristotle, and Kant, he is the product of an enormous subliterature of commentaries: by Max Black, Garth Hallet, Eike von Savigny, Gordon Baker, and P. M. S. Hacker, among others. The quantity of his work, unlike the tiny amount of material produced by Frege and Austin, is enormous and comparable in size to that of Plato and Aristotle. Moreover, it covers the entire gamut of philosophy, from logic through philosophical psychology to considerations of culture and value. It has also had a profound effect on the nonphilosophical disciplines in the humanities and social sciences. Most important, he surpasses Quine in inventiveness and creativity. The later Wittgenstein (in contrast to the author of the *Tractatus*, who was also part of the philosophical solera system) is genuinely original, virtually without antecedents. Von Wright, widely recognized as a careful judicious historian of philosophy, says this explicitly: "The later Wittgenstein, in my view, has no ancestors in the history of thought. His work signals a radical departure from previously existing paths of philosophy."

This is also my assessment; indeed I believe Wittgenstein may well be the most original philosopher since Kant. What now follows are the supporting reasons for this judgment. Let me quote two passages from *Zettel* (1967b) to illustrate the point:

> 395. A man can pretend to be unconscious; but *conscious*?
>
> 396. What would it be like for someone to tell me with complete seriousness that he (really) did not know whether he was dreaming or awake?—
>
> Is the following situation possible: Someone says "I believe I am now dreaming"; he actually wakes up soon afterwards, remembers that utterance in his dream and says "So I was right!"—This narrative can surely only signify: Someone dreamt that he had said he was dreaming.
>
> Imagine an unconscious man (anaesthetized, say) were to say "I am conscious"—should we say "He ought to know?"
>
> And if someone talked in his sleep and said "I am asleep"—should we say "He's quite right?"
>
> Is someone speaking untruth if he says to me "I am not conscious?" (And truth, if he says it while unconscious?" And suppose a parrot says "I don't understand a word," or a gramophone: "I am only a machine"?)

One could write a whole book on these two passages. But their originality is palpable. Who has ever asked, "Can a man pretend to be conscious?" Or who has ever produced this example: "Imagine an unconscious man (anaesthetized, say) were to say "I am conscious"—should we say "He ought to know"? Who has ever said: "And if someone talked in his sleep and said 'I am asleep'—should we say 'He's quite right?' " The answer is nobody before Wittgenstein. Neither Descartes, nor Locke, nor Hume, nor Kant, and certainly not Frege, Russell, Carnap, or Quine. These are powerful, deep questions that uncover the logic of mental talk. And they are not isolated examples. Wittgenstein's philosophy is full of such questions and the implicit replies to them. Unlike some disciplines in which it is the answers that count, in philosophy genius is often measured by the questions asked. By that criterion Wittgenstein has no equal. He posed a host of queries that no one had asked before and that no one might ever have asked had he not lived.

"If you are whistling a tune and you are interrupted, how do you know how to go on?"; "Why is the alphabet like a string of pearls in a box?"; "Does my telephone call to New York strengthen my conviction that the earth exists?"; "Are we to say that the knowledge that there are physical objects comes very early or very late?"; "Does a child believe that milk exists? Or does it know that milk exists? Does a cat know that a mouse exists?" The list is endless.

Another feature of Wittgenstein's thought supports his inclusion among the philosophical greats. As I indicated in chapter 5, he developed a new approach to doing philosophy. Indeed, he said of himself that his most important contribution was to have introduced a new method. (We can contrast him in this respect with Quine, who refined old methods.) His substantive contributions to the theory of meaning, the philosophy of mind, epistemology, aesthetics, and mathematics are all products of this new method. One test of progress in philosophy is whether a new conception induces others to reassess ancient issues in fresh and unanticipated ways—and this effect is usually a function of a new method. From Plato through Kant this has been the case. In this respect, Wittgenstein is highly original. Serious students of Wittgenstein will never approach philosophical issues in pre-Wittgensteinian ways.

Of course, what often makes for dispute in philosophy and for differences in the estimation of philosophers by other philosophers are differences in the judgments about the merits of the methodology being invoked. So there is, as one might well expect, dispute about Wittgenstein's status. But whatever history's ultimate judgment about his style of doing philosophy, there is no doubt that he was an original and profound investigator whose way of exploring conceptual problems has no exact precedent. All the indexes for inclusion among the philosophical gods are thus favorable in his case. I conclude that Wittgenstein, uniquely among those we have discussed in this book, will make the grade.

## Part 2

I now turn to two recent trends in analytic philosophy, both strongly influenced by developments in science. The first concerns two theories about the human mind, and the second deals with perception. Though each trend has older origins, both approaches differ from anything in the tradition. The questions I raise in what follows are whether the apparent novelties represent real advances or are only cosmetic.

### *The Philosophy of Mind*

The last quarter of the twentieth century has seen a profound shift in interest among analytic philosophers from questions about meaning and reference to questions about the human mind. As we shall see, a roughly similar change has occurred in the philosophy of perception. Such processes or states as thinking, judging, perceiving, believing, and intending are mental activities, and their products or objects, such as representations, meanings, beliefs, and visual images, are intimately tied to these mental activities. Generally, beliefs are expressed in propositional terms, for example, that it will rain today. A proposition is generally taken to be a meaningful entity. Or, again, when I perceive something, say, a table, my mental state results in a visual experience of a certain sort. To describe what is believed or perceived thus involves a whole process, part of which involves mental activity and part of which involves the objects or entities connected with such activity.

Traditionally, the philosophy of language concentrated only on the objects thought about or perceived—on the status of propositions, judgments, beliefs, visual images, sense-data, and so on. But this focus has lately been seen as one-sided, and it is now recognized that the mind must always be involved in any investigation into the properties and functions of such objects. Concurrent with this change, another factor has initiated an explosion of interest in the philosophy of mind. This has to do with recent developments in science. Suddenly, science has become aware that the human mind is the last remaining scientific mystery. Of course, for philosophers it has always been a mystery, but now the challenge to unravel its secrets has been joined by neuroscientists, biologists, mathematicians, linguists, computer experts, cognitive scientists, and anthropologists. Thus the ferment about the mind in intellectual circles today is tremendous, and philosophy stands at the center of this vortex.

A large number of scholars still think that philosophy has an autonomous role to play in dealing with such questions. They tend to emphasize the peculiar nature of felt experience, and the fact that each of us has access to his or her own mental experience in a way that no other person has. Pains and visual images, for example, possess a kind of subjectivity that seems to defeat third-person (i.e., scientific) explanations. Roderick Chisholm's *The First Person* (1981); Zeno Vendler's *The Matter of Minds* (1984); Thomas Nagel's paper, "What It Is Like to Be a Bat" (1974), and his book, *The View from Nowhere* (1986); and Alastair Hannay's *Human Consciousness* (1990) are examples of such works. Even some scientists, Roger Penrose, for instance, in *The Emperor's New Mind* (1989), have defended this point of view.

It should be stressed that none of these views is "dualist" in a classical Cartesian sense; none holds that mind and body are two utterly different substances. Vendler, for example, argues in a 1995 paper, "Goethe, Wittgenstein, and the Essence of Color," that visual images are epiphenomenal. They have a physical cause but as felt phenomena cannot be reduced to neural activity. Some philosophers, thinking about the mind from this autonomous perspective, argue that the conceptual model, which claims that the mental-material (physical) distinction is both exclusive and exhaustive, is a bogus dichotomy and the source of much confusion. As Austin once put it, why shouldn't there be nineteen different kinds of things rather than just two? Generally speaking, if analytic philosophers have arrived at a consensus about the mind it is that no strictly Cartesian form of dualism is a serious player in the field today. There is also a growing recognition that the main traditional competitor to any form of Cartesianism, the so-called identity theory, has profound liabilities. Yet the theory is part of an old tradition and has many supporters, both among philosophers and scientists. It is thus worth a brief digression to describe what it is and especially to distinguish it from the two new approaches with which it is sometimes conflated—functionalism and eliminative materialism.

The identity theory, also called "reductive materialism," asserts that mental states are physical states of the brain. The early formulations of this position were "type = type" theories. They held that each type of mental state or process is numerically identical with some type of neural state or process within the brain or central nervous system.

But this formulation quickly ran into the objections that beings with nervous systems other than ours could have mental states and that two human beings who entertain the same belief may not be in the same neurophysiological state. (The notion that systems with different properties could stand in some relationship of identity later became the driving idea behind functionalism, and this is in part why it is sometimes confused with the identity theory.) Type-type identity theory was thus discarded in favor of "token-token" identity theory. This view asserted that the relation of identity holds between particular mental states and particular neurophysiological states, and this is now the canonical version of the theory.

Several compelling arguments support this thesis. Probably the most powerful of these rests on an analogy between felt experience, such as warmth, and a scientific description of this phenomenon. According to the identity theorist, science has shown that warmth is identical with a high level of molecular kinetic energy, just as lightning is simply identical with the discharge of electrons between clouds and the earth and that water is identical with collections of molecules of $H_20$. By analogy, then, mental states are simply certain configurations of the nervous system or certain sorts of neural processes in the brain. We saw, however, in the last chapter that the identity theory with respect to natural kinds is irredeemably flawed. Water is not identical with $H_20$. It can by parallel reasoning be argued—as Kripke has surprisingly done—that felt warmth is not identical with molecular kinetic energy.

But other difficulties are present as well. This thesis, which is a variant of Hobbes's materialism, is still in a programmatic stage. It is agreed that nobody yet knows enough about how the nervous system and brain function to be able to pinpoint the relevant identities, but as evidence continues to accumulate, proponents of the doctrine argue that there is reason to believe that future scientific research will eventually discover these identities. But this supposition also runs into a conceptual hurdle: how is it possible for a researcher to identify someone's felt experience with a given neural process? What possible observation could reveal such an identity? If none could, then how could the so-called theory be verified by adducing evidence in its support? The objection questions whether the identity theory is even sensible.

A final criticism states that the initial plausibility of the analogy upon which the theory rests depends on an ambiguity in the concept of warmth. When the ambiguity is exposed, the theory can be seen to be question begging—to be assuming rather than proving that felt sensation is identical with neural activity. The concept of warmth can be given two interpretations. It can be thought of as something objective, as temperature measured by a thermometer, and also as a subjective sensation. The former, one can agree, is identical with molecular action of a certain sort. But the latter is entirely different in character. Given the same external temperature, for instance, different people may react differently; what one senses as warmth, another may not and so forth. It thus seems that no one-to-one relationship exists between felt experience and external molecular movement. To assume that warmth is identical with temperature is thus to beg the question at issue, namely, whether the felt sensation is identical with high average molecular kinetic energy. For all these reasons, and others, those attracted to a materialist theory of the mind have developed alternative systems that they believe bypass these objections.

These are functionalism and eliminative materialism. We shall now consider the arguments for and against each of them. This will help us determine whether these are genuinely new developments in the philosophy of mind.

*Functionalism.* This doctrine was invented by Hilary Putnam in the mid-1970s (and was disavowed by him about fifteen years later). Putnam realized that the token-token identity theory is open to the query "What do two neurophysiological states have in common if they are both the same mental state?" His answer was that they serve the same function in a human organism. What Putnam meant by this reference to function can be explained by an example. Suppose a batter is hit by a pitched ball and falls groaning to the ground. One can distinguish three phases in this episode: an external stimulus that affects the body (namely, the ball's hitting the player), an internal sensation that the player feels (e.g., a pain), and finally observable bodily behavior (groaning and falling to the ground).

Putnam argues that internal distress, say, pain, characteristically results from an injury to the body and that it in turn causes a behavioral reaction. Pain is thus a mental state, interceding between an external stimulus and subsequent bodily behavior. Functionalism thus asserts that any event that plays a similar intermediary role is a mental state. Such things as fears, beliefs, and intentions are mental because they play a mediating causal role in the overall economy of the human organism. One attraction of functionalism is that it acknowledges the existence of internal mental events in a way that strict behaviorism does not. It also rejects type-type identity theories, and for that reason is usually interpreted as holding that psychology is not reducible to physics or biology. But it does espouse a form of the token-token identity theory, maintaining that each instance of a given mental state is numerically identical with a physical state in a particular physical system. It is thus ultimately a form of materialism that is based on token-token identities.

The main argument for functionalism is that it seems to be an accurate description of how mental states and mental activities function within a total organism. Their role seems to be both reactive and causal. Human beings are exposed to external stimuli; these are processed by the mind and give rise to behavior. This analysis seems to capture both the psychologist's and the ordinary person's intuitions about the nature of mental activity. Indeed, one great advantage of functionalism is that it allows the mind to be modeled by computers. Once it was understood that any sort of system, whether animate or not, could be described in functional terms, it was obvious that the analysis applies to computers. A computer is essentially an information processor. But this, many philosophers contend, is what a human being is. In a computer the software (the program) functions like the human mind. It reacts to external inputs via the hardware and gives rise to certain outputs. The hardware is analogous to the brain. The brain provides the stimuli and reacts to the activity of the mind. The hardware-software distinction thus provides an ideal model for how functionally equivalent elements at a higher level can be implemented by different physical systems at a lower level. One and the same program can be realized by different physical hardware systems; accordingly, it was argued that one and the same set of mental processes can be manifested in different forms of hardware implementations.

Functionalism, as a philosophical conceit, was thus the source of a research program in cognitive science called "strong artificial intelligence" (strong AI), which asserts that having a mind is simply having a certain sort of program. This view is also called "Turing machine functionalism" because it satisfies a test developed by the mathematician Alan Turing for deciding whether a given system exhibits intelligence. In 1938 Turing envisioned a computing machine that would replicate human thought. His machine, which was an abstract mathematical design, could not in fact be constructed because it required an infinite tape. This requirement in practice is no longer considered essential because the memories of modern computers can be extended to meet any demand. Such computers are considered Turing machines—that is, automata that are relatively self-operating after they have been set in motion. They function by transforming information from one form into another on the basis of predetermined instructions or procedures. The ability to reason, discover meanings, generalize, and learn from past experience are considered capacities characteristic of human beings. That machines can exhibit many of these qualities, such as decision making and playing chess, is taken as evidence that machines can think. Thus any entity that can transform inputs into meaningful outputs is said to pass the Turing test and to be intelligent. So far, no computer capable of duplicating human intelligence has been developed, but AI research has led to some important practical results in decision making, natural language comprehension, and pattern recognition.

Parallel-processing computers have impressed many functionalists with their power, adaptability, and the ability to learn. That they can pass the Turing test seems to support the functionalist thesis that they are thinking entities (or, in the language of Descartes, "*res cogitantes*"). Regarding these subtle matters, the intelligent ordinary person remains both impressed and undecided.

John Searle's work is central to disputes concerning the Turing test. In a series of papers beginning in 1980, he claims to have refuted strong AI. His refutation turns on an example that he calls the "Chinese room argument." He envisages a situation in which somebody is locked in a room with a computer and fed questions written in Chinese. Searle points out that one could deal with incoming symbols via a program that allows one to match these with output symbols. The Turing test would be satisfied, yet the person engaging in this procedure would not understand Chinese. Searle's argument turns on the distinction between a formal, or syntactic, system and its semantic content. The program would allow one to satisfy the syntactic requirements while lacking the appropriate semantic understanding.

This argument has been intensively debated since he first proposed it. The consensus is that he is correct, but the issue is still under discussion.

Several other serious objections arise in regard to functionalism. Perhaps the most penetrating is the "inverted spectrum" counterexample. According to this objection, it is entirely conceivable that two human beings could possess inverted color spectra without knowing it. They may consistently use language in the same way, employing the word "red," for example, to describe the same object. Yet the colors each senses may be different from one another. But, according to functionalism, because both sensations play exactly the same causal role in the organism, they are the same sensation. The counterexample shows that similarity of function does not guarantee similarity or identity of felt experience and that functionalism is unsatisfactory as an analysis of mental content. Functionalists have responded to this and other objections with problematic success. Nevertheless, because of its appeal for researchers in the cognitive sciences, and despite Putnam's defection, it is still a widely held theory among philosophers, cognitive psychologists, and artificial intelligence researchers. To my knowledge, no similar view has existed in the history of philosophy. Whatever its merits, it is clearly a new and substantive doctrine about the human mind. As such it represents a serious alternative to such traditional theories as Cartesianism, the identity theory, and epiphenomenalism.

*Eliminative materialism.* Eliminative materialism is a more radical view and is deeply committed to scientism. Its main exponents are Paul Churchland and Patricia Churchland. Paul Churchland's *A Neurocomputational Perspective*, published in 1989, and *The Engine of Reason* (1995); Patricia Churchland's *Neurophilosophy* (1986) and, with Terry Sejnowski, *The Computational Brain*, published in 1992; and the Churchlands' cowritten *On the Contrary* (1998) contain sophisticated and highly developed forms of the theory. What they claim is that a sophisticated scientific theory does not require that there be such things as thoughts, beliefs, and intentions but only neural activity in the brain. This view differs from the identity theory in any of its forms, such as the "token-token" theory. The latter assumes that scientific inquiry begins with different descriptions of the same phenomena, one involving a mental vocabulary deriving from folk psychology and the other a physicalistic vocabulary that is properly the province of science.

The issue for the identity theorist is to show that the former level of discourse reduces to the latter. The eliminativists take a further step. They claim that there is no scientific observable evidence that such entities as thoughts and beliefs exist. Therefore, a mature scientific theory need not be reductionist at all. There exists nothing that has to be reduced to physical processes. The reductionist is thus trying to do the impossible, to reduce nothing to something. Just as chemical theory did not try to reduce phlogiston to the observable but simply dispensed with any reference to it, so thoughts, beliefs, and indeed the entire mentalistic repertory of folk psychology can be eliminated. They instead propose a wholly materialistic theory that describes neural activity in the brain.

Supporters of eliminative materialism argue for the theory vigorously and ingeniously. But it has remained a minority view. There are a number of serious objections to it that a majority of philosophers find compelling. I will mention two.

First, it is difficult to give an interpretation of the doctrine that is compatible with scientific theorizing. The eliminativists are proposing a theory. But all theories have semantic properties; they are either true or false, consistent or inconsistent, supported by observational data, and so on. What would it mean to say that neural activity is logically inconsistent, for example? Because all neural activity is describable by contingent propositions, how could one show that two different occurrences of neural activity are logically inconsistent? Indeed, what would "proposition" and "logically" mean in this case? If a proposition is just neural activity, how can it describe anything? It seems impossible to translate such semantic concepts as meaning, truth, and denotation into the vocabulary of neural firing. In sum, the objection contends that it is a category mistake to ascribe truth or falsity, or any semantic notions, to brain processes.

Second, there is the problem of "qualia." These, the felt sensations we all have, do not have the same problematic status as phlogiston. They obviously exist, and each human being knows that they do. To deny that they exist is tantamount to saying that there are no such things as sounds but only physical vibrations of various frequencies. Just as persons know that they hear sounds, they know that they experience mental phenomena. It is plausible, of course, to hold that such qualia are correlated with neural or other physical episodes, but that is to presuppose that qualia exist. It is argued against the eliminativists that every scientific theory must begin with such indubitable data. The failure to do so is thus to ignore facts that any empirical theory must accommodate. If this last objection is correct, eliminativism cannot be the philosophical theory that gives a satisfactory account of the science of the mind.

Eliminativism has become popular among neo-Quineans. The theory seems to be prefigured in Quine's rejection of mental entities, such as meanings. If one takes a further step than Quine did and rejects his behaviorism in favor of neural activity, one will easily arrive at eliminativism. Again, to my knowledge, no such theory has existed in the past. It is thus something genuinely new in philosophy. Of course, to say that it is new is not necessarily to endorse it as correct. The objections to it are strong, but its persistence among a coterie of philosophers and cognitive scientists means it cannot be dismissed out of hand. We shall have to wait in this case for the verdict of history.

### *Perception*

Sense-data theory has a long history. In its early modern form it can be traced to Descartes, and it plays fundamental roles in the philosophies of Locke, Berkeley, and Hume. It received a considerably more sophisticated treatment in the twentieth century by Russell, Moore, Broad, and Price, but under the attacks of G. A. Paul, W. H. F. Barnes, and John Austin it has essentially vanished from the present philosophical scene. Yet, operating like the solera process, it has been revived and refreshed in a different guise in the 1980s and 1990s.

The central issue in all versions of sense-data theory is whether human perception of the external world is direct or indirect. It is a concern that arises primarily for various forms of metaphysical realism. These hold that the world contains mind-independent entities, and the question is whether visual access to them is mediate or immediate, that is, whether it is conditioned by the intervention of mental entities or even by certain physical factors. The model invoked in these discussions is not necessarily Cartesian, but it does presuppose the existence of minds. The term "external" means "outside of the human mind," so a mind/nonmind contrast is operative in such analyses. What is interesting about contemporary discussions, especially those emphasizing recent work in psychology and neurology, is that they construe the direct-indirect distinction in different ways from their sense-data predecessors. We are thus dealing with an old problem revivified. Philosophers have been sensitive to these later scientific developments, and a burgeoning literature has developed that addresses the question.

Let us begin with a psychologist. In chapter 9 of *The Ecological Approach to Visual Perception* (1979), J. J. Gibson argues that the normal perception of physical objects (e.g., Niagara Falls) is direct. By "direct" he means that it is not mediated by sense-data, or by images of any sort, which he described as "flat pancakes." He contrasts such flat pancakes with three-dimensional objects whose properties, including their three-dimensionality, are seen in normal perception. Gibson agrees that there is such a thing as indirect perception. One looking at a photograph of Niagara Falls is seeing Niagara Falls indirectly, that is to say, by means of the photograph. But in general persons see objects themselves, not images or photographs of them, and that is direct seeing. Though his remarks are in part directed at the early sense-data theorists, his real targets are contemporary cognitive scientists who claim that all perception is mediated by "mental representations." His theory thus opposes any form of representative realism.

He argues that all such theories give an incorrect interpretation of certain scientific facts. According to optical theory, light is reflected off the surfaces of opaque objects, moves through the atmosphere, and is picked up by the human visual system, which includes the eye, the optical nerve, the retina, and the brain. According to this theory, all the steps between the original stimulus and the ultimate effect are causal, and Gibson accepts this. What he rejects is a certain scientific-philosophical interpretation of it. According to him, representative realists contend that each step in the causal process is an intermediary that conditions the character of the signal that is transmitted from the original source to the observer. In their view the last event in the process is directly perceived, and through it is perceived the original source in the external world. This last event is a so-called mental representation, that is, some sort of structure in the brain that reconfigures the external object from the messages it derives from the causal sequence.

Gibson rejects the inference that the elements in the causal sequence mediate normal perception. Instead, he argues that these causal factors should be seen as facilitators, not as intermediaries. Their function is analogous to what happens when one turns on a light. The light does not condition (i.e., affect or distort) one's perception but makes it possible to see the objects that a room contains. There is no reason to believe that one's apprehension of such things as tables or chairs is affected by turning on a light. The analogy applies to all cases of normal perception. We normally see three-dimensional objects without distortion and do not see representations from which we infer three-dimensionality. We literally see the dimensionality of these objects, just as they exist.

Gibson's views have generated a huge literature, much of it critical. One basic objection to his approach is that it has ignored new findings about the brain mechanisms involved in perception, including such aberrant perceptual experiences as the phantom limb phenomenon. Recent work by V. S. Ramachandran on the phantom limb phenomenon—see, for example, "Blind Spots" and "Perceptual Correlates of Massive Cortical Reorganization," both in published 1992, and *Phantoms in the Brain: Probing the Mysteries of the Human Mind* (1998), coauthored with Sandra Blakeslee—is based on an impressive amount of data about how people who have lost a limb feel complicated sensations in "it." They state that their hands are cramped or that some of their fingers cannot extend properly or that there is a pain in a specific area of the limb. Ramachandran's research has identified the loci of such sensations in specific areas of the brain, and as a result he has shown that in normal persons the stimulation of these zones can produce sensations comparable to those in persons who have lost a limb. His inference from this collection of data resembles the demon hypothesis of Descartes. He argues that all human sensations exist only in the brain and therefore that one's so-called perception of the external world is always by means of such representations.

Philosophers have entered this debate at a variety of different levels, usually supporting one or the other of these two positions. They have generated a vast array of arguments pro and con, some of them new and some old. Let me do some special pleading here. I will now describe some of my own work in *Surfaces* (1988) and *Sketches of Landscapes: Philosophy by Example* (1998). I think it casts some new light on these issues, but of course whether that is so is open to debate. In both studies I propose alternatives to all traditional theories of perception, such as direct realism and representative realism. These are overarching, holistic views, each asserting one simple thesis about perception: that all perception is mediated or that it is unmediated. I claim that such doctrines are too simple to do justice to the variegated perceptual data that experience provides, and I support this contention with a number of arguments and examples. Here is one such example.

In the first half of the century philosophers generated theories of perception that were highly compelling. One of these culminated in the thesis that if a perceiver is looking at an opaque object from a particular standpoint and at a given moment, the most the observer can see of that object is a facing part of its surface.

The argument in support of this view held that every opaque object has an exterior and that its exterior is its surface. Because the object is opaque, the observer cannot see part of it from his or her perspective—its reverse surface, for example. It follows that from a given perspective and at a given moment, one could never directly perceive the whole of any opaque object, such as an apple. This perceptual fact was taken to constitute a refutation of direct realism and to imply some form of representative realism. The argument also implies that any judgment about the whole object transcends the available perceptual evidence and thus opens the door to skeptical challenges. But in my opinion the argument is fallacious, and its skeptical implications are to be rejected. I argue that the examples philosophers invoke in support of this view are constrained in their topological and spatial variety. Such things as billiard balls, tomatoes, dice, inkwells, tables, persons, and planets constitute a limited range of items used to support the conclusion that one cannot see the whole surface of any opaque object.

But with a simple change of examples, this holistic theory and its skeptical conclusion collapse. Tennis courts, putting greens, roads, and mirrors are opaque, yet, depending on the contextual circumstances, all of their surfaces can be seen. Any adequate theory of perception must thus take account of the differences between opaque objects that have various topological characteristics—between spheres, cubes, rhomboids, and rectangles (such as tomatoes, dice, etc.) and those that I call "stretches"—putting greens, tennis courts, sheets, lakes, and roads. Depending on its size, and the prevailing visual conditions, all of the surface of a stretch (say, a mirror or a pool of water) can be seen.

When one adds to these differences other contextual constraints, for example, that many objects are moving, that they may or may not have surfaces even though they are opaque, that the observer may also be in motion, that light playing on objects takes many different forms, that particulate matter in the atmosphere produces a host of differing effects, that the observer's visual acuity and distance from the object condition what that person sees, it is impossible to accept a theory that claims there is single thing, such as a surface or part of a surface, that is invariably seen in each of these cases or that one never sees a whole object. An example-oriented, context-oriented description of the vast range of perceptual situations is able to take account of these multifarious factors in ways that no holistic theory can. My example-oriented approach thus shows that neither direct nor representative realism provides an accurate description of the perceptible world. It also offers an alternative to any scientific-psychological account such as that of Gibson, or to any of the philosophical accounts we find earlier in the century in Russell, Moore, Broad, and Price.

I do not claim that my approach solves all the issues of perception; it is clear that some problems of vision (and the other sense modalities) not only involve conceptual and linguistic considerations but an array of psychological, neurological, biological, and computer-based factors as well. But I do think I have produced an alternative to the familiar direct-indirect dichotomy that the tradition has been obsessed with. If I am right, it is a case of new wine intermingling with and revitalizing the old.

## Part 3

Late in the twentieth-century, a number of eminent philosophers announced that philosophy as a mode of inquiry was finished. There was nothing left for philosophy to do. The task of solving philosophical problems was to be left to science. As Hilary Putnam says in *Representation and Reality*, "The way to solve philosophical problems is to construct a better scientific picture of the world. . . . All the philosopher has to do, in essence, is be a good "futurist"—anticipate for us how science will solve our philosophical problems" (1989:107).

Putnam's remark is interesting for several reasons. To begin with, my study of analytic philosophy suggests a contrary assessment. The twentieth century has been an epoch of dynamic philosophical invention and development. To be sure, as the solera system model shows, philosophical practice throughout much of the century has obsessively addressed problems that have ancient origins. It is also true, as his comment reflects, that scientism in post-Quinean forms is still with us. Yet, it must be acknowledged that the creation of mathematical logic, the invention of the theory of descriptions, and the contributions of the modal logicians have cast new light on those old issues. Even in the areas where philosophers have interacted with scientists and social scientists, philosophical approaches have continued and still continue to preserve their autonomy and to make fruitful contributions to the subjects under consideration. The remark is true even of such scientistically inclined thinkers as Russell, Carnap, and Quine. But it is even more obvious in the work of the later Wittgenstein and Austin. The concept of the language game and its import for social institutions, and the role of speech acts in human communication, have initiated research programs in some of the social sciences. Work in the philosophy of mind has influenced the cognitive sciences, and philosophical research has had reverberations in scientific accounts of perception. As we move into the twenty-first century, the evidence is strong that philosophers will continue to generate new ideas. There is thus no reason to believe that all the best ideas lie in the past.

It is also worth emphasizing that Putnam's comment reflects an earlier twentieth-century tradition and does not describe or fit the radical changes that have taken place in philosophical activity in the last decade. The philosophical scene as we enter the new millennium is different in at least two important respects from what it was in earlier decades. First, since the retirement of Quine analytic philosophy has had no dominant figure. Today we have no Wittgensteins, Russells, Carnaps, or Austins. In his 1997 book, *Profitable Speculations: Essays on Current Philosophical Themes*, Nicholas Rescher has compiled an impressive mass of data about the diversity of philosophical practice at the end of the twentieth century. He summarizes the situation this way:

> Once upon a time, the philosophical stage was dominated by a small handful of greats and the philosophy of the day was what they produced. Consider German philosophy in the nineteenth century, for example. Here the philosophical scene, like the country itself, was an aggregate of principalities—presided over by such ruling figures as Kant, Fichte, Hegel, Schelling, Schopenhauer, and a score of other philosophical princelings. But today this "heroic age" of philosophy is a thing of the past. The extent to which significant, important, and influential work is currently produced by academics outside the high-visibility limelight has not been sufficiently recognized. For better or for worse, in the late twentieth-century we have entered a new philosophical era where what counts is not just a dominant elite but a vast host of lesser mortals. Great kingdoms are thus notable by their absence, and the scene is more like that of medieval Europe—a collection of small

> territories ruled by counts palatine and prince bishops. Scattered here and there in separated castles a prominent individual philosophical knight gains a local following of loyal friends or enemies. But no one among the academic philosophers of today manages to impose his or her agenda on more than a minimal fraction of the larger, internally diversified community. Given that some ten thousand academic philosophers are at work in North America alone, even the most influential of contemporary American philosophers is simply yet another—somewhat larger—fish in a very populous sea. If 2 or 3 percent of professional colleagues pay attention to a philosopher's work, this individual is fortunate indeed. (p. 20)

The reasons for this "democratization" of philosophy remain obscure. But that such a phenomenon has taken place is evident. Rescher's account is unquestionably accurate, and there is no doubt that the discipline today presents a different face than it did in its earlier phases. Second, because of such democratization and diversity of interest, there has been a virtual revolution in the topics now being discussed by philosophers. In particular, the kind of scientism that motivated Putnam and his predecessors, Frege, Russell, Carnap, and Quine, is less prominent than it was a quarter of a century ago. One can get a sense of this change by looking at recent issues of the *Proceedings and Addresses of the American Philosophical Association*. This periodical carries the programs of the annual meetings of the American Philosophical Association. In its issue devoted to the Pacific Division meeting held in Berkeley, California, from March 31 to April 3, 1999, the topics discussed included "Race and Rights," "Rawls, Marxism, Feminism, and Postmodernism," "The New Nationalisms," "Dilemmas of Community and Identity: An Africana Philosophical Encounter," "Native Voices and Philosophical World Views," "Reefer Madness: Legal and Moral Issues Surrounding the Medical Prescription of Marijuana," "Philosophically Feminist and Radically Heterosexual: Rethinking Subversive Sexual Politics," "Battered Women, Intervention, and Autonomy," "Consumer Preferences and the Ratchet Effect," "Humility Reconsidered," "Pride, Modesty, and Snobbery," "Violence in Contemporary Society," "Gender and the Martial Arts," "Intersectional Identity and the Authentic Self? Opposites Attract," "Is (Merely) Stalking Sentient Animals Morally Wrong?" and "Feminist Moral and Political Philosophy." This list is merely a segment of the unusual issues addressed at the conference. But the totality of such topics represents a large percentage of the papers presented.

I describe these topics as unusual from the perspective of Putnam's remark. It is impossible to see how any of them could be resolved by getting a better "scientific picture of the world" or why the philosopher should "anticipate" that science will solve them. Of course, scientific information may well be relevant in coming to grips with issues about the medical use of marijuana or the implications of cloning, for example. But it is naive to think that science is the discipline that can or will adjudicate the conceptual, moral, or political issues that these unusual topics raise.

In reflecting on this group of presentations, I wonder whether the very conception of the role of philosophy has not changed recently. It strikes me that the classical problems that the solera model presupposes are being ignored or dismissed by many contemporary American practitioners—perhaps even by a majority of those ten thousand professional philosophers that Rescher mentions. Their concerns are not so much with past, classical problems as with current issues. Clearly, there is a growing feeling, especially among younger academics, that the field should move on to deal with present-day moral, political, and social difficulties. Whether in the end a deeper probing of these matters will ultimately lead to the ancient dilemmas about causality, existence, identity, and the nonexistent remains to be seen.

Many analysts think that they will: that these current interests are only a superstructure, and a superficial one at that, covering the deeper problems that the canon has identified. But if the analysts are wrong, and if these more recent problems continue to have their own autonomy, philosophy will be moving into a new, more applied dimension, and in that sense there will be palpable progress in the field. If, however, these problems turn out to be merely a patina that thinly covers the classical issues, even that will be of interest in showing how immediate, practical, and pressing problems ultimately rest upon deeper traditional considerations. In neither case is science likely to provide a solution to these worries. The prospect for the future of philosophy as a humanistic discipline with important things to say about the inanimate world and its creatures is thus, in my judgment, an excellent one. But as Moritz Schlick once said, "the method of verification" is waiting. We shall thus have to wait and see what the future brings.

# References

## Works Cited


Austin, J. L. 1962a. *How to Do Things with Words*. Edited by James Urmson. Oxford: Clarendon.

———. 1962b. *Sense and Sensibilia*. Oxford: Clarendon.

———. 1970a. "Intelligent Behavior." In O. P. Wood and George Pitcher, eds., *Ryle*, pp. 45–52. New York: Doubleday.

———. 1970b. *Philosophical Papers*. 2d ed. Edited by J. O. Urmson and G. J. Warnock. Oxford: Oxford University Press.

Ayer, Alfred J. 1948. *Language, Truth, and Logic*. 2d ed. London: Gollancz.

Bartley, W. W. III. 1973. *Wittgenstein*. New York: Lippincott.

Blumberg, Albert and Herbert Feigl. 1931. "Logical Positivism: A New Movement in European Philosophy." *Journal of Philosophy* 28 (11): 281–96.

Broad, C. D. 1924. "Critical and Speculative Philosophy." In J. H. Muirhead, ed., *Contemporary British Philosophy*, pp. 77–100. London: Allen and Unwin.

———. 1959. "Autobiography." In P. A. Schilpp, ed., *The Philosophy of C.D. Broad*, pp. 3–68. Chicago: Open Court.

Carnap, Rudolf. 1928. *Der Logische Aufbau Der Welt* [The Logical Construction of the World]. Berlin-Schlachtensee: Weltkries-Verlag.

———. 1937. *The Logical Syntax of Language*. London: Kegan Paul.

———. 1947. *Meaning and Necessity: A Study in Semantics and Modal Logic*. Chicago: University of Chicago Press.

———. 1963. "Intellectual Autobiography." In P. A. Schilpp, ed., *The Philosophy of Rudolf Carnap*, pp. 3–84. Chicago: Open Court.

Chisholm, Roderick M. 1981. *The First Person: An Essay on Reference and Intentionality*. Brighton, Sussex, U.K.: Harvester Press.

Churchland, Patricia S. 1986. *Neurophilosophy.* Cambridge, Mass.: MIT Press.

Churchland, Paul M. 1995. *The Engine of Reason.* Cambridge, Mass.: MIT Press.

Churchland, Paul M. and Patricia Churchland. 1998. *On the Contrary.* Cambridge, Mass.: MIT Press.

Creath, Richard, ed. 1990. *Dear Carnap, Dear Van.* Berkeley: University of California Press.

Darwall, Stephen, Allan Gibbard, and Peter Railton. 1992. "Toward Fin de Siècle Ethics." *Philosophical Review* 101 (1): 115–89.

Donnellan, Kenneth. 1977. "Speaking of Nothing." In S. P. Schwartz, ed., *Naming, Necessity, and Natural Kinds,* pp. 216–44. Ithaca, N.Y.: Cornell University Press.

Dummett, Michael. 1981. *Frege: Philosophy of Language.* 2d ed. Cambridge, Mass: Harvard University Press.

——. 1993. *Origins of Analytic Philosophy.* London: Duckworth.

Fann, K. T. 1969. *Symposium on J. L. Austin.* New York: Humanities Press.

Frege, Gottlob. 1949. "On Sense and Nominatum." In Herbert Feigl and Wilfred Sellars, eds., *Readings in Philosophical Analysis,* pp. 85–102. New York:Appleton-Century-Crofts.

Garver, Newton and Seung-Chong Lee. 1994. *Derrida and Wittgenstein.* Philadelphia: Temple University Press.

Gibson, J. J. 1979. *The Ecological Approach to Visual Perception.* Boston: Houghton Mifflin.

Hacker, P. M. S. 1996. *Wittgenstein's Place in Twentieth-Century Analytic Philosophy.* Oxford: Blackwell.

Hampshire, Stuart. 1970. Review of Ryle's *The Concept of Mind.* In O. P. Wood and George Pitcher, eds., *Ryle,* pp. 17–44. New York: Doubleday.

Hannay, Alastair. 1990. *Human Consciousness.* London: Routledge.

Kripke, Saul. 1980. *Naming and Necessity.* Cambridge, Mass.: Harvard University Press.

Lichine, Alexis. 1971. *Encyclopedia of Wines and Spirits.* New York: Knopf.

McGuinness, Brian. 1988. *Wittgenstein: A Life—The Young Ludwig, 1889–1921.* Berkeley: University of California Press.

Malcolm, Norman. 1984. *Ludwig Wittgenstein: A Memoir.* New York: Oxford University Press.

——. 1989. "Wittgenstein on Language and Rules." *Philosophy* 64 (247): 5–28.

Marcus, Ruth B. 1993. *Modalities.* New York: Oxford University Press.

Martinich, A. P. 1984. *Communication and Reference*. New York: de Gruyter.

Mates, Benson. 1981. *Skeptical Essays*. Chicago: University of Chicago Press.

——. 1996. *The Skeptic Way*. New York: Oxford University Press.

Mendelsohn, Richard L. 1996. Commentary. *Inquiry* 39 (2–3: 303–305.

Monk, Ray. 1990. *Ludwig Wittgenstein: The Duty of Genius*. New York: Free Press.

Moore, G. E. 1903. *Principia Ethica*. Cambridge, U.K.: Cambridge University Press.

——. 1922. "The Refutation of Idealism." *Philosophical Studies*, pp. 1–30. London: Routledge.

——. 1959. *Philosophical Papers*. London: Allen and Unwin.

——. 1965. "Visual Sense-Data." In R. J. Swartz, ed., *Perceiving, Sensing, and Knowing*, pp. 130–37. Berkeley: University of California Press.

——. 1968. "An Autobiography." In P. A. Schilpp, ed., *The Philosophy of G. E. Moore*, pp. 3–39. Chicago: Open Court.

Nagel, Thomas. 1974. "What It Is Like to Be a Bat." *Philosophical Review* 83 (4): 435–50.

——. 1986. *The View from Nowhere*. New York: Oxford University Press.

Pascal, Fania. 1984. "A Personal Memoir." In Rush Rhees, ed., *Recollections of Wittgenstein*, pp. 12–49. New York: Oxford University Press.

Penrose, Roger. 1989. *The Emperor's New Mind*. Oxford: Oxford University Press.

Putnam, Hilary. 1977. "Meaning and Reference." In S. P. Schwartz, ed., *Naming, Necessity, and Natural Kinds*, pp. 119–32. Ithaca, N.Y.: Cornell University Press.

——. 1989. *Representation and Reality*. Cambridge, Mass.: MIT Press.

Quine, W. V. O. 1934. *A System of Logistic*. Cambridge, Mass: Harvard University Press.

——. 1940. *Mathematical Logic*. New York: Norton.

——. 1941. *Elementary Logic*. Boston: Ginn.

——. 1950. *Methods of Logic*. New York: Holt.

——. 1953. *From a Logical Point of View*. New York: Harper and Row.

——. 1960. *Word and Object*. Cambridge, Mass.: MIT Press.

——. 1969. "Epistemology Naturalized." *Ontological Relativity and Other Essays*, pp. 60–90. New York: Columbia University Press.

——. 1970. *Philosophy of Logic*. Englewood, N.J.: Prentice-Hall.

——. 1974. *The Roots of Reference*. Chicago: Open Court.

——. 1985. *The Time of My Life*. Cambridge, Mass: MIT Press.

——. 1986. "Autobiography of W. V. Quine." In L. E. Hahn and P. A. Schilpp, eds., *The Philosophy of W. V. Quine*, pp. 3–46. Chicago: Open Court.

——. 1991. "Two Dogmas in Retrospect." *Canadian Journal of Philosophy* 21 (3): 265–74.

Ramachandran, V. S. and Sandra Blakeslee. 1998. *Phantoms in the Brain: Probing the Mysteries of the Human Mind*. New York: Morrow.

Rescher, Nicholas. 1997. *Profitable Speculations: Essays on Current Philosophical Themes*. Lanham, Md.: Rowman and Littlefield.

Rhees, Rush, ed., 1984. *Recollections of Wittgenstein*. New York: Oxford University Press.

Russell, Bertrand. 1919. *Introduction to Mathematical Philosophy*. London: Allen and Unwin.

——. 1956. *Logic and Knowledge: Essays, 1901–1950*. Edited by R. C. Marsh. London: Allen and Unwin.

——. 1963. "My Mental Development." In P. A. Schilpp, ed., *The Philosophy of Bertrand Russell*, vol. 1, pp. 3–20. New York: Harper and Row.

——. 1969. *The Autobiography of Bertrand Russell: The Middle Years, 1914–1944*. Boston: Bantam.

Ryle, Gilbert. 1949. *The Concept of Mind*. London: Hutchinson.

——. 1970. "Autobiographical." In O. P. Wood and George Pitcher, eds., *Ryle*, pp. 1–15. New York: Doubleday.

——. 1971. *Gilbert Ryle: Collected Papers*. Vol. 1. London: Hutchinson.

St. Augustine. 1960. *Confessions*. Translated, with an introduction and notes, by John K. Ryan. New York: Doubleday.

Schilpp, P. A., ed. 1968. *The Philosophy of G. E. Moore*. Chicago: Open Court.

Schlick, Moritz. 1918. *Allgemeine Erkenntnislehre*. Berlin: Springer.

Searle, J. R. 1969. *Speech Acts*. Cambridge, U.K.: Cambridge University Press.

——. 1995. *The Construction of Social Reality*. New York: Free Press.

Sluga, Hans. 1993. *Heidegger's Crisis: Philosophy and Politics in Nazi Germany*. Cambridge, Mass.: Harvard University Press.

——. 1998. "What Has History to Do with Me? Wittgenstein and Analytic Philosophy." *Inquiry* 41 (1): 119–21.

Smart, J. J. C. 1962. "Sensations and Brain Processes." In V. C. Chappel, ed., *The Philosophy of Mind*, pp. 160–72. Englewood Cliffs, N.J.: Prentice-Hall.

Stebbing, Susan. 1968. "Moore's Influence." In P. A. Schilpp, ed., *The Philosophy of G. E. Moore*, pp. 515–32. Chicago: Open Court.

Stevenson, Charles L. 1945. *Ethics and Language*. New Haven, Conn.: Yale University Press.

Strawson, P. F. 1960. "On Referring." In Antony Flew, ed., *Essays in Conceptual Analysis*, pp. 21–52. London: Macmillan.

Stroll, Avrum. 1988. *Surfaces*. Minneapolis: University of Minnesota Press.

——. 1994. *Moore and Wittgenstein on Certainty*. New York: Oxford University Press.

——. 1998. *Sketches of Landscapes: Philosophy by Example*. Cambridge, Mass: MIT Press.

Szabados, Béla. 1999. "Was Wittgenstein an Anti-Semite? The Significance of Anti-Semitism for Wittgenstein's Philosophy." *Canadian Journal of Philosophy* 29 (1): 1–28.

Vendler, Zeno. 1967. *Linguistics in Philosophy*. Ithaca, N.Y.: Cornell University Press.

——. 1984. *The Matter of Minds*. Oxford: Clarendon.

——. 1995. "Goethe, Wittgenstein, and the Essence of Color." *Monist* 78 (4): 391–410.

von Wright, G. H. 1984. "A Biographical Sketch." In Norman Malcolm, ed., *Ludwig Wittgenstein: A Memoir*, pp. 1–20. New York: Oxford University Press.

Warnock, G. J. 1969. "John Langshaw Austin: A Biographical Sketch." In K. T. Fann, ed., *Symposium on J. L. Austin*, pp. 3–21. New York: Humanities Press.

Wasserman, Gerhard D. 1990. "Wittgenstein on Jews: Some Counter-Examples." *Philosophy* 65 (253): 355–65.

Whitehead, Alfred North and Bertrand Russell. 1910–1913. *Principia Mathematica*. Cambridge, U.K.: Cambridge University Press.

Wittgenstein, Hermine. 1984. "My Brother Ludwig." In Rush Rhees, ed., *Recollections of Wittgenstein*, pp. 1–11. New York: Oxford University Press.

Wittgenstein, Ludwig. 1922. *Tractatus Logico-Philosophicus*. London: Routledge and Kegan Paul.

——. 1958. *Philosophical Investigations*. 2d ed. Oxford: Blackwell.

——. 1960. *The Blue and Brown Books*. Oxford: Blackwell.

——. 1967a. *Letters from Ludwig Wittgenstein, with a Memoir by Paul Engelmann*. Oxford: Blackwell.

——. 1967b. *Zettel.* Oxford: Blackwell.
——. 1969. *On Certainty.* Oxford: Blackwell.
——. 1973. *Letters to C. K. Ogden from Ludwig Wittgenstein.* Oxford: Blackwell.
——. 1974. *Letters to Russell, Keynes, and Moore by Ludwig Wittgenstein.* Ithaca, N.Y.: Cornell University Press.
——. 1980. *Culture and Value.* Oxford: Blackwell.
Woolf, Leonard. 1960. *Sowing.* New York: Harcourt-Brace.

### Further Reading

Arrington, Robert and H. J. Glock, eds. 1996. *Wittgenstein and Quine.* London: Routledge.
Ayer, Alfred J., ed. 1960. *Logical Positivism.* Glencoe, N.Y.: Free Press.
Barnes, W. H. F. 1950. *The Philosophical Predicament.* London: Blackwell.
Bergmann, Gustav. 1954. *The Metaphysics of Logical Positivism.* London: Longman.
Biletzki, Anat and Anat Matar, eds. 1997. *The Story of Analytic Philosophy.* London: Routledge.
Broad, C. D. 1923. *Scientific Thought.* London: Kegan Paul.
Casati, Roberto and Achille C. Varzi. 1994. *Holes.* Cambridge, Mass.: MIT Press.
Caton, C. E., ed. 1963. *Philosophy and Ordinary Language.* Urbana: University of Illinois Press.
Chisholm, Roderick M. 1957. *Perceiving: A Philosophical Study.* Ithaca, N.Y.: Cornell University Press.
——. 1997. *The Philosophy of Roderick M. Chisholm.* Edited by Lewis Edwin Hahn. Chicago and La Salle: Open Court.
Churchland, Paul M. 1988. *Matter and Consciousness.* Cambridge, Mass.: MIT Press.
Cremaschi, Sergio. 1997. *Filosofia Analitica e Filosofia Continentale.* Firenze: La Nuouva Italia.
D'Agostini, Franca. 1997. *Analitici e Continentali.* Milano: Cortina.
Davidson, Donald. 1980. *Essays on Actions and Events.* Oxford: Clarendon.
——. 1984. *Inquiries into Truth and Interpretation.* Oxford: Clarendon.
Donnellan, Kenneth. 1977. "Reference and Definite Descriptions." In S. P. Schwartz, ed., *Naming, Necessity, and Natural Kinds*, pp. 42–65. Ithaca, N.Y.: Cornell University Press.

Dreyfus, H. L. 1979. *What Computers Can't Do: A Critique of Artificial Reason*. 2d ed. New York: Harper and Row.

Egidi, Rosaria, ed. 1995. *Wittgenstein: Mind and Language*. Dordrecht, Germany: Kluwer.

Feigl, Herbert and Wilfred Sellars, eds. 1949. *Readings in Philosophical Analysis*. New York: Appleton-Century-Crofts.

Feyerabend, Paul. 1987. *Farewell to Reason*. London: Verso.

Frege, Gottlob. 1950. *The Foundations of Arithmetic*. Translated by J. L. Austin. Oxford: Blackwell.

———. 1960. *Translations from the Philosophical Writings of Gottlob Frege*. 2d ed. Translated by Peter Geach and Max Black. Oxford: Blackwell.

———. 1964. "On the Scientific Justification of a Conceptual Notation." *Mind* 73, no. 290 (April): 155–60.

———. 1964. *The Basic Laws of Arithmetic*. Translated and edited with an introduction by Montgomery Furth. Berkeley: University of California Press.

———. 1996. "*Nachgelassene Schriften* (Posthumous Writings)." Translated and with commentary by Richard L. Mendelsohn. *Inquiry* 39 (2–3): 308–42.

Garavaso, Pieranna. 1998. *Filosofia della matematica*. Milan: Guerini.

Garver, Newton. 1994. *This Complicated Form of Life: Essays on Wittgenstein*. Chicago: Open Court.

Gibson, Roger F. 1982. *The Philosophy of W. V. Quine: An Expository Essay*. Tampa: University Press of Florida.

Glock, H. J., ed. 1997. *The Rise of Analytic Philosophy*. Oxford: Blackwell.

Goodman, Nelson. 1951. *The Structure of Appearance*. Indianapolis, Ind.: Bobbs-Merrill.

Grice, H. Paul. 1989. *Studies in the Way of Words*. Cambridge, Mass.: Harvard University Press.

Haller, Rudolf. 1988. *Questions on Wittgenstein*. Lincoln: University of Nebraska Press.

Hannay, Alastair. 1971. *Mental Images—A Defense*. London: Allen and Unwin.

Hempel, Carl G. 1996. "Problems and Changes in the Empiricist Criterion of Meaning." In A. P. Martinich, ed., *The Philosophy of Language*, 3d ed., pp. 26–38. New York: Oxford University Press.

Hintikka, M. B. and Jaakko Hintikka. 1988. *Investigating Wittgenstein*. Oxford: Blackwell.

Jackson, Frank. 1977. *Perception: A Representative Theory*. Cambridge, U.K.: Cambridge University Press.

Janik, Allan and Stephen Toulmin. 1973. *Wittgenstein's Vienna*. Cambridge, Mass.: MIT Press.

Kneale, William and Martha Kneale. 1962. *The Development of Logic*. Oxford: Clarendon.

Kraft, Victor. 1953. *The Vienna Circle*. New York: Philosophical Library.

Kripke, Saul. 1977. "Identity and Necessity." In S. P. Schwartz, ed., *Naming, Necessity, and Natural Kinds*, pp. 66–101. Ithaca, N.Y.: Cornell University Press.

——. 1982. *Wittgenstein on Rules and Private Language*. Cambridge, Mass.: Harvard University Press.

Kuhn, T. S. 1962. *The Structure of Scientific Revolutions*. Chicago: University of Chicago Press.

Lazerowitz, Morris. 1964. *Studies in Metaphilosophy*. New York: Humanities Press.

Lehrer, Keith and J. C. Marek, eds. 1997. *Austrian Philosophy Past and Present: Essays in Honor of Rudolf Haller*. Dordrecht, Germany: Kluwer.

Linsky, Leonard, ed. 1952. *Semantics and the Philosophy of Language*. Urbana: University of Illinois Press.

Lycan, W. G. 1987. *Consciousness*. Cambridge, Mass.: MIT Press.

Malcolm, Norman. 1977. *Memory and Mind*. Ithaca, N.Y.: Cornell University Press.

——. 1977. *Thought and Knowledge*. Ithaca, N.Y.: Cornell University Press.

——. 1986. *Nothing Is Hidden: Wittgenstein's Criticism of His Early Thought*. Oxford: Blackwell.

Martinich, A. P. 1996. *The Philosophy of Language*. 3d ed. New York: Oxford University Press.

Meinong, Alexius. 1960. "The Theory of Objects." In R. M. Chisholm, ed., *Realism and the Background of Phenomenology*, pp. 76–117. New York: Free Press.

Mill, John S. 1843. *System of Logic*. London: Longmans, Green.

Naess, Arne. 1968. *Scepticism*. New York: Humanities Press.

Nozick, Robert. 1974. *Anarchy, State, and Utopia*. New York: Basic.

Pap, Arthur. 1949. *Elements of Analytic Philosophy*. New York: Macmillan.

Paul, G. A. 1965. "Is There a Problem About Sense-Data?" In R. J. Swartz, ed., *Perceiving, Sensing, and Knowing*, pp. 271–87. Berkeley: University of California Press.2

Pears, David. 1987. *The False Prison*. 2 vols. Oxford: Clarendon.

Popkin, R. H., ed. 1999. *The Columbia History of Western Philosophy*. New York: Columbia University Press.

Popper, Karl R. 1945. *The Open Society and Its Enemies*. London: Kegan Paul.

———. 1958. *The Logic of Scientific Discovery*. London: Hutchinson.

Popper, Karl R. and J. C. Eccles. 1985. *The Self and Its Brain*. Berlin: Springer.

Putnam, Hilary. 1977. "Is Semantics Possible?" In S. P. Schwartz, ed., *Naming, Necessity, and Natural Kinds*, pp. 102–18. Ithaca, N.Y.: Cornell University Press.

Quine, W. V. O. 1966. *The Ways of Paradox and Other Essays*. New York: Random House.

Ramsey, William, Stephen Stich, and David Rumelhart, eds. 1991. *Philosophy and Connectionist Theory*. Hillsdale, N.J.: Erlbaum.

Russell, Bertrand. 1903. *The Principles of Mathematics*. Cambridge, U.K.: Cambridge University Press.

———. 1912. "Knowledge by Description and Knowledge by Acquaintance." *The Problems of Philosophy*, pp. 46–59. London: Oxford University Press.

Searle, J. R. 1983. *Intentionality: An Essay in the Philosophy of Mind*. Cambridge, U.K.: Cambridge University Press.

Smythies, J. R. 1994. *The Walls of Plato's Cave*. Aldershot, U.K.: Avebury.

Strawson, P. F. 1952. *Introduction to Logical Theory*. London: Methuen.

———. 1959. *Individuals: An Essay in Descriptive Metaphysics*. London: Methuen.

Stroll, Avrum. 1999. "Twentieth-Century Analytic Philosophy." In R. H. Popkin, ed., *The Columbia History of Western Philosophy*, pp. 604–66. New York: Columbia University Press,

Swartz, R. J., ed. 1965. *Perceiving, Sensing, and Knowing*. London: University of California Press.

Tarski, Alfred. 1944. "The Semantic Conception of Truth." *Philosophy and Phenomenological Research* 4 (1): 341–75.

———. 1956. *Logic, Semantics, Meta-Mathematics*. Oxford: Clarendon.

Urmson, James. 1956. *Philosophical Analysis*. Oxford: Clarendon.

Wisdom, John T. 1952. *Other Minds*. Oxford: Blackwell.

———. 1957. *Philosophy and Psychoanalysis*. Oxford: Blackwell.

Wittgenstein, Ludwig. 1929. "Some Remarks on Logical Form." *Proceedings of the Aristotelian Society*, supp. vol. 9: 162–71.

——. 1966. *Lectures and Conversations on Aesthetics, Psychology, and Religious Belief.* Edited by Cyril Barrett. Berkeley: University of California Press.

——. 1981 and 1992. *Last Writings on the Philosophy of Psychology.* 2 vols. Oxford: Blackwell.

Wright, Edmond, ed. 1993. *New Representationalisms.* Aldershot, U.K.: Avebury.

# Index